Developing Coaching
LEADERS

WWLJ
Publishing

Contact information for WWLJ Publishing– www.scottclancy.ca or email scott@scottclancy.ca

ISBN: 978-1-7388677-0-7 (paperback)
ISBN: 978-1-7388677-1-4 (ebook)
ISBN: 978-1-7388677-2-1 (audiobook)

Ordering Information:
Special discounts are available on quantity purchases by corporations, associations, and others. For details, contact scott@scottclancy.ca or visit www.scottclancy.ca

Publisher's Cataloging-in-Publication Data

Names: Clancy, Scott, 1966- .
Title: Developing coaching leaders : the fundamentals and techniques that make leaders
    extraordinary / Scott Clancy.
Description: Cobourg, ON : WWLJ Publishing, 2023. | Includes bibliographic references.
    | Includes 10 b&w charts and diagrams. | Summary: The author uses his extensive
    military leadership and sports coaching backgrounds to lay the foundations for
    leading and coaching teams to success. Pragmatic examples, tools and processes
    provide readers with a road map to learning great leadership and coaching skills.
Identifiers: ISBN 9781738867707 (pbk.) | ISBN 9781738867714 (ebook) | ISBN
    9781738867721 (audiobook)
Subjects: LCSH: Coaching (Athletics). | Leadership. | Mentoring. | Mindfulness
    (Psychology). | BISAC: SPORTS & RECREATION / Coaching / General. | SELF-HELP /
    Personal Growth / Success. | EDUCATION / Leadership.
Classification: LCC GV711.C53 2023 | DDC 796.07 C--dc23

Developing Coaching
LEADERS

*The Fundamentals and Techniques that
Make Leaders Extraordinary*

Major General (ret)
SCOTT CLANCY
OMM MSM CD

PVAC - AIAW

To Leaders now and in the future:

Never underestimate the impact of your actions.

The exponential expansion of your meaningful engagement
will make our world extraordinary!!

Contents

Section 1
FUNDAMENTALS

Section 2
TACTICS, TECHNIQUES, AND PROCEDURES

Section 3
PROVE IT!

Introduction

My commanding officer and all his majors were glaring at me. You could have heard a pin drop. But I, a young captain, was riveted by the senior colonel in front of me and didn't hold back with my honest but highly provocative question.

"What is forcing all of our good people to quit the military?"

The colonel didn't miss a beat in answering my question.

"*Leadership!*" he said, motioning to the still-glaring bunch of senior officers off to the side. "Managers and bureaucrats, even good pilots, but not inspiring leaders."

He didn't stop there. As he continued talking, he made a point to listen and answer each and every question we had. The young officers like myself were eager for guidance, but we masked it with an air of confident apathy—or even cynicism—for much of the military hierarchy.

I felt different after the colonel left. Connected. Inspired. I felt like I could trust him and therefore trust our mission. He hadn't just led us in those moments; he had coached us, listened to us, and even critiqued us and our leaders, frankly and fairly.

I caught hell for asking that question. But I could not have cared less. My head was full of sparks and electrons, swirling around a new world that had just opened for me. I had a ton of learning to do about leading and coaching. In answering my question, this colonel had given me the answer I knew was true, but also the challenge to lead better. It put me on a path to be authentic, leading people by enabling their talents, but also to never lose sight of the crucial mission and its vital role for the nation. It wasn't only that one word, *leadership*, that inspired me; it was the rest of the colonel's answers as well. I saw him coaching us to be better leaders in that moment, and from then on, I knew I wanted to lead people to be their best. Until then, I had thought coaching was about putting someone through the paces in practice and that the crucible of the situation would force them to learn. Until then, I had seen leaders, both good and bad, as being that way merely because of their personal nature and character. They would lead because they were charismatic and had good technical skills. But, as the colonel spoke that day, the lightbulb went off for me that the colonel was employing immeasurable knowledge and a multitude of skills to show up as a leader as he gave that presentation. Some of those skills pertained to leading, while others were all about coaching. But the colonel was humble about his own knowledge. His approach, tone, vocabulary, and message were not a highly crafted "pitch" but an authentic expression of a true professional who always knew that a lifetime of learning might still come up short in a critical moment. The path I had just embarked upon would place me on a lifelong journey to perfect my skills around leading and coaching.

What's the question you *want* to ask, the one that starts leaders coaching?

The military is commonly thought of as an organization that produces good leaders. I have had the pleasure of serving with many *great* leaders, but I have also been exposed to some who led poorly. I watched, learned, and was given the privilege of leading military and civilian personnel. I always considered myself a student of leadership. Simultaneously, I had the pleasure of coaching my sons, other youth, and, finally, cadets at the Royal Military College (RMC) in a variety of sports, but mostly basketball. So…I have led, and I have coached. And although in my experience they are not the same thing, there is significant overlap in the skills and techniques that these two roles, coach and leader, require. They are also approached very differently within the military and sports realms. But this overlap was intriguing.

I think, to start, we need to have a common frame of reference for what coaching and leading are. A good friend of mine, Steve Nash,[1] gave me a great leadership quote that I use often: "Leadership is an emotional trust relationship." I like how this applies to coaching as well. Therefore, our first definition will be that **leadership and coaching are emotional trust relationships**. This describes what they are, but it doesn't completely define what leadership and coaching do. Therefore, alongside this, I would say that **a leader is anyone who is attempting to move a team toward a goal.** The size of that team is not important, and I postulate that part of our exploration of coaching and leading side by side will lead to a conclusion as to whether a team of one would fit this definition. Defining coaching is a much more difficult thing. **Coaching, for me, is about maximizing an individual's performance with the intent to achieve aspirational goals but centred on individual development.**

As a senior officer in the Royal Canadian Air Force (RCAF), I was constantly discussing leadership with everyone around me, from superior officers, peers, subordinates, business leaders, senior government officials, and academics to my family. As a basketball coach and father of two high school basketball players, I found myself engaging with players, other coaches, officials, managers, and parents on the finer details of coaching. Both new

---

1   No, not Steve Nash the NBA MVP (yes, another Canadian), but imagine the excitement at the first tryout for his girls' basketball team when the other parents heard that Steve Nash would be coaching!

and experienced leaders and coaches share a deep desire to improve their skills and knowledge. They would often express to me their struggles in dealing with low employee loyalty and an overall disconnection between themselves, their employees, and the vision or goals of their organizations. In turn, these same leaders and the people who worked with and for them commonly stated that leaders struggle to connect and follow through with employees in interactions beyond transactional performance-oriented feedback. Finally, most leaders feel that they are assigned leadership positions and are left to "figure it out" for themselves, with little or no guidance or coaching along the way. The sink-or-swim mentality of corporate or bureaucratic processes layered on top of a flimsy organizational hierarchy manifests a de facto model of leading where you either have it…or you do not.

The more that I discussed leading and coaching, I realized that even many *good* leaders and coaches could not explain what they were doing to be successful in their field and with their teams. I was exposed to many who were not successful as well. But both groups would cling to the idea that you either have it or you don't, that leading or coaching are innate skills or character traits. I don't believe this. Nor do I believe that "just doing it" works. "Fake it till you make it" will only take a leader so far. You will need a deeper understanding to progress beyond binary transaction-based leading. Similarly, a lot of well-intentioned coaches and leaders have a smattering of positive ideas about leading and coaching that are only "meme deep" ("Be authentic," "Servant leadership," etc.). One cannot help but think that this is not excellence by design, but by accident.

I believe that the shortfalls that leaders have in coaching skills and knowledge specifically have led to chronic employee underperformance that stems from people feeling undervalued by the organizations they work in. People cannot relate, or do not associate, their individual development with their current roles or jobs, much less with their leaders or their bosses. Their uninspired workplaces have workplace cultures oriented toward performance, where the people working there see through the veil or jargon to organizations that have drifted from core objectives, goals, and, ultimately, values. Bad leaders affect the health of the people that work for them and cost their organisations time and money. This lack of leadership can have catastrophic consequences, especially in the military, health care, and first responder arenas, ultimately costing lives.

We can do better than this. We have to. Our countries, our communities, our teams, and our people deserve more. The world needs better leaders and coaches. I think this book can help you be both.

On my journey of learning, I have found that effective leaders typically coach well, and effective coaches lead well. To me, this means that maximizing skills in one role or perspective can translate directly to being better in the other. What this means to leaders is that to be extraordinary, you need to lead *and* coach simultaneously. Organisations that will excel in any situation, dealing with all the challenges placed in front of them, will therefore *Develop Coaching Leaders* (that's what you came here for, right?).

Have you thought of the question you want to ask yet, the one that starts leaders coaching?

Here are some: So, how can this be achieved? How do you systemically solve underperformance? What about those organizations where the objectives and values have been steadfast and true? Why are they experiencing the same problems, and what is the fix? Is workplace culture the problem or is it a result? Isn't our modern workplace culture merely a representation of society as a whole? What is the link between people's desire to develop themselves and organizational demands on performance? How do you develop people who are "self-starters" that get stuff done on their own initiative? How do you inspire people?

To assist leaders and coaches, this book will provide a framework of fundamentals and techniques, then show how to practically apply them to leadership and coaching situations. This is not a "do what I did" biography couched in a how-to book. I have tried to be honest about where I succeeded and failed so that my experiences can serve as examples, but the focus is clearly on the skills and knowledge required to lead and coach well. I think that, by returning to our fundamentals in leading and coaching, developing trust, connecting with our people, connecting them with the mission, and being self-aware enough to realize that we are constantly learning how to apply these fundamentals, we will become better leaders and coaches and start to answer that list of questions above. This book provides insights intended to spark our individual learning as coaches and leaders.

I want this material to appeal to as many leaders as possible, from those taking on a role for the very first time to seasoned individuals. Indeed, I think that many people are leading and coaching long before these formal roles or titles are assigned to them. There are some complex ideas that I wanted to explore based on my experiences as a coach and a leader. There are also basic elements and stories of success and failure that were inspired by looking back as I learned to coach and lead. New or aspiring leaders can hugely benefit from being exposed to mature concepts and ideas alongside the basics. In fact, when this happens, the rudimentary elements gain more importance, and the refined ideas are easily seen to be rooted in first principles. Much the same, seasoned leaders can find a harmony between some of the ideas that would appeal to them right away, while benefitting from reviewing the basics to ensure they don't lose sight of that which is important.

There are a couple of ways to read this book. Reading this from front to back might not suit everyone. My wife Val had the idea of dividing this book into a very comprehensive list of small chapters rather than a lower number of longer ones so if you want to read about a specific item, you can just jump to that content. *Aha!* [2] You are in control, so read the book any way that you want. That being said, I recommend reading the first chapter before diving in to understand how the book is structured. It is pretty intuitive—from there, dig in anywhere you would like.

The world needs better leaders and coaches. Be both!!

---

2 Humour note: When my wife discovers that I have left the front door unlocked, she shouts out "*Aha!!*" with a wry smile on her face, if only so that we both know that she is doing her pre-bed rounds and that our nervous nelly approach to safety—including checking candles, the fireplace, lights, our dog, and the front door—has all been taken care of. The more I discover the nooks and crannies of her character, the more she endears herself to me.

CHAPTER 1

From Coaching Hoops to Training Troops

There is a common set of problems that leaders and coaches face, no matter their experience level. These problems are the following:

- Leaders and coaches drift/depart from the fundamentals of coaching and leading,

- They cease to develop themselves and their teams professionally and personally,

- They manage people rather than leading (inspiring) and coaching (mentoring) them, and

- They focus on productivity or business outputs to the detriment of their team.

Does this resonate with you, your team, your organization, or even your family? The downstream results of these problems have wide-reaching implications, and we see them rampant in our business, sports, and military organizations: low to nonexistent employee loyalty, low initiative and lack of innovative work, transactional dealings with employees and supervisors, and team members who are uninspired, disconnected, and generally apathetic to the work and the workplace.

One may say that not all these problems are caused by leaders. This is true, although many are. More still are exacerbated by poor leaders who are unable to deal with the complex issues and the overwhelming scrutiny placed on them in our workplaces and on our teams. But most importantly, every single issue, I believe, can be drastically improved upon if not resolved by good leaders and coaches.

Many leaders get their first dose of coaching as parents helping out with our kids' teams. I loved coaching basketball, especially with youth. But the more I saw of coaching, the more I saw people drift from the basic principles I believed were foundational to good coaching. Winning, performance, and accolades seemed more important to many than the impact on society that youth sport can have through character development and instilling values. I am sure that most of you have seen and experienced this as well, either from within youth sport or as parents and coaches. Even more revealing was that coaches confided in me that they really did not have any formal training and relied on their experience and their natural attributes to guide them. These influences formed their coaching techniques. In other words, if something got them success (winning), they repeated it. *Wow!*

Got some questions for those folks? Does this explain some attitudes you have seen or experienced, either as parents or in youth sport? What behaviours are being re-enforced here?

As much as I loved coaching, I had wanted to be in the military ever since I was a little boy doing the changing of the guard on my front lawn. At the height of my career, I was given the privilege of leading the most precious resource of our country in the most noble cause: Canadian military personnel in the defence of the nation. Finally, I was blessed with the privilege of leading combined troops from the Canadian and United States (U.S.)[3] militaries within NORAD.[4] The more that I led in the military, the more I realized that there was an inherent link between the *way* in which I was leading and the techniques that I used to coach. My personal journalling started me reflecting on my sons' experience with basketball, my associated coaching, and some of their experiences with other coaches. But what I had taken for granted before now became obvious to me. Much of my work as a **coach** was based upon fundamentals of **leadership** I had picked up throughout my military career.

What are these two titles, "coach" and "leader"? Are they skills? Headspaces? Functions? Roles? Philosophies? More importantly, how are they linked? Are they mutually supporting? It's clear that there is overlap. But… how do they overlap? Are they just different perspectives on the same set of skills? When I tried to answer these vexing questions, a truism emerged: better coaches make better leaders. Those leaders at the top of the pyramid in the military organizations I was exposed to were all coaching their teams well. Contrarily, those who I saw underperforming or leading poorly had fundamental flaws not only in the way they were leading but in the way they coached—or did not coach—their subordinates and teams. *Aha!* **Leaders need to coach.**

In my other role as a basketball coach, my experience led me down a different path than I would have anticipated, especially in retrospect. On the basketball court with small kids from 8 to 13 years of age, coaching seemed more like leading. Yes, these were kids. No, I was not treating them like re-

---

3   Humour note: In this book, I will always state Canada first and then the U.S. second, not only in respect for my roots but as an inside joke with a mentor and friend, General Tom Bussiere. While Tom was in command of the Alaskan NORAD Region (and I was serving as his deputy), he would always say "America… and Canada" and then break into a large smile, even though in many instances the only Canadian in the room was me. Tom is a descendant of Île d'Orléans French-Canadian great-grandparents and is a shining example of the staunch allies our U.S. counterparts always were.

4   NORAD stands for the North American Aerospace Defence. It is a bi-national command between Canada and the USA. NORAD command is in Colorado Springs, and it has three subordinate military regions: the Canadian Region, the Continental Region, and the Alaskan Region.

cruits. But they had literally next to no basketball IQ. They needed directed guidance: "Just do as I say and do as I do." I would demonstrate things. I wanted the kids to imitate, practise, be corrected, and finally understand the skills they were learning. But, at the outset, I needed them to do as I said. Even when I bridged into college-level hoops, I found myself telling a 6'7" 23-year-old, "Just do as I tell you. Yes, it is uncomfortable. But that is what 'right' looks like. Now do it until it becomes second nature." **Coaches need to lead.**

The symbiotic relationship between coaching and leading is inherent in the phrase **Coaches Need to Lead; Leaders Need to Coach.** To make the phrase come alive and be helpful in solving common problems, there needs to be focus, detail, and examples to explain it. The solution therefore is to provide the insights, aide-mémoires, checklists, and explanatory examples to entrench fundamentals of coaching and leadership.

We all typically have positive experiences in leader-follower relationships where we are being coached by mentors and supervisors. Most of us have that specific teacher (or instructor) or two that truly believed in us and inspired us to learn. We think back to "legacy" coaches, the ones that entire generations of players remember and who taught us so very much about ourselves through the venue of sport. In the military, we often reminisce about fantastic leaders who seemed to always know how to react and who could be so many things to so many people.

For me, those positive experiences involved being led through a solid example while being coached to find the unique path that was my own leadership journey. The best coaching and mentoring sessions (in retrospect, of course) were the most uncomfortable. They dealt with my shortcomings and what I needed to do to improve upon them. But the coaches guiding me through them also walked that fine line in ensuring I was developing and growing and that whatever coaching items we discussed did not change the expectation they had concerning my performance. All this led me back to the same question: Were they coaching well or leading well? But more than that, what were the techniques that enabled them to be effective in the coaching and leading role? What were those things that led me to be inspired and connected and that established mutual trust?

Clearly any solutions I propose would have to be rooted in tips, hacks, techniques, and processes that demonstrate the application of fundamentals in practical situations and circumstances. But more than that, solutions about how to lead and coach can only go so far. Another key difference to me was that effective coaches and leaders were focused on developing me in these roles. Therefore, the solutions must be intimately linked to how leaders and coaches develop skills and knowledge in their teams in these two pivotal roles. Good coaches and leaders mastered elements of both sides and approached situations with a more robust set of tools to achieve success. The more tools in your toolbox, the better a coach—and therefore leader—you will be.

It is probably true that my reflections on mentor/coach experiences are significantly biased by my military roles and experiences. It might be easy to point to a specific individual who shaped my own views on mentoring and coaching because they coached me, and many others, so very effectively. But the reality is that I was influenced by so many great leaders in my military career, leaders who took the time to coach me, even though they themselves were so very busy and were sought after to resolve crucial problems. I had the pleasure of being an Air Force officer and having access to the entire spectrum of the RCAF. But, as a tactical helicopter pilot, I also spent *soooooo* much time with the Canadian Army, living on army bases, teaching tactics at the Army Staff College, and having the pleasure of sitting at Army Council for two years as the Commander 1 Wing. Although these two arenas shaped my leadership, it was my roots in the tactical aviation community that truly taught me how to coach and mentor. The tactical helicopter (tac hel) community was and is full of individuals at all ranks who had a true sense of who they were and how to develop young leaders through example and patience. (And with the pranks we pulled, they needed patience!)

Within a military context, there is a lot placed under the banner of "leadership": tactical/individual prowess, technical skills, flying ability, organizational skills, management skills, program management skills, and even personal relationships and character all seem to be "leadership" functions. I think that that is a cop-out. It allows many people to think that all these skills, including leadership, are like character traits. It is limiting. There is no space to grow. By exploring all these elements, breaking them down, and examining their components and how they interrelate, we can employ techniques to maximize them.

Therefore, we will also explore the links between competence and trust, management practices and individual development, and even innovative and comprehensive scheduling and prioritization processes I implemented in a global organization using coaching and leading techniques. I will share this framework of techniques and then demonstrate how to practically apply them with real-world examples.

I find that most leaders and coaches intuitively want to do the right things, but either they find it a tough trial-and-error slog or they are not sure how to explain why they are having success—or, more often, troubles. Many dealing with challenges do not have a framework of fundamentals, nor do they have the techniques to enable resolution. This process isn't so much about reinventing yourself from the ground up as it is about reflecting and adding skills and knowledge to your toolbox. By putting into context those things you are already doing, you will develop as a leader and as a coach. Moreover, you will learn to develop your team better to ultimately replace you. That is why I keep going back to the language in the definitions of leadership and coaching: "emotional trust relationship," "move a team toward a goal," "maximizing an individual's performance," and "centred on individual development." I weave these words here between the definitions of leading and coaching because I think they illuminate just how interconnected coaching and leading are.

Some of the symptoms of our core problems are a loss of employee loyalty and a general disconnection of the people on our teams with the goals and values of the organization we are affiliated with. This book is not going to eliminate the desire for social welfare in the workplace, where advancement, life balance, and opportunities are expected and movement beyond the organization, or even between jobs, is the norm for those seeking the right environment. But this book *will* provide tools that maximize the knowledge and skills of coaches and leaders, and this can translate into personal loyalty.

To be clear, I do not believe in trying to change the constant flow through of people. Your best (or worst) recruiter is every ex-member of your team or organization. Imagine if this were what your ex-team members were saying to others when they talked about your team or organization: "You *have* to work/play/serve there! I learned *sooo* much and developed *sooo* fast from those leaders and coaches. It was foundational to my development. They made *me* into a leader and a coach."

While coaching youth basketball, I invariably ended up in high-pressure moments in tournament or playoff games that were win-or-go-home situations. In many instances, the teams would be so evenly matched that the game would come down to the final seconds of play.[5] Coaching under this pressure and maximizing the potential of the team meant in many ways just repeating the guidance, "Control your emotions. Trust your training. Do exactly as we practised. Do exactly as I say." For many military leaders, the highly effective leadership approach I often saw was "Follow me, I will show you the way." When we look at military leadership down at the small

---

5   The joke around our house (yes, initiated by my lovely wife and her awesome dad, Mac) was that all basketball games come down to the last two minutes… so why not just play the last two minutes? Or at least, let's just watch the last two minutes! At the two-minute mark of every March Madness game, Val shouts out, "Game is starting!!"

combat unit level, much of leading is by personal example and specific direction in times of crisis. Bullets are flying, and decisions need to be made with little or no time to seek clarification on already imperfect information. Both examples, that of the coach in the high-pressure moments of a game and that of the small unit combat leader, involve coaches and leaders leading. But in both cases, it is also clear that the coaching they have done with their teams leading up to those moments is just as important as, if not more important than, how they direct in those crucial seconds. Moreover, if they haven't set the team up well prior to those moments, there is a good chance that even the best direction will not—or will not be able to—be followed through upon.

There is obvious crossover in the concepts of coaching and leading. Let's go beyond the theory. Let's develop pragmatic and practical techniques for what works from a coaching or a leading perspective. Let's answer your tough questions (have you thought of them yet?) and then use checklists and aide-mémoires that enable practical application of fundamentals in a variety of situations. The book is organized in easy-to-read chapters and sections that allow for focused study. There are practical examples drawn from the military and sports fields that show these techniques working. More importantly, I share some of my own personal struggles in developing these skills as a leader and coach, which will hopefully allow you to learn from my mistakes.

Many of you will identify as either a leader or coach, not as both. I ultimately want to convince you that these roles are symbiotic. However, they also provide a powerful tool through which to see the concepts that we are exploring. "Coach" and "leader" are two different paradigms.

Let me explain. In the RCAF, there has been a debate over the order of these two elements:

MISSION   PEOPLE

Is it "Mission First; People Always"…OR…"People First; Mission Always"?

One train of thought is that if you always enable your people, then the mission will take care of itself. The immediate counterpoint is that the sacrifice that is about to be made to accomplish the mission is the people themselves, so how is that taking care of people? How do you square that?

The opposite side of the debate is that the mission comes first, and the people are the key component to accomplishing this. The nuance here is that when push comes to shove, the mission must take precedence over the people. In combat, this seems to make perfect sense. But in day-to-day peacetime operations—not to mention the corporate civilian world—this paradigm is what allows organizations and leaders to brutalize personal lives and demand more out of people than those people can realistically achieve. "People always" is the afterthought. Everything is viewed through the paradigm of mission accomplishment. This lens doesn't consider whether the paradigm is situationally dependent.

PARADIGM

LENS TO LOOK THROUGH

Figure 1.1: Paradigm—A Lens to Look Through

In the end, the language that we use in command/leadership positions to support whichever of the "people/mission" paradigms you ascribe to is important because the *debate itself* serves a dual purpose of demonstrating a deep caring for the people and helping the commander hone their cognitive skills for when it comes time to assign priorities between people and the vital mission. More than anything, this debate highlighted to me the relationship between coaching and leading concepts, again through two different perspectives: "I lead you" versus "I coach you."

As my study into coaching and leading progressed, an interesting pattern emerged (at least, I think it was interesting). What I began to see was a series of items, skills, tools, situations, and functions that were associated not only with coaching, but, by association, with leading. However, not all these items seemed to apply cleanly, or in the same fashion, to both. Some applied significantly more to one than another. *But*, more than anything else, by exploring each item I got a better perspective on the relationship between coaching and leading. The two perspectives[6] are really two different paradigms through which to view the skills and knowledge surrounding leading and coaching.

By looking at these items, first through the lens of coaching, then through the lens of leading, the benefit of coaching and leading techniques and skills comes to light—specifically, the applicability of not only the individual item or technique, but of being able to employ it from a coaching or leading perspective.

Because basketball and the military are the foundations of my experience, I chose to group the elements that will be explored into two groups: **fundamentals** and **TTPs**. *Fundamentals* are the basketball coach's roots: passing, footwork, shooting, defence, etc. Fundamentals will group all the elements that I see as foundational to leading and coaching together.

---

6   "Perspectives" is the word my wife Val sees being used the most this year as a "buzzword." In 2021, it was "pivot." Her analysis and predictions on buzzwords would be a very interesting read.

Each item will be explored and analyzed for its applicability to leading and coaching through each lens. *TTPs* is a long-used military acronym that stands for **T**actics, **T**echniques, and **P**rocedures. TTPs will group those items that get more into the specifics of applying foundational elements to coaching and leading. Some of the TTPs are processes that support the rudiments. Others are tactics or approaches to coaching or leading in specific situations. I feel that TTPs are more "technique-y" than fundamentals, but they will also be explored and analyzed through the same two lenses: their applicability to coaching and to leading.

Taking the time to analyze each element through both the lens of coaching and the lens of leading will show significant overlap between the worlds of coaching and leading. I also hope that our journey will highlight the mutually supporting nature of these two paradigms. And, in many ways, looking at a fundamental- or a TTP- through one or both lenses can drastically help a coach or leader approach a situation differently.

The last chapter will sum things up with deductions that show good practices through each of the two lenses, especially focusing on how, for leaders, adding coaching skills makes us better. In the section "Prove It!", I will make some more overarching deductions on the overlap and applicability of the various fundamentals and techniques and explore the links between them and more systemic or comprehensive approaches.

Finally, it is worth mentioning that I think I am more of a leader than a coach. Although I dabbled in coaching basketball for youth teams and at the Royal Military College, I would in no way consider myself a professional "coach." However, I stop short of saying I am not skilled in this arena due to the significant overlap in skills between coaching and my 37 years of experience in the RCAF. Therefore, the focus of our journey will be slightly biased toward leaders who are adding coaching skills to their repertoires. In addition, recognizing my blind spot at the start means that I will augment my personal opinion on some of the fundamentals and TTPs with that of my "collaborators." I have specifically chosen my collaborators because I value their opinions. They are as varied as experience can be. They are coaches, artists, office workers, law enforcement, military officers, friends, family, and aid workers. They are my foil, and they make me stronger. Some of them are quoted here; many more have shaped my thinking and the thoughts of this book via our dynamic interactions. Hopefully, they make our journey more enjoyable by countering my dogmatic ideas and presenting that most powerful perspective, the opposing point of view.

Let's *go*.

Section 1

FUNDAMENTALS

A thick finger was waving at me. Behind it was a powerful and wise face.

"No! Look at your feet!"

My feet? What the hell did my feet have to do with this complex wrist grab I was trying to master?!

Fundamentals. In most sports, most academics, most pursuits in life, fundamentals are everything. Similarly, when you're a coach and leader, laying the foundation for individual and team development means focusing on fundamentals. When we focus our teams on the basics, many people will feel uncomfortable. But to lay the right foundation, you need to get comfortable with being uncomfortable. Once the team has seen the right way to do things, coaches and leaders should ensure that they practice it so often that the uncomfortable becomes muscle memory, to be done without thinking. The team now knows that the fundamental is the right way to do things.

Often, we see teams and individuals going through the motions and having moderate success. Just as often, when we look closely, we see that corners are cut and the attention to detail is not there. A return to the basics and fundamentals is also about the precision and discipline to do something the right way - the first time.

Attention to detail and discipline were fundamental coaching and leading skills I garnered from my military service. But I had never seen them so vividly applied by a coach as I did while studying a martial art. I have two wonderful sons, Mathew and Ryan. While we were stationed in Winnipeg, both boys started taking tae kwon do. After their classes, I saw adults commence training in the Korean martial art of hapkido. All of this was done under the tutelage of Grand Master Park. I decided that hapkido was something I wished to study. A year or so later, while I was trying to learn the intricacies of a wrist grab, Grand Master Park tapped me on the shoulder, waving his finger at me, and proceeded to point at my feet.

Master Park showed me how to adjust my balance, changing my posture just slightly. The ensuing reaction from the guy whose wrist I was holding indicated an immediate shot of pain up his arm. I was focused on my hands and arms, but Park, a true Grand Master, focused on how the fundamentals of balance, body position, and posture wove together to achieve the desired effect.

Mastery of the basics, the fundamentals, will open the door to allow for in-depth applicability to complex systems. In basketball, if the "basic" is the screen, then the complex system is the "flex" offence. In helicopter flying, if the "basic" is hovering on night vision goggles, then the complex system is a night air assault onto an enemy position under fire. The basic concept of the screen or hovering teaches a foundational building block and allows the individual or team to understand how to deal with the myriad of situations that could develop at that primary level. If these basic concepts are not understood, then the jump to combining multiple "basics" together in a dynamic situation cannot be truly understood, only mirrored. Effective leaders and coaches will enhance the IQ of the team at the fundamental level, demonstrating how these basics can be combined to achieve success.

In this section, "Fundamentals," all the chapters discuss skills and concepts that I believe are at the core of coaching and leading. As a coach and leader, whether you are new in the role or seasoned, you will be able to see the baseline of what you need to be successful in your role. These core truths represent a standard to be adhered to. When leaders and coaches drift from this standard, it leads to systemic problems within organizations. Even those organizations that have great values and focus cannot thrive nor allow their people to develop to their potential without their leaders and coaches ascribing to these fundamentals. The chapters themselves will provide theoretic overviews of the concepts and skills along with practical examples and pragmatic aide-mémoires.

CHAPTER 2

Trust

Team members need to trust that a leader or coach knows what they are talking about, can develop them in the right ways, has their best interests at heart, and, finally, will enable their personal success alongside that of the team. If these standards aren't met, team members will feel disconnected from the team and the organization. They will do their jobs but nothing more. And, more importantly, they will not feel valued, and their own health may suffer.

The starting point for developing trust is remembering that coaching and leading are *emotional trust relationships.* This means that when establishing trust, it needs to resonate emotionally, and, as with all relationships, it is a two-way street. In the military, the trust between leader and subordinate is on a visceral and basic level: "I am placing my life in your hands." Military leaders who forget the nature of this relationship can get lost in the bureaucracies and theories of management and business-style leadership.

You might be leading a team at work but find that the goals and purpose of the organization resonate with just a very small percentage of that team. When I was a young officer, I thought that I had to self-motivate and that anyone else who didn't have that same drive was just not seeing clearly. I obviously had a lot to learn. But I had the benefit of a couple of key mentors who took the time outside of their purely leadership-based roles to coach me about my own journey to leading. I wish I had recognized what this coaching was doing for me at the time. When the team and the individual are coached, the focus shifts from tasks to individuals' personal improvement. This is more personal and can create that "why," that purpose, that drive, that shows those individuals that this task may only be the first in a long series of steps on the road to their own growth. For leaders and coaches, seeing the path, or road, from the perspective of those being coached or led, and how it serves their personal growth while achieving organizational goals…that is powerful. Coaches and leaders who invest like this in the development of their teams will create trust. Trust is the emotional glue that binds "People" and "Mission" together.

Wait a minute. Did I just blur the lines between leading and coaching?! Yup, that is what I see when I reread the previous paragraph. I think that in many instances we need to approach team interaction through different lenses or roles. When we're at work, we are leading a team, but we are coaching (or mentoring) an individual to maximize their potential. Both develop trust. Both are relationships. And they can exist together. The leader provides direction, vision, and the organizational tools needed to succeed. Leaders are also required to provide that inspiration. This is where we can cross over to being coaches. Many jobs, tasks, or projects are lacklustre to individuals and teams. By coaching the individuals and showing how they can personally excel through the accomplishment of team goals, the leader is providing that emotional inspirational element of "purpose" at the individual level.

When I was stationed in Alaska as the deputy commander of the Alaskan NORAD Region, my boss was General Tom Bussiere. He is, in my opinion, a great and compassionate leader. Tom knew within a short time of his arrival in Alaska that the NORAD mission did not resonate with the large team we had spread out across the vast state.[7] So he embarked upon a series of town halls, informal gatherings, across our enterprise to speak personally to every single soldier, sailor, aviator, civilian, and marine within his command. What blew me away—besides his determination to reach everyone personally—was the manner in which he articulated his vision.

Each time he spoke with an audience, he asked everyone who was a leader, even if they only supervised a single person, to raise their hand. Now, the military is a very hierarchical institution. Almost everyone at each town hall was supervising someone in some way. Tom placed the responsibility of explaining the NORAD mission to subordinates on each and every leader. He explained our region's leadership role in the mission as that of the front line in defending North America. He insisted that each leader be able to explain in detail how their subordinates' specific daily tasks related to the accomplishment of that mission. He stayed in each room for hours answering any questions relating to this shared responsibility. For those not familiar, it can be a struggle to understand the link between the work of a military or civilian clerk in an office in Fairbanks, Alaska, and that of a fighter jet on the tail of a Russian bomber over the Arctic Ocean a thousand or so miles away. Tom pledged to each audience that, if they struggled with making the link, they could call him and he would help them out. "This is a sacred trust," he explained. "Leading is not a right, it is a privilege, and this explanation is your duty as leaders."

What Tom was doing was more than establishing a connection between the team members and the mission, which we will talk about in a little bit. He was tying in their leadership and the privilege of leading, not merely to the specific task that they were doing, but to the systemic product of the team. By painstakingly ensuring that all levels of leadership within the organization could explain to their teams the "why" behind the tasks, he

---

7   If you layered Alaska over the rest of the USA, it would stretch from Texas to Minnesota and from California to Florida. Texas is currently the second largest U.S. state. If you cut Alaska in half, Texas would become the third largest state.

was placing them in a coaching position. He was connecting how they performed in their jobs to the most important mission possible, the survival of our countries. He inspired them not only with his commitment to the mission, but, more importantly, with his commitment to each and every leader in the organization. By highlighting each leader's role in leading and coaching their teams, he laid a foundation of trust.

I wish I had better understood the value of trust during much of my military career and my coaching experience in basketball. In all my formal leadership training in the military, trust had never been broached as a topic. In all my coaching classes and experience, trust had never been a subject of discussion. To make matters worse, I didn't realize until much later in my career how important trust was. I didn't reflect on it.

This last part is key and applies to trust, but also to almost everything else in leading and coaching. It is one thing to acknowledge that something is important or even essential. It is something else to reflect on that and internalize its importance. It is not that I was resistant to the concept of trust. It was just not something we discussed. The concept of trust was pervasive across every team I was a part of. How much did I trust the other pilots I was flying with? Their judgment and their skills? Were they writing cheques their skills could not cash? What about my senior leaders? Did I trust them with risky decisions where our lives were at stake? Questions of trust can be elephants in any room that, when not openly discussed—or, for coaches or leaders, personally reflected upon—will leave a glaring gap in the relationship with your team, ultimately undermining your role. Whether you are a newer leader or coach or a more experienced one, my advice is to start with trust development as *the* fundamental to pay attention to. I didn't, and I was worse off because of that.

How do we begin to develop trust as coaches? Charles Feltman's *The Thin Book of Trust* outlines four distinctions of trust: care, sincerity, reliability, and competence.[8] I like this breakdown. When I was coaching youth basketball, I thought that the best starting point was competence. I believed that I needed to establish my knowledge of the game, especially the fundamentals involved, and make sure that my players trusted my knowledge. As I look back, I now know I could not have been more wrong. When I was coaching my oldest son's first team (11-to-13-year-olds), we went to our first tournament and got our behinds handed to us, despite months of practice. Although the boys had good fundamentals, their inexperience—and my lack of an organized offence—meant we looked like kindergartners. But the boys just knuckled down, we introduced an organized offence, and the team got better. What I had inadvertently done is start with care, sincerity, and reliability instead of competence; I just hadn't realized it. Looking back, the other coaches might have been more competent, but when I watched them yell, criticize, and remove players from the floor for mistakes, I knew I didn't want to be "that guy." Making mistakes was the perfect opportunity for my players to learn. They wouldn't get better by sitting on the bench, but by rising to the occasion. When I coached through the mistakes, offered advice, and demonstrated my belief in my team, they became better people and, very often, better players. Care, sincerity, and reliability were more important to the development of the players than competence was. (Later, I did have to study to get better at coaching the specifics of basketball…but that's another story.)

In the military, I always thought that leader competence was much tougher to downplay. There is a baseline of competence (flying, tactics, mission planning) that is expected to underscore trust in one's leader, and that is what subordinates count on when their lives are on the line. It is the price of admission to leading, the "ticket to the dance." In other words, without that baseline competence, the rest seems superfluous. But when I compare this requirement of competence in the military context against Mr.

---

8   Charles Feltman, *The Thin Book of Trust: An Essential Primer for Building Trust at Work* (Bend, Oregon: Thin Book Publishing Company, 2008).

Feltman's breakdown of trust into four distinctions, my black-and-white competency requirement seems blurred. In other words, I do not think that task-oriented competency, although expected, is enough to inspire people to follow you in combat. There is a linkage between a leader's competence in achieving a task and the reliability that they demonstrate in executing that task now and in the future. More importantly, there is a moral component to that reliability. For me personally, not only was I trusted because I had demonstrated task-based competency, but my bond with subordinates was that I would employ that skill to their best interest no matter what. The more I led teams, the more my word meant in executing that which I had the competence to do, and therefore the more I was trusted.

The paradox between that crucial competence and the other distinctions of trust still exists, however. I have worked for and with many individuals who were "nice people." But they were not experts at their jobs, and the cost, or potential cost, in terms of lives and security would fundamentally compromise the essence of trust. Conversely, I have served with a great many leaders who had extraordinary technical competency, flying, or tactics, but I would not trust them to lead or manage a group of people outside of their area of expertise. I struggle to this day with how to lead and coach people who do not possess the right balance of distinctions. What I have come to realize is that there is a minimum baseline of competence that is required to develop enough *credibility* with subordinates that they will trust you. That *credibility* is the key to engendering the trust required to coach or lead. But in business and in many normal leader or coach relationships, do we not ignore most of these distinctions and trust people within the confines of their specific responsibilities? Are not most of our relationships competence-based ones? I trust the grocery store clerk to ring through my groceries, but that is where that trust ends. I hate my boss, but I trust them to pay me for the hours I spent clocked in…but that trust only goes so far, and I would not trust them with my savings or my life. *Aha!*

Is trust an "all-or-nothing" thing?

In order to begin to lay that foundation of trust, we need to deal with the perception that trust is a binary thing. Consider the following: Is whether or not you trust someone a yes or no question for you–you either trust them or you don't–or do you trust different people to different degrees? When I ask those whom I am coaching or mentoring, most people respond that trust is indeed an all-or-nothing thing for them. But when I begin to break it down for them, it seems that they have not thought through the idea of degrees of trust, some of which they are given no choice about. For example, if you don't trust your boss, then you cannot trust anything at all about that individual, including their guidance on how to accomplish a task. This environment will inevitably impact your performance and may force you to leave the team. The reality is that you have no choice but to trust an individual in certain areas unless you are willing to suffer the consequences of acting on your notions of all-or-nothing trust. There are people who deliver highly technical and competent performances but who we know would stab us in the back for their own personal benefit if given the opportunity. They have no "care" for the team or the people around them, and, therefore, we will place limits on our trust for them, but there still remains a *residue* of trust. My experience in coaching teams has made me realize that, once we lift the thin veneer of all-or-nothing trust, people are much more open to the realities of the various distinctions of trust. Seeing trust as more complex than all or nothing, and having various components or distinctions, is also a very beneficial perspective through which to discuss this essential element of leading and coaching as they pertain to trust, thereby allowing for a very frank conversation about our team and the culture in the workplace.

Here is a good hack. At an upcoming meeting, ask your team, "Is trust all or nothing?" Ask some leading and probing questions about yourself as a leader and coach. "Do you trust the guidance and direction I give you?" "Do you think I would undermine your personal performance to get ahead or blame a mistake I made on you or the team?" "If you made a mistake or had a breakthrough idea, do you trust me enough to confide in me about it?" "If individual needs are going to be compromised by organizational performance goals, can I be trusted to have a frank and honest conversation with you about that?" Be ready to listen, take notes, and ask more probing questions. I suspect the feedback you get will be focused on specific examples that you will need to address. Do *not* defend right away but listen (more to follow on listening). This simple process will begin laying the foundation of trust.

When coaching sports, the trust a coach places on a player during execution is implicit since the coach cannot be on the court. The tools that the coach has at their disposal to shape and hone behaviour to maximize the performance of the individuals is finite. Once the players are on the field of play, they are in control. As a seasoned aircraft commander or as an instructor pilot, crawling into an aircraft beside a co-pilot is always putting your life in their hands. During many flights as an aircraft commander, I never touched the controls. And if I did, it was just for a moment. These co-pilots needed the experience, and they were only going to get it if they actually flew. So, *fly!* But there is an inherent trust there. Not just in the individual, which one cannot understate, but also in the instructors and schoolhouses that brought that individual to that point.

That systemic trust is endemic in every military organization. I trust the technicians to do their work and ensure the aircraft are airworthy. I trust the system that qualifies them and sustains their technical certifications. I trust the leadership to ensure they, and the other members of the crew, are not too tired to complete their missions. I trust the flight safety system of zero blame that creates a culture of reporting that highlights all incidents and issues so that they can be discussed without fear of repercussions from the chain of command. Finally, I trust the individuals themselves for their professionalism and dedication to ensuring that they are rested, are not distracted, and have read the most up-to-date information/intelligence/

bulletin and that, if they are not ready to fly, they have the moral courage to say something.

Flying 15 feet above the ground, travelling about 100 miles per hour, is no time for anything to go wrong. In reality, things *will* go wrong. But the best way to make sure your training and procedures work is to set yourself up for success in every instance. In this way, the odds are on your side. Survival in this environment—and we have not even mentioned how the enemy will negatively influence survival—will depend on trust.

Coaches and leaders need to trust the training and associated institutions to produce quality individuals capable of executing the tasks at hand. This is key to trusting the individuals working for them. In addition, all coaches and leaders, military or otherwise, must realise that they are in the second row. It is the team members that are executing the various functions directly. Many leaders and coaches must rely exclusively on members of their teams to affect the execution of their missions. And the higher up the hierarchy they go, the more removed they are from those moments of direct influence on the mission. Instead, all the real influence that coaches and leaders have is in setting the conditions for that success. This is where the hard work is. Laying out a vision, explaining it deeply, breaking down its various aspects, drilling and practising those distinct elements, preparing each person within the team for their individual role, setting the behavioural, organizational, and bureaucratic rules so that the focus can be on the mission, and always guiding and correcting while challenging and expanding horizons. Am I talking about coaching or leading? *Yes.*

In 2016, when I was promoted to brigadier general, the vice chief of defence staff and my personal mentor, Lieutenant General Alain Parent, saw the importance of the concept of trust and created a program to expose the general officer corps of the Canadian Armed Forces to the nuances of trust. He started by getting us all copies of *The Speed of Trust* by Stephen M.R.

Covey.[9] This book was my first real exposure to trust as a facet of leading. I read it…and I was hooked. For the first time, I was reflecting on the concept of trust. Internalizing its importance. I saw myself as developing trust in some of the areas discussed, but in others, in my personal life and professional life, I was failing. I had drifted from my core values and was retreating behind platitudes and processes. I was not authentic. By this I mean that in some areas of my life, I was not acting in accordance with my true values.

Many of us in highly demanding jobs drift from the value of following through on what we promise to our families. We use our jobs to excuse missing things, not getting things done, or being late or not home when we said we would be. Personally, I had drifted from the value of my word. I would let the constant excuse of overwhelming work mean that I did not have to be authentic and straightforward. This allowed me to avoid difficult conversations or to merely deflect blame when confronted. I decided I needed to change. If I was going to be late, or if I had to change things, I would stop and acknowledge the consequences this would have on my personal life. This meant that, in many cases, I would accept the professional consequence of going home before the work was completed. I would also open up difficult conversations about timing with Val. I was fearful because I never wanted to disappoint her. In reality, when I was more open, she was able to help me resolve many of my dilemmas from a loving and supportive place, often providing solutions that my previous entrenchment or ignorance had not let me see. She could trust that if I said I was going to be somewhere at a certain time, I was there.

Next, I embarked upon a path of defaulting to trusting everyone at 100%; instead of making them earn my trust, they received it automatically and could only lose it. I made this part of my introduction to my teams from

9   Stephen M.R. Covey, *The Speed of Trust: The One That Changes Everything* with Rebecca R. Merrill (New York, New York: The Free Press, 2006).

then on. This was a crucial change and competed with my innate beliefs about proving trust via competence. Instead, I accepted people for their skills and got to know their strengths and weaknesses, but would always trust them. This directly led to people in my teams openly letting me know when they didn't know if they could do something or were overwhelmed by their jobs or even my direction. I trusted them, so now they trusted me with their vulnerabilities. We could have open and honest conversations surrounding what was feasible and what was not.

Knowing that trust is not binary, and thereafter exploring the various elements of trust, made me look back on other times in my career when I had trusted people in the performance of their duties, but always questioned whether I would trust them with non-work-related issues. Horrible people have led awesome teams in combat. The competence element of trust can only take you so far. I had experienced first-hand innumerable people, ones who I would not follow out of curiosity, placed in charge of organizations that they could not even fathom how to wield. In the profession of arms, a lack of competence results in the direst of consequences. The various components of trust included competence but were not limited nor defined by it. In the latter portions of my career, once I had reflected more about trust, I began to see the components of it everywhere. I found myself using it as a benchmark for assessing leaders, climate and culture, and morale. As a fundamental of leadership and coaching, trust could not be more pervasive.

My oldest son, Mathew, when working in his first job out of university, operated using "certainty" as his barometer for checking with his bosses on an issue. If he was uncertain as to a policy or approach, he would ask. However, if he was certain, then he believed that he was empowered to merely execute. Having been exposed to the military and military leadership growing up and while working in the Canadian Parliament, Mathew also had insight into why military hierarchical concepts of command and control do not work very well outside of combat. In the military, the approval process for just about anything—even just what form is to be used to gain approval—is highly refined. In contrast, in many other workplaces, this process is very loose, if it is even codified at all. Hence the idea around "certainty." The looseness or latitude that this provides leads to the development of judgment by the team members. That judgment leads to the development of trust between the team and their leader or coach. As team members, you trust that your bosses have your back just as you have their best interests at heart. They, in turn, trust in you because the judgment you are demonstrating enables a level of agility and performance without intimate oversight that directly benefits the mission and the team.

Another hack: in a meeting, ask the following questions: "Do you feel you have the authority to be able to take action when you are certain doing so is in the best interest of the organization?" "What are the approval processes that are preventing or slowing you and the team down from doing the work that needs to get done?" "Do you feel that you are professionally trusted to do your job and make decisions?"

We have spoken a bunch about trust and competence and have broken down trust to being more nuanced than merely yes or no. All this to establish trust between us, as leaders and coaches, and our teams. But is that trust not a two-way street? Using Charles Feltman's distinctions of trust again, I believe that the two-way street of trust gets significantly undermined by a lack of reliability. Reliability is about being able to count on someone to deliver on what they promise. I also believe that the antidote to this pervasive lack of reliability is accountability. Accountability from an individual and team to its leader or coach is foundational to trust. I think that leaders and coaches who establish trust through sincerity and care for their teams and the individuals that comprise them have only taken trust so far. To me, it is obvious that every team is going to hold leaders and coaches accountable for their overall performance and for their specific actions supporting the team. This is a good dynamic. We speak often about how performance goals often dominate discussions with leaders and coaches to the detriment of the team and the leader/coach-team dynamic. But we don't often speak about how to execute that accountability and why doing it well is essential to trust. The simplicity here is key.

"This is your job/role/position. The requirements of holding this job/role/position are 'X.' You have not done this. Why?" The ability to correct errors is directly linked to accountability. If errors are not corrected, if they are left to fester, they will undermine not only the performance of the team, but the trust that the team has in the leader to manage the team and move it toward its goals. Leaders who do not get held accountable for their actions cannot maintain credibility when holding subordinates or team members accountable. Coaches need this level of accountability from their players while holding themselves to a similar standard. If the standard is to come to practice mentally and physically prepared to focus and to work hard, then coaches as well as players must be held to this standard. Organizations, specifically the leaders and coaches at the head of organizations, that are going to learn from the inevitable mistakes that they make need to be accountable for change. This is a commitment to constantly improving, not just for production outputs, but for the benefit of the people in the team. Individuals and teams that are held accountable for improvement will truly learn from their errors.

The issue here will be the level of consequences for mistakes and *how* you as a coach and leader conduct yourself with tact, tone, and understanding. I wish I made this connection as a young leader. I was a rather loud "in your face" or "overenthusiastic" leader. Even as I toned down with age (no, really—I did), I valued frankness and directness over tact and empathy. My personal energy and desire to be the best I could be were also often misinterpreted as anger or frustration.

Funny enough, it was my role on the basketball court that made me think about this more deeply. A mistake on a basketball court should result in a player being given extra drills to correct the error, not being benched for the remainder of the season. However, a mistake in combat that leads to a loss of life may result in a court martial rather than a mere administrative warning. Care needs to be taken. If individuals or teams feel that there are significant institutional or personal consequences for mistakes, then they will be less likely to buy in at a personal level and put themselves out there for the team or leader. They will not take risks; they will be driven uniquely by the specific direction or tasks that are given to them. Most importantly—and, potentially, most dangerously—they will not highlight errors for fear of repercussions. On the opposite end of the scale, organizations, leaders, coaches, and teams that do not have adequate consequences for errors will not have due regard for standards, safety, authority, and even the mission. Both undermine the fundamental of trust.

In coaching, we want individuals and teams to improve. There is a symbiotic relationship between individuals and their teams. If an individual develops and is more effective, this translates to the team improving. The individual's enhanced skills can not only increase their own output but can translate to better overall performance by others. Players who hone better skills inspire others to do the same, but also enable others. By seeing how another player gets open to receive a pass, I become a better pass-maker. Similarly, if the entire team begins to perform at a higher level by developing team communication or enhanced operating procedures, this inspires individuals to develop themselves. However, if individual errors are punished with more time sitting on the bench, then players will not commit to putting themselves out there and will only be second-guessing when they will be punished for their errors. This applies to team dynamics as well since reduced playing time and errors will be seen as uniquely negative unless coaches frame them as learning experiences and tailor the consequences to be positive.

Don't get me wrong, there need to be consequences for mistakes. This is how we learn as humans. But they need not be soul- nor inspiration-crushing. In fact, mistakes should be used to draw teams together and help them unite behind the "improve" banner. Instead of removing someone from the task (or the court), explore the ability to pair them with someone who is doing the task well and direct additional practice to improve. Supervise and follow up to ensure improvement. Provide personal insights and techniques if you have access to them. Use other members of the team to support and assist while making it clear that improvement needs to happen.

In leading, if the team or individuals feel like the institution or the leader (or both) will only punish them for not conforming to specific direction or trying to achieve the mission in a better way, then they will stick to the specific task they have been handed and do their best within the specific work, human resource, administrative, and logistic constraints that were handed to them. If the team fails, it's not their fault; they were just doing as they were told. Trust is non-existent.

How do you develop that trust through accountability? Leaders and coaches must set intentions formally, correct errors with tact and empathy, and, finally, challenge teams to learn while rewarding those that take the extra time to figure out a better way to make the team more effective in achieving desired goals. Identify those who apply their individual skills diligently, even if they fail multiple times, all while trying to improve. Make sure that these individuals are heavily incentivised to continue to improve. Ask yourself how much you would sacrifice current production, mission accomplishment, or games won now if it meant that you would have the best, highest-performing team next year. Now go out and incentivise that! Hold the team accountable for the things that will get those results. Hold individuals accountable for their words, actions, and behaviours, but do so in a way that will engender mutual trust between you as the coach or leader and individuals as solid members of the team. This is the trust distinction of sincerity.

Accountability requires standards and reporting frameworks that everyone is aware of. A reporting framework is a system of feedback on a recurring timeline that is programmed to see output as compared to the goals, objectives, and vision of the team or organization. These frameworks cannot be just words. They need to have specific deliverables and timelines. Review of the deliverables needs to be done on a specific routine and discussed with individuals and the team. Excellent organizations will review their accountability frameworks to tweak the deliverables and ensure their alignment with the core values and organization's vision. At an organizational level, this framework would look like a monthly or quarterly wrap-up of what was accomplished compared to the objectives that were set for that performance or output. But, more importantly, how do these outputs compare to the core values of the organization? This is where I think leaders and coaches struggle the most with trust. What are your core values? Do they include player development? Or character development? Winning? Or do they include preparing players to compete at a higher level? What are your team's core values? How about your company values? Is the bottom line of the organization dollar-driven? Is it not fair then that the employees within the organization will see their personal value through the exact same lens, dollars earned? The more time I spent thinking and working through the core values of the organizations I was a part of, the more decisions and direction became very clear to me. Spend time thinking about the core values and results that link your own team and their performance. Spend even more time talking and listening to the team on this subject. But once these values are clear, do not stop there.

Performance or accountability frameworks need to drive down to the individual level as well. Here, I tend to disagree with some contemporary HR logic that states that performance reviews are not effective. I think they are an essential part of the accountability framework. But they cannot be one-sided. The beginning of each performance review should be spent setting individual goals in collaboration with the team member. Those goals must involve personal and professional development in addition to performance goals. This is a linked discussion. On numerous occasions, I have set objectives for personal or professional development that were clearly going to impact an individual's productivity in the short term. Recognizing this formally is about entrenching the importance of the individual's development as part of the team and is foundational to the accountability underlying trust.

Holding individuals and teams accountable for their specific outputs and effort is similar in leading and coaching. In coaching sports, I have noticed that the emphasis of the coach shrinks back to the individual and their personal development. The amount of time spent in the gym, the number of shots that get put up, and the player's skills in footwork, shooting, passing, and defending are what are considered important. But the reality is that this measure of things done only goes so far, whether in sports, business, or life. Teams need to be held accountable not merely for the work that they are doing but for the effect that they are achieving with that work. It is not good enough to measure how many games have been played, how many points have been scored, how many Russian aircraft have been intercepted, how many flying hours have been clocked, or how many exercises have been executed. These things are indeed important, but a true measure of accountability is to compare these performance-related items against what desired effect is being achieved by this performance. Within the NORAD enterprise, the focus of our accountability could not be solely on alerts conducted, but rather on how well we were deterring our adversaries, advancing the strategic framework for procurement within both nations, and even maintaining security within the continent. Timelines, deadlines, strategies, and feedback mechanisms abound in this arena. Our people, and the trust we have with them (and they with us as leaders and coaches), can get lost in this heady space.

In sports, the overall effect—wins, losses, performance relative to other teams—is important, but is perhaps only one barometer against which individual effort is measured, rather than the focus. Whether that translates into victory on the field of competition, well, that is another matter. As a coach, deciding on exactly what it is you truly value (skills, character, integrity, camaraderie…) will shape everything else you do. The fact that I never coached a super winning team nor had the pressure of professional sport on me might be biasing my opinion here, but stick with me. I always used to tell the boys, "Right time, right place, doing the right things. If the ball goes in the hoop, that is a bonus." My thought process was always that if they applied themselves to those fundamentals, then the actual "winning" was the work ethic, love of the sport, basketball IQ, personal character building, and camaraderie that game success only accentuates. The score was never a measure of winning to me, but effort sure was. This clarity made it easy to create emotional relationships with those I was coaching, relationships where we held each other accountable and trusted each other deeply. Team to coach, player to coach.

Wow, there is a lot linked to trust! So much that I never considered. Even if trust being so important seems self-evident when revealed to us, we are not actively aware of it at any moment while leading and coaching. Looking back on our experiences with other leaders and coaches is beneficial in framing our ideas of trust. As developing coaches and leaders, we must look back on our own behaviours and ask ourselves how specific events, things we said, and interactions we had either created or broke emotional trust relationships. Lastly—and this is something I never did until later in my career—take some time to acknowledge and reflect on the events in crisis where trust was implicit. Then ask yourself, "What were the 101 things that were done and said leading up to that event that laid the foundation of trust?" I have issued many orders for people going into harm's way. Laying the foundation of trust is essential for success in those moments.

Trust is fundamental to coaching and leading. There are very common threads that weave throughout the distinctions of trust that enable both coaching and leading. Although at an organizational level at work I led by inspiring the team to achieve lofty and somewhat elusive objectives for national security, at an individual level I always worked to understand the people and their contributions. I knew who was working late and putting in the effort. I knew what it took to be in these staff positions with the pressure of performing and producing on the ethereal goals that general officers pontificate upon. So, when I was at their level one on one, we would have much the same conversation as we would have if I was coaching. (In fact, I think I *was* coaching). "Look at what you have accomplished. Look at the work you have put into this! Look at how far we have brought the team in such a short time! Look how your work and your words are directly influencing the key decision-makers in both countries. Things may or may not change. Our job is to make sure that the key decision makers have the right information and are poised to make the best decisions." Highlighting these things, giving honest and individualized feedback by coaching each individual, is reaffirming of the sincerity, care, competence, and reliability that the individual places in the leader. It paves the two-way street of trust.

CHAPTER 3

Vision

Why is my team disconnected and unmotivated?

Why is our workplace culture oriented around doing the bare minimum and then going home?

Is there an inherent link between a team's purpose and an individual's purpose or inspiration?

There can be many answers to these questions, but leaders and coaches sit at the cornerstone of all the solutions. The creation of a vision for any organization is the centre pillar to providing it with purpose. Vision exposes the essential nature of the mission. It is "start with why," it is "find your purpose," but most of all it is what forms the connection between the individual, the team, and what they are to accomplish. It is the seed for inspiration.

Up until the very end of my career, I always believed that I was horrible at visioning. As a leader in the military, I always had the benefit of senior leaders who had a vision of where we were going. In my mind, I never needed to make anything up.[10] I just adopted my boss's vision, made sure

---

10 That said, when I led the air component to the joint force in Haiti after the earthquake in 2010, I had a T-shirt I would wear with my PT gear that said, "I Make Stuff Up." My chief warrant officer kept telling me that I couldn't wear it because it panicked the troops!

that it was translated into what my teams needed, and executed like my life depended on it. In coaching basketball, I was never self-aware enough to know that the vision I created for the teams I coached was embedded in the manner in which I was coaching. My vision was to create young men (I almost exclusively coached boys' basketball) who loved the game and were given an opportunity to learn life lessons that made them better friends, family members, and citizens. But I never came out and said that!

In 2002, as a young major, I had a relationship with my boss at the time, then-Lieutenant Colonel Alain Parent, that would end up being life-changing. He became one of my closest mentors and a personal friend. He was designated as the incoming commanding officer to our tactical helicopter schoolhouse in Gagetown. I was also due to be posted that summer. He told me he was bringing me with him to his command as one of his subordinates in the role of the unit operations officer. I was flattered. Then, a few short weeks later, he showed me his vision for the squadron, how he was going to lay that vision out to the team, and how it connected within the larger workings of the Air Force. What struck me first was not my role within this vision and how I could further it, but rather that he had created this vision, while I felt I had *none* of the inherent creativity, perspective, or sheer talent it would take to create similar visions of my own. What followed that was a lifelong quest to seek out the best ideas from those who were better at creating "visions," taking the best of what they had to offer and discarding that which did not seem right to me.[11]

Over time, I kept getting sent into new roles and jobs where I had to shape teams and inspire them to achieve very lofty goals. What I found was that when I was able to get right down to their level and explain things to them, when our organization's vision resonated throughout the various

---

11   I would sometimes use the word "plagiarize," though not in the pure academic context (and this is not an admission of any academic misconduct!). Instead, I knew that a deep study of what worked and what did not, from lessons learned, podcasts, military history, and analysing leaders I worked with, would be the best way for me to fill the void in my creativity that I felt I was lacking.

teams, we had success. Where I could not articulate and translate that vision, we struggled. And I do mean "we," myself and the team. This is the
inherent link between vision and connection.

Creating a good vision for a team is not as simple, nor perhaps as complicated, as one might think. I return here to my basketball roots. Here is a
drill. It may feel uncomfortable. Just do it until it becomes muscle memory.
Perhaps do it by yourself or as part of your team. As a fundamental, let's
break it down and walk through how to create a vision.

1. What do you need to accomplish? What specific tasks have been
   assigned to you and your team? What tasks are implied in the
   accomplishment of those assigned tasks? Write them down. Now
   stop and think. Deduce or draw out the core or essential tasks (one
   to three) from both above lists and think about them in priority.
   To help, ask the question, "If all else fails, what must be done no
   matter what?"

2. What is your boss's intent? No, this isn't asking what tasks you
   were assigned, but the intent—what do they seek to accomplish?
   Where was your boss going by assigning these tasks? What is your
   boss's boss's intent, or the organization's intent, and how does that
   intent relate to the tasks you have been assigned? How can you
   incorporate these more ethereal ideas into the accomplishment of
   your tasks? This is about the vision first. Don't let the "how" creep
   in until the vision is complete.

3. How do the people you are working with/coaching relate to the
   tasks, the organization, and the overarching intents above? How
   can you organize, plan, and articulate the accomplishment of your
   tasks in a way that lets them all see themselves as part of not merely
   the tasks, but the organization's intent? (This is a great space for
   collaboration.)

4. Now for the "how." Break down the job/tasks. Start with the

"end state" and work backward. What do the tasks look like pragmatically? Daily, weekly, monthly, yearly. How do the various pieces relate to each other? How does the organization look at the end once the mission is accomplished? Can you envision how this gets laid out or what it will take to get there? Are there options?

5. How can you ensure that this vision is captured, professed, bought into, supported, adjusted, and sustained? How do you weave it into the culture of your team? What daily/routine practice, beyond the accomplishment of the mission, can you use to reinforce that vision and have the team take it on?

When I was that young major, I had thought (wrongly) that I lacked the creativity to be able to have a vision. What I don't think I understood was that creativity is not only intuitive bolts of lightning. Much creativity is about putting in long hours of practice and study to hone and have a base from which to be creative. I always felt that with my dedication and devotion to serving, enabled by a strong work ethic, I could accomplish just about anything (thanks, Mom and Dad). So, I put in the hard work. Here is how I approached developing my skills at visioning:

1. Who is a leader in your field/organization/arena right now? What approaches, tips, and tools are they using that resonate with you? Use them. Contrarily, who is underperforming, not leading, or failing in the same areas? What things do you need to avoid following in their missteps, and how would you fix or approach things differently?

2. Break down the things you have to do. Look at each of the component parts, understand each one, and understand how they fit together. Analyze how others in related fields approach these broken-down tasks.

3. Stop thinking about the entire enchilada. Make a plan. Know the overall timelines. Prioritize hard. Then do the first thing that needs

to get done. Head down. "Get 'er done."

4. Treat your plan like a job. Because it is! Performance tracking and keeping things accountable to the team are the things that keep everyone authentic and reinforce trust.

5. Get ready for adversity.[12]

6. Develop a mantra that personifies your leadership within this vision.

> ◗ **MANTRA:** When I took command of an air wing of the RCAF, I knew that I needed a mantra that personified what was most important to me: preparing the people of the wing for combat. My mantra was simple:
>
> # FLY–SHOOT–SPEND
>
> **Fly:** When in doubt, fly more. Real capability would not be forged without a baseline of competence and skills that can only be achieved while in the aircraft.
>
> **Shoot:** Be lethal. Focus on the tactical skills that the Canadian Army and Special Operations Forces would need to enable their mission in combat.
>
> **Spend:** Do not allow our people to be limited by the bureaucratic constraints of our military institution. The staff must fight those battles so that the only true limitations for our people are their imagination and their own physical capacities.

7. Who will you lean on? What is your circle of inner support? Who do you confer with personally and professionally as this gets hard (friends, family, key co-workers, mentors, coaches, leaders)?

Setting a vision as a leader within a military or civilian organization is not

---

12 Brené Brown's work on "effing first times" (FFTs) assisted me greatly in preparing for and recognizing them when they come up! Her work highlights needing to recognise when you are dealing with something for the first time and the emotional and logical false expectations you will set for yourself at those times.

the same as setting a vision when coaching… or is it? I learned just as much about setting a vision from being a coach of my sons' teams.

My last year coaching my son Ryan's basketball team, I had been coaching them for several years, so I knew the young men and their parents well. It was a great bunch. The league had decided to create two teams for Ryan's age group because there was such an interest in playing, and my old assistant was coaching the other team.[13] At our first practice, I met the boys at the entrance to the gym and told them to stay there. I told (asked) the parents to go inside the gym. I then asked the boys a few questions. But the big one was "What are the things we want to accomplish this year?" It was a simple question, and once they started talking, they couldn't stop. Here are some of the things they came up with:

1. Be friends at the end of the year.

2. Be competitive in every game.

3. Beat the other team from our city.

4. Play together as a team.

5. Be good sportsmen.

6. Practise hard.

7. Give everybody an opportunity to play.

8. Still love the game at the end of the year.

I told Ryan to go warm up the team, and I spoke to the parents. I read them the list that the boys had made. I told them that I would tailor my coaching to that list. I highlighted that our only scoreboard-related goal was to beat the other team from our city.

---

13 Ryan still chafes at this decision to this day. "Finally, we had the talent to make a great team, and they decided to water down the talent by making two teams." Obviously, I still had some work to do in coaching him on why he was playing.

Flash forward a month or so, and we met the other team from our city in an exhibition game. But to our boys, this was the only game that counted. In my opinion, the other team had more raw talent, and they were positioned to beat us. But they didn't want the win like our boys did. And they were cocky. I also had a habit of coaching the boys on the bench more than the boys playing on the floor. This is because I wanted to involve everyone, and this approach significantly increased the players' game IQ. I would then use substitutions to adjust what was happening on the floor. Boys coming off the floor got personalized coaching from me at that moment. They got my direct attention. We talked about the adjustments that I was making, and I praised them for their play. Finally, I made it clear they were getting a quick rest but then they were going back in, so they needed to be ready. This allowed for everyone to learn—and to lead. The leadership came from the boys playing on the floor, as they were the ones getting players together and holding each other accountable.

Throughout the game, our smaller and under-matched players won little victory after little victory. Defence—true "be the help" focused, grit- and determination-driven defence"[14]—is a great foundation, and it is what I praised the most. It showed the deepest selflessness and character. The other team stuck to its top few players while I made sure everyone on our team played hard and had lots of minutes. This kept our floor and bench intensity high.

In the last five minutes of the game, we were behind, and the boys came to me during a time out and said "Coach, let's play our best players." Winning here was one of their objectives. It was a team decision. So, we put in our best, but it was not going to be enough. When we were down by one, with less than two minutes left, I made a substitution. We had a player who was an exceptional athlete, a goalie in competitive hockey. His dad wanted

---

14   In basketball, while playing man-to-man defence, if one player gets beaten, another will come off of their assigned player and "help" their teammate who has just gotten beat. This allows for a more aggressive defending of the offensive players and is the personification of team defence.

him to play more than one sport (hockey can be a bit all-consuming if you are Canadian), and this young man loved basketball. Moreover, many of his school friends were on our team. But this was his first year playing. He didn't have the same technical skills as many of the other players. Fitness-wise, however, he was the fastest and quickest on the team. I went to him and said, "I am putting you in." I grabbed my son Ryan and this young man, Joe,[15] and said, "Boys, we need the ball. Joe, forget everything about team defence. Get me the ball." The bench was electric! Ryan and Joe were like whirling dervishes on the court, double team, rushing from one side to the next. And the rest of the team had enough IQ and good communication to adjust to this style. I was very proud! And then an amazing thing happened: the other team coughed up the ball. Ryan had the ball with mere seconds left, and speedy Joe took off down the other end of the court. Ryan tossed him the long ball and the clock wound down. Joe laid up the ball and sank the winning basket. The buzzer went off and the bench went nuts! Joe was hoisted (kinda) on little shoulders (12- to 13-year-olds). The boys were gracious with the other team. But what I remember most was Joe's dad coming up to me at the end of the game and saying that Joe would never forget that day. In reality, none of us would.

This win stood out to me not only because it was the goal the team had set for themselves for that year, but because, for the rest of the year leading up to that point, in practices as well as in games, the team had never wavered on their other goals. Their focus on being competitive without worrying about score is what allowed them to care in the one moment that the score meant something to them. Their barometer for personal performance was not gauged against another team's prowess but rather against their own effort and determination. This allowed them to have a spirit of cohesiveness that clearly enabled them to rise to occasions that perhaps were beyond the mere sum of their athletic talent. Character, good solid character, is built

---

15   Name changed to protect the innocent.

on a foundation of solid values, a base from which structure and vision can grow.

I had seen too many win-focused teams, too many poorly led organizations. I wanted those young men to grow as people. Leading them to set their own vision allowed them to be accountable. It set boundaries for all of us: players, parents, and coach. We owned our triumphs and our failures. More than once, we had to remind ourselves collectively or individually that sportsmanship was independent of whether that quality is reciprocated in other teams, parents, or officials. Our approach to officiating was always "Show respect and put the ball in the hoop so much that it doesn't matter." The boys held each other accountable for effort, not for the score. "Right place, right time, doing all the right things." Whether the ball went in the basket…well…that was not quite so important.

This is what inspired the team. This was the vision in application.

At the end of the season, we held a party at one of the parents' houses. One parent had made books for each of the players, and for me, based upon the hundreds of photos he had taken throughout the year. I cherish that book to this day. But during this party, we parents watched those kids laugh and play and romp around. We all took great pride in having met the objective we all cherished most: they were friends at the end of the season.

Visioning is not only the purview of those at the top of large organizations. Each leader and coach can create visions that inspire their own teams to exceed their own thoughts of potential. I have even seen small directorate teams establish such great visions that entire organizations adopt them and expand on these awesome ideas and the related implementation practices. Disconnected teams? Ask them what inspires them and where they are lacking inspiration. Ask them where those voids are in their "why." Then establish a vision to fill those voids, whatever they are.

CHAPTER 4

Teaching = Leading = Coaching

We all have had that fantastic teacher or instructor, or maybe a slew of them, who inspired us to be who we are (or at least let us know that we could be more than who our peers made us feel like we were right then). They were leading us to a better version of ourselves. They were inspiring us to achieve. They were coaching us through the hard parts, knowing that we had great things inside of us all along. But *we* had to do the work. They couldn't do it for us.

Many of us also had fantastic coaches or leaders in youth sport or community programs. As they guided us through all those activities, they taught us key lessons about values, skills, behaviours, and, above all, ourselves.

Teaching is a human interaction. Therefore, it is bound by the same factors as all human relationships. Great teachers understand this and help you define what success means to you (they encourage you to try), allow you to learn from your mistakes (they create a safe space for you to face failure), and guide you in moving forward (they help you learn). In trusting these teachers, you can take the chances that allow your creative spirit to guide your learning. The focus of great teachers is on the relationship that enables that learning.

For coaches and leaders, my advice is to start with teaching the "why." Teach the "why" behind that which is being done. This can and should be done continuously. Next, never give up an opportunity to teach the lessons learned from your current organization or pertinent lessons from history. Finally, don't always focus on teaching that which did not work—also focus on examples of things working well. Always bring it back to the "why" for your team or organization. Teaching these things sets the foundation for true understanding.

A focus placed only on output will not allow the team, or individuals, to be able to see your vision through the "noise" of executing the task. I would often see this with inexperienced (or control freak) coaches in basketball. "You go here, you go here, pass this here, she shoots." And when you ask the players why? "Because coach said so." Ugh! Teach the "why": "Let's talk about creating space. Now read the options you might have, find opportunities like this, adjust like this, and remember these fundamentals at this point. Are we all understanding?" By encouraging learning, we also inspire and motivate.

In my military experience, we were always training. Most military training is building blocks designed to start at the smallest grouping (section, aircraft, vessel, etc.) and to place those organizations in ever-evolving, dynamic, and complex situations that replicate that which soldiers will face in combat. The situations they are put through are what teach them. Yes, there are observer-controllers that ensure they are doing things right, and the chain of command is always watching. But the beauty is that the good organizations recognize their own mistakes, correct them, and then repeat the training until it's right. I know that this is the premise behind adult learning, but we inherently lose sight of the fact that we are always teaching, even when we are in a situation where we personally must perform. Others learn from how we handle being corrected and adjusting our approach. Oftentimes I see leaders cease teaching and coaching when they themselves are being assessed. It's like the scrutiny they are under means that they should stick to strictly performance-related behaviours. In reality, we are always learning. Every single real-world crisis I was involved in as part of my service with NORAD became a teaching moment or a scenario that we would replicate for future team members at all levels to learn from. Indeed, after almost every real-world event, the most senior leaders would get on conference calls and discuss, critique, empathize, and support the decision-maker(s). The *best* leaders during real-world crisis events are still coaching their teams along. "Keep the information flowing. Be focused in your analysis. The priority right now, team, is…" Thereafter, they never miss an opportunity to teach by highlighting errors and applauding solid performance.

There is always a trade-off between teaching and time available. I was always going over every single meeting's allotted time. I always believed in explaining why, explaining how things came about, giving my teams insights from senior executive meetings where I was the only one from my team present, and making linkages to put the whole picture together. This is teaching. I know I bored a lot of folks, but everyone understood what they needed to get done and why. And if they were confused, they just needed to ask.

When I discuss the idea of taking this time with busy business executives or government and military leaders, the excuse I always hear is "I don't have time." Well, that is crap. If we knew that taking two minutes out of each meeting to have a teaching moment was going to guarantee a higher success rate, larger financial return, safer operation, or better chance of victory in an upcoming game, we would do it in a heartbeat. Those who put the time in to professionalize the people they are coaching or leading will build resilient and effective organizations that everyone wants to be a part of. They feel enabled and understood because they have internalized the purpose of what is being done and believe that by contributing to the mission, they make themselves better, and, by extension, their organizations get better as well. *Purpose* is a powerful thing and clearly justifies the time required to professionalize the team.

We give people purpose by teaching them. Doing so continuously creates a learning culture. Implementing a learning culture is about valuing that mistakes are recognized and people willingly own up to them so the team improves. Start creating a learning culture in the teams you are leading and coaching by demonstrating that you do not know everything and that you are at the forefront of trying to learn to improve. In the military, we always used to try to assess whether a unit or formation was a "learning organization." It was not only that they had the requisite tools and were going through the process of conducting After-Action Reviews (AARs) properly,[16] but, perhaps more importantly, that they truly got to the root of the issues and sought resolution, not by listing items on spreadsheets for future action but by truly making changes. This can only be driven by coaches and leaders.

Teaching has a domino effect. I always say that, as a coach or leader, you should "be trying to create people to replace you." You teach so that others can be better than you are. Through continuous teaching, we end up creating the leaders and coaches of the future—hopefully better than we could ever be. In so doing, we are pushing over the first domino. This is easy in the military context, as the endless hierarchical turnover and bottom-fed system mean that promotion and advancement are at the core of every leader's progression. But, as coaches, we need to be creating more coaches for the next generation, as opposed to focusing on building star athletes. When we continuously teach, we keep on setting up and knocking over dominos. Those dominos spread into a beautiful mosaic of coaches and leaders who teach purpose to their teams.

On a team, create leaders who know about concepts and can adjust with-

---

16 AARs are a tool used in the military to review the execution of a mission or task, exercise, or operation, or even the daily function of a unit or part of a staff. More on AARs in the chapter "Feedback Loops."

out detailed overwatch because they know your "why" (vision and intent). This is known in military spheres as mission command. At its core, it is teaching-focused.

CHAPTER 5

Self-Awareness

Self-awareness is fundamental to your development as a leader and coach. Improving self-awareness is similar to developing a strong set of core muscles for physical training. Every physical exercise requires strong core muscles. How do you improve self-awareness? Do the work! Don't take shortcuts. This is your core.

I don't know how self-aware you are (or think you are). I believe that those who are self-aware are always seeking other ways to test their biases and perspectives. Those who aren't self-aware are usually either too timid to explore those things or, on the other end of the scale, are perhaps allowing ego and pride to prevent them from seeing the gap. Self-awareness was probably my largest blind spot as a leader and coach.

Now, I am sure that anyone who knows me and is reading this right now will say, "No shit!" From the time that I was a young officer, I was outspoken, brash, overbearing, and perceived to be somewhat insensitive. It's okay. Being self-aware also means admitting that I needed to change. I had leaders all along the way who told me these things. They were also gentle enough with me to balance the fact that I had a huge capacity to work and an intellect that made people accept some of these faults to gain the benefit of working with me. In fact, at my retirement in 2021, Lieutenant General Alain Parent characterized my entire career as "shock and awe," stating that everyone I worked with was shocked at the outset of our relationship and then grew to be in awe of what I could accomplish. I don't recommend that approach to anyone, but there is nothing here I did not know. We can have a long discussion about whether I was merely being myself or was just too stubborn to admit I needed to change, but it's not about me—it's about you. What I am saying is that, although I was aware of these character traits and how I was being perceived, this was not the self-awareness that, in the end, was the most revealing to me.

Does any of this resonate with you? Or have you done enough work on yourself to know who you are at your core and have practices in place to check in and reassess? Are you self-aware enough to intuitively know how the people around you are reacting to you and your behaviours and words?

As I came closer to the end of my career, my professional self-study turned from the fields of military and international planning and execution of operations toward a more inward study of self-improvement with the purpose of benefiting those I was leading and serving with. The nucleus of this was that I had always been an avid fitness person. I tried to work out and be physically and mentally fit. I became enamoured with triathlons, although I struggled with them.[17] I loved the training and its diversity. But this meant I had to pay attention to eating habits, an aspect of fitness I didn't understand well. So, I started reading and researching. I tried Cross-Fit (and wrecked my shoulder), but I was very impressed with some of the training regimens and concepts it presented. I incorporated all of these into my personal workouts to stay strong. This entire time, the mental mindset of the endurance athlete was being developed alongside the skills it takes to be a high-performance individual in any field. There was a parallel between athletics and performance, especially in the mental sphere. Then I saw a book written by the guy who invented "SEALFIT," Mark Divine.

---

17 My friend Todd would call them "complete-itions," the idea being that you win if you finish, and you are only competing with yourself.

It was in reading Mark Divine's book *Unbeatable Mind* that I first encountered the concept of the "monkey mind." The idea is simple enough. We are wired as humans to have emotions and thoughts. As the human brain evolved over millennia, it relied on being very critical of oneself as a survival mechanism. Even the smallest of errors could be fatal or could result in not obtaining life-sustaining food and water and these self-critical internal emotions and negative thoughts can take us over. But recognizing that these emotions and thoughts are *not* our actual selves, but rather our subconscious selves, is the first step in being truly self-aware.

To me, this was an incredible concept. I led significantly through my emotions. I let my mouth go wherever my emotional mind took it. This idea opened the door for me to understand that it was possible to control the monkey mind. I started a regimen of meditation to assist in this. Secondly, and this may come as a surprise to many, I had significant self-doubt and truly did not like myself in many ways throughout my career. I would brood and turn my decisions and mistakes over and over in my mind. I remember that when my dad, Doug Clancy, would take a bad shot on the golf course, he would say, "Oh, Douglas!" in a very self-deprecating fashion. I felt "Oh, Scott!" very often. The only person I have ever opened up to on this is my wife Valy,[18] and she knows only too well how deeply I would criticize myself. Recognizing that my thoughts were just that—thoughts—and that our genetic engineering to see every single fault or flaw was a hunter-gatherer survival mechanism allowed me to be calmer, see the thoughts for what they were, and realize the true power in controlling—no, harnessing—one's emotions.

Then I read Susan David's book *Emotional Agility*. Wow! She explained how emotions and reactions don't *have* to be tied together. I know, seems

---

18 Val is also known as "the Valy-girl," so I tend to refer to her as "Valy." When she was a kid, everyone would call her "Muffy." Her brother Sean couldn't pronounce her full name, "Valerie," when he was very young. Their dad, Mac, would tell the story of "Little Miss Muffet," so Sean started calling her "Muffy."

obvious, but I am merely a dumb tac hel guy at heart. She introduced to me the idea of creating space between my emotions and the reactions or behaviours that stemmed from them. In Susan David's words, "The space between stimulus and response is *choice*. Create space for the choice that is more in line with your values and true intentions. (Vice a reaction) At the beginning, at least recognize the need for that space."[19] My mind immediately went to four or five times in recent memory where I had had an emotional reaction that I had immediately regretted. The idea of creating space and choosing a reaction that was more aligned with my true intent was empowering. However, and to quote the Grinch, "But how?!"

This was a watershed moment for me in being self-aware. Self-awareness up to that point had meant accepting myself for who I was. For someone who was pretty comfortable in their skin, at least outwardly to the people working with me, that just meant knowing that I was a loud, brash, energetic person who was prone to outbursts. This realization that I was *not* my emotions meant that I had to be more reflective about who I was and why I was behaving in certain ways. I needed to question that which for five decades I had just accepted as my own character. I was choosing to behave in these ways. I needed to reflect on who I wanted to be and how I wanted to behave. What did I value, and why? How could I behave in a way that was more in line with these values? This was very humbling. I questioned even more deeply how I got to be where I was and all my so-called success, if it was based on flawed values and behaviours. But it was also liberating. I did not need to be the way I was. I saw differences in how I was socially and with my family versus how I was at work. I wanted to be more balanced and aligned. But where did I start?

I started by identifying triggers to my emotions, those things, situations, and even people that triggered my emotional reactions. I drew upon lessons I had learned in dealing with personal and professional trauma and in work-

---

19   David, Susan PhD, *Emotional Agility,* Avery Press, 2016.

ing with individuals suffering from post-traumatic stress disorder (PTSD). I needed to understand and be cognisant of the triggers that caused me to react and to avoid them. I needed to walk away from situations that were triggers. I was finding ways to create that space.

There is a physical element to this that all the experts on the topic speak about. When strong emotions occur, most of us have physical reactions as well. Our faces can get flushed, and we can sweat or get anxious or even have knots in our stomachs and aches in our muscles. One of the best ways to identify when you are triggered is to recognize how you physically feel when you are getting emotional, which allows you to be mentally aware that it is happening. I really, really cannot get a handle on recognizing my physical symptoms of being triggered. I know that a deep regimen of meditation can assist in this, so I continue to pursue that.

Knowing that I struggled with recognizing emotional reactions coming, I did what I know best: I started planning. I knew that I needed to walk into situations prepared for possible emotional triggers, set intentions, and thereby keep my emotions under control because I was expecting them. I would review my calendar for each day and write my intentions on the tops of pages in my notebook. Other times, before a meeting started, I would take a minute or two to set my intentions and write them down on the page in my notebook relevant to the meeting. This became an integral part of my prep for meetings.

Now, I am not saying that this always worked. In fact, the reality is always that the emotional reactions we regret the most are the ones that surprise us. But what this newfound understanding also allowed me to do is connect afterward with how I would have rather reacted in a fashion that was more reflective of my true values. I used this as a method of going back and apologizing, stating why I had a certain reaction, what emotion it was reflecting, and how I truly felt. The whole idea was to approach the reaction/behaviour in a more intentional fashion.

I think there is also another portion to this process: validating the underlying emotion. As I looked back on my feelings, whether I was able to create the space or not, I was developing a better sense of myself and my emotions. Some of them made perfect sense. Others made me question my thoughts and emotions and explore them through journalling and talking things out with Valy. She has always been my best sounding board, confidante, and supporter. I began to realize that there were a few buttons that people could easily push to wind me up. I hated incompetence. If people were working hard to better themselves and learn, that was okay. But, especially in senior leaders, I could not abide incompetence. It was a trigger and could really get me into trouble. Next, situations where my personal schedule and support of Val collided with work demands where she was undoubtedly going to pay a personal price were a trigger. Planning for these conflicts diminished that probability and therefore prepared me for the possibility. It allowed me to discuss the conflicts with Val, and that decreased my stress and allowed me to create space. While I did all of this, looking back on events and situations, it wasn't sufficient to merely identify and avoid triggers while creating space. I needed to validate the emotions that went along with each trigger, or else I did not *feel* like I was making progress.

This leads to my next piece of advice: "Fake it until you make it!"[20] The process of creating space and setting intentions works, but it doesn't *feel* right at the beginning. No kidding! You are going against millennia of genetic coding. Like any new skill, practise this until the uncomfortable feeling has its own muscle memory, as you then know that that is what right looks like. At one point, it will begin to "feel" right.

A few things that you also need to be cognizant of as you become more self-aware. The more purposeful the work, the more emotionally charged

---

20 Yes I know that earlier in the book I said that fake it till you make it would only take a leader so far. But when used as a mindset of repeating a known skill until that skill becomes a learned behaviour, I think this works.

the environment, the closer your emotions will be to the surface and the harder it will be to create space. It's much the same as if you are physically and mentally fatigued. As a coach and leader, use the skills for setting intentions prior to encounters to inoculate yourself from reactions.[21] Keep asking questions and don't point out personal flaws, but rather flaws in ideas or in execution. Always highlight that you are constantly trying to understand. Reinforce the concept that opinions are important. Always reserve the right *not* to have an opinion and walk away from a situation that you cannot deal with. There were times in the middle of very frustrating meetings when I would merely shut down. I would stop asking questions, stop the discourse. In some cases, I would even stop the meetings. I had a phrase that I used: "What's next?" It meant, "I get whatever we are talking about, and the conversation on this is now complete. Let's move on." I am not saying that this is a great reaction, but it is better than having an emotional outburst.

One of my major motivators to go through this process had nothing to do with myself. As I mentioned, I was a mentor to a significant number of people in the organizations and communities that I was a part of within the military. On the court, the young men that I interacted with would look up to me. Therefore, by placing the emphasis on being a positive example for the teams I was leading and coaching, I was inspired to make personal progress along the lines that Simon Sinek professed, "Only when we know ourselves, can we understand others." I love Simon's work. What I started to realize by helping others is that the common element in many emotionally charged situations was fear, especially fear of failure. Because I knew that fear, I could help my team by avoiding that emotional trigger. I recognized that I set standards for a significant amount of the team's work on a daily basis. Therefore, I could disarm their fears by being vulnerable about what we shared in terms of fears with the work. By being honest about

---

21   See the chapter entitled "Setting Intentions."

what I was afraid of, I opened the door for the team to share their fears. We had disarmed the emotional trigger of fear and could now get through whatever we needed to because we were connected with our true selves, not our emotional reactions. The team knew that, as a leader or coach, I was on their side no matter what, and we could all deal with our fears openly.

Fear, however—fear of failure and the mortal consequences that come with that failure, especially at senior military levels—weakened my ability to cope with my emotional reactions and, ultimately, my service to the nation. I had lived in this space for my entire career. Preparing for and making possible life-and-death decisions is an integral part of the profession of arms. It is the sacred duty of the officer corps. As I aged, especially in the final few years of my service, I found that I was taking more and more of the work very personally. Although I was learning to create space and set intentions, I was simultaneously losing my ability to compartmentalize my decisions from the possible downstream effects on national and international security, let alone the lives of people I was sending into harm's way. This was the point that led me to decide that it was time for me to leave the military. The process works, but, at a certain point, you need to remove yourself from the environment that is creating that stress if it is going to overwhelm you.

Merely understanding the roots of our emotional reactions begins the process of self-awareness. Knowing that we have an internal monkey mind that is constantly telling us how bad we are can begin the journey to disarming that internal voice. By next striving to create space between the emotional reactions that our system is engineered to have, we can access who we truly want to be. Our words and actions need not be reactions, but rather true expressions of the values we believe in as coaches and leaders.

CHAPTER 6

Connection

The coach or leader plays a crucial role in the connection of people to purpose. In the military, it may seem easy. The common duty to the nation would seem to provide an instantaneous connection. I remember that in my first week as an officer cadet at the Collège militaire royale de Saint-Jean, all of us recruits were gathered into a very large theatre. We were asked a simple question to be answered via a show of hands: "Why did you join?"

They started with, "Who wants an education paid for?" At least half of the 225 recruits put their hands up.

Next was, "Who wants a guaranteed job and work experience?" Almost all the rest put up their hands.

I looked around sheepishly. The next few questions were about playing college sports, getting out of their small towns, and things of that nature. Lastly, they asked, "Who wants to serve their country?" I felt like I was the only one with their hand up. Maybe that sense of connection in the military is not as simple as we say?

On sports teams, the branding of the team and seeking the win often fill the same void. But these seemingly powerful agents are not always enough, especially when they cease to resonate within an individual. Seeking and gauging that connection in every interaction is critical. As a coach of basketball, it was my personal love of the game, and my childlike desire to have fun, that I used to foster the connection with the kids I was coaching.

For coaches and leaders, I recommend using the venue/vessel of the "thing" you are coaching to establish that connection (sport, skill, tactic, lesson, leadership opportunity). There is already a basis, as the two of you are already in that venue or vessel together (basketball tryout, basic training, project, etc.). This is the framework or platform for the establishment of a mutual purpose, a connection. There is a credibility that is established, and an expectation not only of performance, but of personal improvement. "If I do things the way you are showing me, if I employ these methods, not only will I have success, but I will also be better. I will have improved." Next, the coach needs to weave personalized and tailored coaching in and around this framework of knowledge. Here are my two favourite coaching verbal skills: inquisition and suggestion. No, they are not medieval mind techniques!

I got these techniques from the application of cockpit resource management skills as a pilot in the RCAF. In an aircraft, civilian or military, the only person whose situational awareness matters is the aircraft captain (AC). The aircraft is going to do what the AC decides. Therefore, if you are a member of that crew, your job is to affect the situational awareness (SA) of the aircraft captain. History is fraught with accidents where it was clear that a member or multiple members of crews knew that things were going poorly but did not speak up. The reasons for those barriers to communication have been as varied as one can imagine: rank, power, sexism, culture, ignorance, animosity. Being a two-way street, it behooves aircraft captains to understand the dynamic at play and set the conditions to break down those barriers. The two best communication techniques that I have encountered to do this are—you guessed it—inquisition and suggestion. In an aircraft, this can look like this: "Shouldn't we turn inbound upon intercept of the on-course heading?" (inquisition or question) or "If we turn inbound now, we will be set up on final." (suggestion). Both of these are examples of a crew member trying to increase the SA of the AC. However, the same tools can be used by the AC: "Can you give me the radial we should commence the inbound turn?" or "Let's review the final portion of the approach; I want us all to be clear on it."

As a coach, using questions ("Do you find it difficult to coordinate the layup on the left side?") and suggestions ("If you slow it down and work backward progressively from the shot, it will be easier to master") is, in my experience, the best way to break through those barriers and start the flow of communication. When I was an early coach, it was not how I coached the team that made the biggest difference; it was how I personalized my coaching to each player that made the difference.

Setting these conditions for connection and trust, we must as coaches and leaders always be conscious of those items that are barriers to that communication. These items, in my opinion, are the smallest indicators of larger issues that need to be addressed to maintain or establish that healthy leader or coach relationship. Now, just because someone is not receptive (or appears not to be), that is not necessarily an indicator of a larger organizational problem. As leaders and coaches, we need to be on the lookout for systemic organisational issues. In my example of aircrew in an aircraft, when crew members shut up and don't communicate because they have no respect for any aircraft commanders on a unit, or specific individuals, this needs to be addressed. The reasons for not communicating may relate to differences in their rank, power dynamics, or other duties outside the aircraft. But these are symptoms of larger systemic issues. As well, and sometimes more importantly, if crew members are looking the other way as powerful people make mistakes, this can be dangerous and have dire consequences. Delineating between individual items and organizational/cultural ones can be tough. Again, ask questions and make suggestions.

Here are a couple more guidelines. First, engaging each person individually is important. Personalize your coaching; tailor it to the individual. Some people respond to high bars for performance and public demonstrative critiques. Others need personalized, quiet, and reflective methods. I would again use query and suggestion. "Do you see how the screen will react?" "Glance backward as you move past the screen; that will help you read the defensive reaction." In sports, breakdown drills and the use of assistants can be very effective here.

I had a mantra that was "Always praise in public and critique in private." Like everything, I see with age that this doesn't always apply. On a basketball court you cannot privately correct each and every error. And in military training, one of the powers of team cohesion is that your informal leaders and the rest of the team are as effective, if not more effective, at inspiring performance through their own influence. So, some public critique can be good. It just must be measured. Always remember that humiliation, or shame, is never the tool of a good coach or leader. Critiques of character or attitude are the danger space here. Performance and behaviour are where you critique. When you coach, you are trying to elicit from the individual what is keeping them back from that performance. So, although the performance or behaviour might be critiqued publicly, these core issues need to be private conversations. Remember, whether *you* know what's holding them back is not important. They need to find it in themselves. I would again ask questions and make small suggestions while offering key insights. But always remember to do so from a caring space. Leaders—and I have experienced this first-hand and practised this perhaps too often—can be gruff and brusque in their demeanour while simultaneously demonstrating deep caring for their people. Technique here is everything.

When I was coaching Ryan's basketball team, there was a young man on the team who hogged the ball, didn't listen to the other players/coaches, was late to practice, didn't have the right shoes or showed up with snow on them (dangerous), and, finally, displayed negative emotional reactions to the other coaches and to me personally. I put up with this for a year (and it drove my assistant insane). The next season, tryouts occurred, and there he was. From a performance perspective, he earned his place on the squad. But his attitude was not good. So, I sat down with him and his mom. I said that I would take him on the team, but he was on probation. He had to be on time, properly prepared and dressed, with a good attitude, or he would not play.

So, we started the year. His on-court play was the same, and he gave attitude every time he came off the court. (I had a fair playing time approach to all the teams I coached.) But, at our first tournament, he showed up halfway through the first game, wearing indoor soccer shoes, wiping snow off their soles. I benched him. He was furious. His mom had travelled to bring him (hours of driving) and, and, and…

After the game, I sat and listened. His dad and his mom both worked. His dad spent significant time away from the house for work, and his older brother had just left for university. He felt lost, obviously, but he also felt he could not control being late. I listened, then asked him some questions: Did he have everything ready and standing at the door well in advance of when they had to leave? Had he spoken to his mom about needing to be on time? Had he let her know this was important to him? Had he asked her how he could help to ease up her burden so that they could actually arrive on time? If he needed help getting to practices/games, had he spoken to other players or to me? Maybe we could help…we were a *team!*

The next tournament, his mom asked if he could come with Ryan and me. For sure! Ryan and I talk about nothing except basketball on the way to tournaments—habit. So, this young man started to engage in conversations about leading on the court and off, attitude, dedication, practice, the art of good passing, favourite players, epic moments in games…and there was an immediate change in every aspect of his participation. He turned that energy into positive things. He became a force on and off the court. He cheered harder, rebounded superbly (rebounding is 10% technique and

90% heart), and, finally, smiled more than any other young man on the team. The next year, the team elected him and Ryan as co-captains. To say that I was so very proud of them both is an understatement. I watched those two young men lead and stir up the team before and during games, but especially in the hardest and darkest game and practice moments. They held each other and the team accountable. They kept fostering that connection that coaching planted. Until that young man connected himself with the basketball, with the team and its vision, he could not recognize the innate leadership and foundational character traits he had within himself.

I had another young man on those teams. He was tall and lanky and had all the physical traits of a great ball player. But he was not outgoing, nor receptive to coaching. I spent a lot of time in practice getting the "reps" needed for good shooting. I tried to adjust some of the oddities in how he shot (flat, no arc). His response: "This is my shot, and I am not interested in changing it." More than anyone, he could physically dominate plays and lead the team to come back or get out of a hole. I would say to him, "Lead! Everyone is a leader." He would shrug it off. Accepting coaching and mentoring is about establishing a connection. I could not.

These are the dynamics of an emotional trust relationship. It takes two, and some are not able to work, through no fault of either. I could not establish a connection.

CHAPTER 7

Connecting with the Material

You as a coach must be connected with the material you are coaching. You need to know it cold, or at least be working really hard at understanding it.

Now, this does not mean the best players or masters of a technique/skill are the best coaches. Far from it. We have all seen how performance coaches who have limited knowledge of the actual techniques of their sports mentally coach teams to great heights. But most of the rest of us will be coaching or leading in a situation where all those functions fall to one person. The reason why you must be connected to the material relates to the fundamental discussed in chapter 6 of connecting with the people being coached. There is a credibility issue here. But fear not, as I am of the belief that it is not in the high-end technique-y space that you need to place your main efforts. Instead, start with fundamentals. A clear understanding and focus on fundamentals will always establish enough credibility to start.

When I first started coaching Mathew's basketball team, it had been decades since I played in college. But I clearly knew the fundamentals: ball handling, shooting, passing, defence, footwork. When we arrived at our first tournament, we got pummelled. I got an earful from the parents and the kids. So, at the next practice, what did I do? More fundamentals. That is all I knew how to do. But I also started to study. I realized two things. First, the kids did not have enough basketball IQ to merely "play." They needed the framework of an offence. Secondly, whatever framework I gave them needed to be rooted in the fundamentals that they were familiar with. So, I instituted an offence.

In my second year coaching, it was clear that the kids had grasped even more of the game, so my assistant taught them a full court zone press. But the reason it was so successful was because they knew the fundamentals so well and could read where the offence was reacting. By this time, I was also coaching at RMC. I watched the coach there walk through the reasons why zone defences do and don't work. Then he walked through a high-IQ method of approaching and breaking any zone (E2C4, find the dancer). With the ball, you must engage two defenders (E2), while you must also see the other four players of your team (C4). The tenets of the zone mean that there is now one defender guarding two players, and/or one of your four players will be further from any defender. This is the dancer—find the dancer. By finding the dancer and feeding the ball to them, the zone must execute the maximum shift. Do this two or three times, and the movement of the zone is so vast that gaps and holes will open, providing ample opportunity to drive and shoot. It all starts with the fundamentals of space: creating space on the floor and using that space. The kids loved it. Yup, I went straight back and taught my young kids this high-IQ element because it was easy to understand, and they could see how it achieved huge effects. I don't like zone defences because I think they do not allow players to understand the more dynamic elements of the game, especially defensive team play. But zones are a reality of the game and varying defences can be a good coaching technique.

So, knowing a tool, method, or skill allows for a deeper connection to the material for those you are leading and coaching. But the real trick is being able to adapt it, and adapt your coaching or leading approach, to the receivers of that information to establish that connection. In trying to teach the concepts of space, I think I angered my assistants, and I even walked out of a practice, I got so frustrated. The kids, on the other hand, picked up the concepts better than the other coaches or even I could. The translation of that skill or method will enable the coachee to connect with the material, see its applicability, and see how the discussion/interaction with the coach allows for the individual to improve.

What is the role of your credibility to the receiver of this leadership or coaching? I think it's essential. But your credibility as a coach or leader is not entirely dependent on your skill or knowledge of the material the team is dealing with. It is also dependent on the trust relationship you have built. Large organizations that have gateways for advancement and standards verification for leaders and coaches will guarantee certain credibility due to the mere fact that the individual is in that position. As leaders and coaches climb organizations, the requisite skills will also deepen and become more generic. Many coaches and leaders stick to a given field of study/expertise but recognize the generic applicability of leading and coaching skills across boundaries of competencies. Personally, I always saw this as an opportunity to share my love of the material and what I knew of it with the people I was leading and coaching. I was sharing my passion and enthusiasm. That is infectious.

As a coach and leader, remember to try to understand the receiver's approach to the information and material you are providing. Use the tools of reading and listening as well as active examples, discussion, and details, all with the intent of creating an emotional connection with the material. More importantly, if it is not obvious, then focus on how you can present info in ways that inspire that connection. Self-discovery is often the best way for individuals to truly grasp and retain concepts. Putting them in situations that reinforce that learning is key and can last forever.

The key abilities we need to hone as coaches and leaders to ensure that connection with the material are proactive self-study, asking good questions, and good listening skills. Develop an ability to guide discussion toward the right tools. Finally, remember that if you can't explain something in simple terms, then you don't know it well enough. Go back to the study portion and keep learning.

CHAPTER 8

Communication... Listening

So...as a senior military leader and basketball coach, I always thought I was a good communicator. I was very sure that my team knew exactly what I wanted and what needed to be done. But those aren't the same thing, are they? As I get older, reflect, and get some distance and perspective on things, I am not so sure that I was indeed a good communicator. Volume and quantity of words may fit the bill, but not as often as other, more relevant, communication skills. The highest amongst these is listening.

Picture communication as walking across a bridge. The bridge is the idea or concept that you are trying to get across. But you build that bridge in the mind of the person with whom you are communicating. The bridge can be a multiple-span, lever-controlled drawbridge, or it can be a simple stone bridge. Either way, the more you simplify and reduce the bridge down to understandable portions, the easier it will be for you to get to the other side and reach your listener. But the listener controls the far bank. Figuratively, the far bank is shrouded in fog. If they don't understand, then the gap remains uncrossed, and your bridge goes nowhere. So, during communication, while you are attempting to transmit your ideas, you need to listen—iteratively (back and forth). By synthesizing that which you perceive the other person or people to have understood, you can adjust your bridge, its form, in order to better span the gap to the listener. To speak well, you need to listen well. To listen well, you must be able to synthesize and communicate with the far bank of the river.

I have been a senior officer for too many years not to realize that I tend to be TRONLY. That is an aeronautic term for an aircraft that has a broken radio that can "transmit only"—no reception capability. In this sense, I am communicating my points but not necessarily taking in that which is being fed to me by the listeners. When you fall into this pattern as a leader, this is reinforced by the perceived gap between the people you are leading and yourself due to a myriad of factors, not the least of which is rank. Coaching, on the other hand, is colloquially seen to be a much more intuitively communicating role, a more positive flow between coach and coached, almost a different mindset. As a coach of very young basketball players, I drew *not* upon my military communication experiences to interact with kids, but rather from my own childish, fun-loving nature. (To all my military counterparts…yes, I have one of those.) I was able to be down at their level, to see body language and verbal interactions as expressions of their side of the "bridge" that I needed to cross. When I came to their level and empathized with them, we crossed the complex gap to develop language, concepts, and understanding that I came to recognize as "basketball IQ." By doing this with many young people that I coached over multiple years, we developed a lexicon and understanding where we could evolve our language. The communication bridged beyond "you go here, pass the ball to him, and he shoots." It became "see the space, engage the screen, read the reaction together, talk it up."

The fundamentals for listening begin easily. First, remember and remind yourself that there is a difference between listening and waiting for your turn to speak (body language here—Mathew snapping his fingers, waiting for you to stop speaking). Next, look at the person; make eye contact. Take notes on what they are saying if it is complex. Repeat what they have said back to them. Synthesize it in other words if necessary. Ask good questions to clarify their points. Ask more questions that relate to your side of the bridge, that expose common elements or clarity of logic that can bridge the gap. Finally, if you "get" something, say that. *Aha!*

I think that asking questions is about something larger in the communications sphere. It is not merely about listening, but it does begin here. If we listen well, this does not necessarily mean we completely understand. In addition, we need to ensure that the other person gets that we understand—both sides of the bridge. By becoming adept at asking good questions, we will cement listening into mutual understanding. Note that I did not say "agreement" but "understanding." Take the time to absorb what people are saying and ask the right questions. If you are still unclear, say that and ask if they can explain it another way. But ask questions.

"Listening means taking someone's reality to heart." Shamma Al Mazrui[22]

I think that another foundational thing enabling communication that many coaches or leaders, myself included, do not do well is setting a common framework of language, linked to the vision for the team, that everyone buys into. If this isn't done, then many of the conversations we have turn into confrontations, debates. (We will get to the difference between discourse and debate in a second.) By establishing a common framework (e.g., "I have a three-word mantra: FLY—SHOOT—SPEND."), the team can communicate on the values, objectives, and end goals in a straightforward way. In the bridge analogy, by establishing a framework of language, you are laying out the blueprint for the bridge design. This will allow the team to relate to the conversation.

In achieving success in mentoring senior military officers, I remember

---

22 Simon Sinek, "Episode 41: Hope with Shamma Al Mazui," December 7, 2021 in *A Bit of Optimism*, 33:24, https://simonsinek.com/podcast-episodes/hope-with-shamma-al-mazrui/

many of us struggled with what we meant by "dedicated" or "institution-al leader" or "potential for the next rank." I remember one specific merit board where we consumed most of our time discussing the framework lex-icon upon which the individuals being assessed would be ranked. Once the framework lexicon discussion was complete, the ranking was very efficient, and, more importantly, collaboratively agreed upon quickly. The frame-work of language made quick work of categorization of the elements that we valued most. The bridge was built here.

Differences in how receptive people are to the conversation will dictate how successful getting your point across is. You create success here by hav-ing buy-in and accountability baked into the organization/team so that when you have tough conversations, the framework and language are there. When coaching basketball, the expectation is that we run hard because there are fresh legs on the bench. But if you are dogging it on the court so that you can extend your minutes, then you are letting down the team by not giving 100%, and you are letting down your teammates as they are itching to be on the court. The language of accountability allows you to an-chor your communication in already accepted paradigms and foundations. "You believe in what we are doing here, right? You want to be part of this team. You asked me to put you in that position. But when you stop getting back on defence during the transition, that is not what we do. Past is past. Good defence gets us good offence." Then stop short of judging and ask questions surrounding the topic. "I don't see the real you coming through here. What's up?"

Listening Tools Summary

→ Read back, repeat, or reword what was said to you in order to confirm understanding.

→ Ask questions to confirm understanding.

→ Compare and contrast with actual situations—but again, ask questions. "How would this apply in a situation where...?" Don't try to undo, but to honestly understand.

→ Be focused on understanding, not on expressing a point of view. (This takes work!)

→ Don't just see understanding as a binary intellectual process—"Yes, I understand the concept." Be deeper about this. Empathize. Empathy—"I feel how hard this is for you." Connect beyond the experience to the underlying emotion. Acknowledge the emotion and do not attempt to diminish its impact. "Can you explain how we can make this easier?"[23]

→ Asking *good* questions is at the heart of communicating.

→ Solicit opinions. Organize meetings this way. Build agendas incorporating this as well as time to discuss. "What do you think?" Value those opinions.

Looking back on my career, I began to see how listening was an essential skill in coaching and leading. Moreover, I could see how my journey dealing with my personal deficiency in listening might help others. This was about my shortfalls as a communicator in my role as a leader. Obviously, I had a blind spot there. I wanted to better explore that blind spot, so I sent this question to a few of my colleagues and asked for their critiques: "Does my overbearing personality, predilection to interrupt, over-preparation for

---

23 Brené Brown, *Dare to Lead* (New York: Random House, 2018), 136–157.

meetings, and not taking the time to listen to entire presentations (I would drive to the heart of the issues and hijack every presentation) hamstring communication?"

Clearly, I was not prepared for the response, but I think that it is very revealing:

Colonel Trevor Teller, RCAF

My experience as your chief of staff (COS) was characterized by a team that was willing to speak up, and, from where I sat, the need was for commander's intent to be provided by you. We got that! But when you were in the room, you would sometimes "hijack" the meeting/briefing more through strength of personality and a deep understanding of the issues. This manifested as team members not always getting a chance to speak. It was interesting to watch those team members who were not comfortable with you as you expressed "the opposing point of view," as they would occasionally shut down[24] and I would get their points afterwards. At the end of the day, we needed a commander, and we got one.

I remember sitting beside you in your "in-brief" as the wing commander. Written at the top of your notes was "Listen, listen, listen." I could always see that this was a bit of a challenge for you, given your ability to synthesize information and conceptualize problems through different lenses. Sometimes meetings need to be hijacked. Sometimes the staff came to me afterward and gave me the bits we needed to advance planning. But we always got direction. From a personal perspective, I very much enjoyed working for you, but I did have a privileged platform for communications. I carried that same platform between myself and the rest of the staff as the COS. It all worked well. And don't forget…we were &^%$#@ busy!

---

24   *Aha!!* Valy told me a great story of when she was involved in a team-building exercise and she offered a solution to the problem. The team immediately dismissed her solution and she shut down. That is exactly what was happening here, and it's the worst thing that can happen when trying to build our bridge.

Major General David "Oscar" Meyer, USAF

Bottom line is no! However, depending on your technique of the day, it could be. The ultimate driver was that we had a limited amount of time to get your direction to the team. Your preparation allowed you to focus on the key points that you wanted the team to understand. I view this more in line with necessary time management that ensures effective communication. The alternative would be to hear the entire presentation and then not have enough time to give critical feedback. For Coach [Major General Pete "Coach" Fesler] and others briefing the four star or higher political levels, they would only come up for air when they specifically planned to allow conversation. Otherwise, the brief got derailed and did not achieve the objective.

Major General Pete "Coach" Fesler, USAF

Our natural tendency, having seen most of this before (and to save time), is to drive directly to that core issue and start digging. This can be good and bad. On the positive, it can keep a staff from drifting. It keeps them focused on what matters. It certainly saves time, both for us and the staff, and helps us avoid running down rabbit trails. It helps the staff understand the core issues.

However, I think the negatives outweigh the benefits. On the downside, interrupting during a briefing can deflate members of your team who have put significant work into the product that they are presenting. Remember, our rank and knowledge were intimidating. They believed that we probably knew more about elements of this topic than they did. They were nervous to come talk to us, and they worked hard to make sure they didn't stumble. Interrupting them was like making the team practice for the big game and then, at game time, telling them, "Never mind, I'll just play for you." Interrupting can also result in the team shutting down. They can feel like they failed, or that you just don't understand, and they stop listening.

It can also have a negative impact on the mission. You and I, by personality and experience, were moving very fast. Our background allowed us to make intuitive judgments. We got to where we were by usually being right when we made gut calls, but this created blind spots for us. When we interrupted our teams, we very well may have missed some key points that they were going to make. If you interrupted me to get to the key issue, and I felt we had missed a key point, I'd jump back in. We were near peers, so I could. They [others] might not jump back in. We could be intimidating, and they would defer. Having missed that key piece of info, we might have driven the team down the wrong path.

I think that a hybrid approach is probably the sweet spot. If we can allow the team to finish their presentation and then drive to the core issues, we gain the benefit of their preparation, give them the chance to show what they know, and also give ourselves time to make sure our preconceived position was accurate. It will cost us some time, but I think that lost time will be made up by ensuring that we are on the right course. I am not suggesting we accept their position. Just let them finish and then let loose with the corrections, questions, and direction.

....

Well, that was humbling! But revealing. As a coach and leader, reflecting on this made me circle back to the listening tools summary that I outlined above and then use the analogy of the bridge to hold in my mind and set intentions for listening prior to a meeting. Achieving that balance between time management, getting to the essential elements of a topic/issue, and ensuring that the individual or team is heard…that is the sweet spot.

Good communication when leading is about getting information, analysing it, making a decision, and expressing that decision. This process is not just a two-way street; it is also iterative. Focused iterative communication is usually discourse or debate, and there is a difference between the two. To be a good communicator, you need to understand whom you are speaking with and why, understand the medium for the communication and its limitations, and understand your relationship to both those you are speaking to and the medium. In a discourse, be able to identify the difference between that which is true and that which is helpful. Even if something is true, it might be inflammatory and not assist in moving the discourse forward. Restraint is important here. This applies especially to that which you are going to bring to the discourse. Recognize that you do not have to resolve differences of opinion. In fact, when differences of opinion remain, that may actually highlight mutual understanding. And, in my humble opinion, people watching good discourse, where opinions are encouraged and challenged, achieve a much higher degree of understanding. Finally, remember that you do not have to *have* an opinion.

According to Bob Gower, renowned coach and communications expert, discourse is talking to someone, trying to learn from them, while testing theories. Debate, however, is not about trying to convince them of something, but just trying to make the other look or feel bad in order to "win." [25] I think we all agree that discourse is healthy and debate not so much. But how do we create the environment that welcomes the kind of diversity of thought that we need in modern organizations and teams?

I learned the hard way that we need to use language that reinforces diverse opinions without being threatening. When I was a young major, I had to execute a planning session to deploy forces on short notice. In the middle of this planning session, one of my peers proffered an idea that was rooted in a deep misunderstanding of what it took to deploy forces to this mission on short notice. But instead of using this as an opportunity to teach, coach, and develop together, I pigheadedly just dismissed it offhand with a final rude quip about his point being a stupid idea. Not only was my approach

---

25   Robert Gower, "Rules of Engagement: 5 Steps to Better Arguments," LinkedIn, September 15, 2020, https://www.linkedin.com/pulse/rules-engagement-bob-gower/.

wrong, but the language and tone were now the focus of discussions—including discussions with my boss—when the focus should have been on how wrong this idea was. Not only that, but the individual still thought that he had a good point. I could have used different language, tone, and approach, perhaps raising the idea of discussing it at a break, to handle the situation much better. Instead, I let my ego and character get in the way of just listening and having a clear discourse that valued the individual while discussing the value of the point they raised.

Here are a few more communication tools that I have picked up over the years:

1. Especially in heated situations and crucial times, you can also employ the tool of changing tone to take the edge off a heated debate. Soften your volume and change your tone from stern and serious to something else.

2. I do enjoy using humour to take the edge off a heated debate or tough conversation and to remind us all that, whatever we are talking about, our relationship with each other is more important than our disagreement.

3. When discussing especially complex or controversial items, take a step back by stating the common elements in both or various positions/options. By stating the common elements, we develop common ground. Much discourse focuses on highlighting only the differences in our positions, but in many instances, we share more in common than we disagree on. Stating this common ground ties the team together to finding a common solution.[26]

---

26 As Canadians—and especially for me as a Canadian spending a significant amount of time working for and with Americans—we would constantly highlight the differences between Canada and the United States. However, I would often remind my teams that it was like having a twin brother or sister. We identify ourselves by our differences, but to almost any outsider, we are identical. We like the same music, we have the same respect for the rule of law, and our multicultural societies struggle between our value-based desires and the realities of our class-based, disproportionally white-dominated systems.

4. I also try acknowledging each side's perspectives of the other. "This is huge. Jane, I hear you note where Bob's plan falls down." Then, "Bob, I hear that you value how Jane's team has resolved some of the planning issues." Again, we are establishing common ground as the team sees "team" as more important than "solution."

5. Do not attack an opinion or difference to the point of judgment of someone's character. (See my example of saying an option was stupid above.) Furthermore, allow for the diversity of thought to allow for varying opinions as compared to a template. Opinions and options need to be as varied as the personalities and characters that have them. A Democrat can believe in gun ownership rights and a Republican can believe in strong unions. By accepting that variance, we accept the diversity of thought that comes with the inherent flexibility of mind.

6. Body language—pay attention to yours. It can change everything. Eye contact: are you facing the person who is talking? How is your posture? Head, arms, eyes? This is important in today's virtual world as well. In the first week of my arrival in Alaska, my commander had to go to Hawaii to get briefed on his upcoming new job. There was a weekly secure video update to the commander of NORAD/ USNORTHCOM. I would be on the Video Tele Conference (VTC), but it was my boss from Hawaii who would be doing the talking. The instant the conference ended, my phone rang. It was my boss. "Hey, Scott, when the commander is talking on the VTC, you need to be looking at the camera and not talking to anyone else in your room on your end." It seemed that my inability to speak without flailing my arms all over the place had created quite the visual spectacle, especially while I was muted and speaking to someone in the room with me. This was noticed by everyone, including the four-star general! I learned about body language from that. So, lean in when you are listening hard. Have a

furrowed brow if you don't understand. Don't roll your eyes if you think something is stupid. Don't fold your arms and stare off into the distance when someone is talking. And, above all else, be aware of how the people around you are perceiving your body language.

CHAPTER 9

Finding a Style

My initial reaction to the idea of finding a leadership style is…don't. Just the idea of finding a leadership style always seemed a tad faulty to me. Instead, I preferred advice like, be you. Be authentic. When asked about it, I would say that there are some leadership fundamentals to follow but that finding a style is not one of them. My short-sightedness was that I never truly reflected on and analyzed my leadership "style," but I sure had a ton of superiors and peers tell me what they thought my style was. It was fascinating to me. I never found the exploration of a personalized style helpful as a young leader. The reality that I saw was that the situation and the people were going to dictate the approach. And when I asked those same superiors about style, they seemed to give me rote textbook approaches to situations. Not helpful. Or perhaps I was just not mature enough. They were, however, able to tell me very clearly what was *not* working. That did help.

Then, when I was enrolled in the USAF Air War College course, one of the leadership assignments was to create a command philosophy. I was a colonel by this time with 28 years of experience in the military. This was an assignment that was supposed to have us assess the values that were at the heart of our leadership and that we used as guiding principles, not just in a single command or situation, but in all of our commands. It was defined by what we thought was the most important about *how* we wanted to lead. I was assigned a USAF brigadier general (now-Lieutenant General Richard Scobee) to assist me in this endeavour. I struggled with it. What then-Brigadier General Scobee said to me was, "Think of this as a narrative of your value system within command. Kind of a mantra, or paradigm, that lets others know what is important to you in the realm of leadership and how you see things."

After soul-searching and thinking on this, I was finally able to complete the assignment. My command philosophy is based upon three things: "professionalism," "mission command," and "lead by example." "Professionalism" was based upon my desire to always be the smartest tactician in the room, to lead via an expertise of operational effectiveness. I had seen too many leaders advance in the past who I would not have followed into combat because they were inept or incompetent. "Mission command" reflected that I would lead via intent, that I would inherently trust my subordinate leaders and my staff, and that the "how" would be a matter of ownership by lower echelons. And "lead by example" was self-explanatory; I would set a personal and professional example that not only exemplified the values and ethics of the CAF, RCAF, and tac hel, but that also demonstrated that I shared in the personal deprivations of the troops.

I wish I had done that exercise much earlier in my career and repeated it more often throughout. But that singular exercise defined more to me about *how* I wanted to be as a leader and coach than anything else I had done in my professional development prior to that. I would thereafter encourage those working for and with me to do the same.

One of my friends was a huge sports fan. His command philosophy was "Be the 12th man" (referring to the invisible hand of the crowd and morale in sports). It was a powerful paradigm that he used very effectively to inspire maximum effort and cohesion amongst his people facing daunting tasks and heart-breaking tragedies. Another individual had a two-tiered ap-

proach, which was "Make the most of each day" and "the power of posi-
tivity." She led her teams in maximizing outputs and creating very positive
work environments where everyone knew exactly what they could do to
achieve very lofty goals.

But coaching…wow…that was a different process. What style did I want
to have? Well, I knew what I *didn't* want to do. I did not want to focus on
winning. I did not want to have good players and bad players, nor small
players and tall players. I wanted everyone to learn everything, and I wanted to create a love for the sport of basketball that would last my teams' entire lives. I wanted them to have *fun!* Finally, I wanted to be able to expose
these young people to life lessons and character-building experiences that
they could take with them for the rest of their lives. I had seen the crucible
of competitive sport and knew that it had significant similarities to the
crucible of combat. So, I had a few pillars that emerged:

1. Practise hard; games are easy. (I loved practices but disliked games/
    tournaments.)

2. Coach the bench.

3. Criticize in practices; cheer on in games.

4. Character trumps wins… in every sense.

5. Fundamentals over Xs and Os.[27]

6. Basketball IQ lasts forever.

7. Use simple phrases to cue big concepts.

8. Make sure it's fun!

Whether as a coach or a leader, sit down and connect with your values
and the values of the organization or team you are a part of. I would start

---

27 Xs and Os refers to the drawings on chalk and whiteboards that coaches use to explain plays and
    player movements about the sports field or court. Generically, it refers to all the specific techniques
    of the game.

by grabbing a blank paper and writing out what you believe your core values are, then what you think the values of the organization are. To start writing, ask yourself what you "value." In life, what do you value? Logic and intellect? The rule of law, fairness, and order? Respect for people? Chances for development for everyone? How do you lead your life? Are fun and experiencing things important? Do those exposures force growth, personally and professionally? Service? To others or the greater good? Making a good living? Setting up your kids for success that perhaps you didn't have? Leaving behind a legacy? Being a thought leader?

Now shift to the organization that you are coaching or leading in. What do they value? Is what they profess different than reality? How do you rationalize that?

Now look at the two lists—your values and the organization's values. What jumps out at you? Where is there alignment? Where can you help the organization foster the correct values? Ask yourself how those values will lead to explaining the "how" that you want to approach your role. Keep these close and allow them to infect everything that you do. Then communicate, communicate, communicate on those values, drawing every practice, meeting, or engagement back to them.

CHAPTER 10

Adjusting Approaches

I always considered how a leader adjusted their approach to be a core metric when evaluating leadership competence. Adjusting approaches or style is based upon two main variables: the situation and the personalities of the individuals involved. In my mind, how well a leader could assess, vary, and adjust their approach was a direct indication of their strength as a leader. It was a direct indication of how many people their inspiration and organization skills would reach. It was a direct indication of their mental agility. I would go so far as to state that honing your ability to make adjustments is even more important than finding your own style.

But this is not just choosing an autocratic versus free rein approach as one moves from a combat situation to leading a group of engineers innovating a solution to a wicked problem. There is a time and a place for leaders, even in combat, to step back and allow subordinates to figure it out. They have the tools and must provide those solutions. At higher levels of command and leadership, resisting the temptation to get down in the weeds is difficult, especially when one is going to be held accountable for every mistake that subordinates make. Micromanagement has historically been one of the overarching killers of any innovative spirit. But the line between fostering innovation and making sure the entire team is aligned with the vision can be…blurry. Varying technique, even with the same team, trying to solve the same problem but on a different day, is a real thing. I have been very open to free-flowing discussions on one day and then realized a day later that the team was stuck and moved into being very directive to keep them going on the timeline. Different meetings will take on different flavours or approaches. In a brainstorming session on the campaign to foster capability and deterrence within the NORAD/USNORTHCOM enterprise, for example, all options and discussions were welcome. But the team expected something very different from me at my bi-weekly priorities meeting, where I was very directive even though I listened to my division chiefs.

It is important to understand how the approach of a coach or leader needs to be reflective of the personalities involved. You need to know yourself and those you coach or lead. This requires an investment of time. Focus on the individual and get to know what drives them/motivates them.

Here is where accountability can be tricky. Standards usually need to apply to everyone, but not everyone buys in or allows that framework to resonate with them. For others, these standards can work against them. This is especially true with individuals who lack the necessary background or baseline skills but who have been thrust into the team regardless. There is such a huge gap between those individuals and the other team members that the framework is completely unachievable. They can barely understand what is going on. If not coached and led well, they will flounder and be lost. In many cases, they shut down.

Style or approach is not fixed. It's like a quiver with a variety of arrows. What works for 14-year-old boys might make 14-year-old girls very sad, and vice versa. What works for highly motivated and disciplined military professionals will not work for an eclectic group of local volunteers. Within a group, not everyone will respond to you. Recognize that. Be open to that and see the signs—body language, engagement, tone of voice, and comments. Some coaches will have better success just coaching the team as a homogeneous group. Others will have a stronger connection with individuals. Communication is the main tool to figure out what is working and what is not. By varying your style, being open to coaching, or leading in different ways for different people or situations, you open up the tailoring of all your frameworks to maximize the potential of the individual.

When my younger son's team was all between 11 and 12 years old, I knew that some of my players didn't have the same maturity as the others. They were all a set of goofy boys that, if left to their own devices, would end up laughing and joking around. But some of them took criticism very differently. My son Ryan, whom I love beyond words, must decide to do something before he applies himself to it. If he doesn't decide, he just goes through the motions. Once he decides, he applies all his focus and energy, and nothing can stop him. He's stubborn as the day is long and wicked smart (I have no idea where he gets it from!).[28] But Ryan was also very used to my style of coaching. He had experienced it in our laneway hoop since he had been old enough to throw a basketball. Some of the other boys on his team were much more amenable to a softer and more instructive approach. There were times when Ryan would test my authority and smarts as they pertained to a specific approach or drill because he had not decided whether he bought into it or not. That pushback got him running a lot more lines than many of his teammates. But he also had the pleasured life of arguing with his dad/coach on an issue for hours (outside of practice) until he decided that I was right or that arguing his point was only a matter of an opinion and that it made sense that we chose one way and went with it. But he had to choose!

Style needs to adapt to the situation as well as to the team or individual. What works in a group setting during an informal brainstorming session will not work in a time crunch or crisis situation. You don't coach a team that is being pummelled the same way you coach a team that is winning.

---

28 "Wicked smart" said with my mom's Boston accent, the same way she would say "baaaaathroom" or "out in the yaahhhd."

In either instance, I was always trying to coach the positive, pull out the successes, and minimize the errors. For a situation where we were woefully behind, I might focus on the individual skills and the opportunity that we had to rise to an occasion and get better. Focus on defence and frustrate them with our effort and determination. On the court, the team would hear positive reinforcement of specific techniques that they had practised, and they would see the small successes of following that guidance. For a team that is winning, the focus needs to also be on the details. I would mix up the players often, force them to run offences through complete cycles, and practise the unfamiliar options that would result. I would also change up players into positions that they did not often get a chance to play—big men handling the ball, smaller boys playing in the post. They all had been taught all the positions, and they all practised them. This kept them all sharp and working and learning hard. Above all else, I taught them how to win with humility by reminding them what it was like when they were losing.

I will cover more about adjusting style or approach to specific situations in the "TTPs" section. But there are a certain number of things that a leader or coach needs to do to prepare for and decide in advance what approach to take. Certain meetings need to be approached differently. Crisis operations with split-second decisions need to be approached a certain way. Debriefing assessments, dealing with grief, disciplining individuals, or asking for assistance all are situations in which a coach or leader should set intentions in advance with how they wish to approach their own style. This will set the best tone and provide the best circumstances for success.

CHAPTER 11

The Role of Authority

Most leadership theory will recognize the dynamic between formal and informal authority in any group. It is perhaps starker in military organizations since the "ask" of performance can include the unlimited liability of one's life, but the dynamic at play is the same. A leader with the formal authority to demand performance in the completion of a paid job will butt up against the reality that, without the people working for them, they cannot complete the task. The people within this same group may think that without them there is no group and the task will not be able to be completed. However, nobody is irreplaceable, and, without leadership directing that performance, there is a good chance that the group will be ineffective, and this will have detrimental consequences for each individual. Not to mention that the individuals in the group signed on and accepted a job knowing full well that they had a boss! Even in the most abstract sense of authority, one needs to accept that being a member of any team requires performing within the expectations of their superior.

The social dynamic at play here can be very complex and bridges instantly into culture, diversity, roles, responsibilities, ethical norms, and healthy workplaces. At the outset, the fact that came home to me very early on in my military career was that good leaders set the tone and enabled the very best in culture, diversity, and ethical norms. I also noticed very early on in my coaching experience that it was team coaches who set the tone for the group. Finally, in assessing my past experiences in both leading and coaching, I came to the realization that the coach or leader could set these positive standards in very short order, with long-lasting effects. But I also found that, once corrupted, the values and culture that were held dear by the entire group could be dashed instantly through poor coaching and leading.

One would think that within military organizations, informal leaders or informal leadership would take a back seat to the formal brand due to the heavy reliance on the chain of command and a rigid military hierarchy. I disagree. It was obvious to me that, even within any organization, informal leaders emerged. Some carried huge sway due to the roles they were assigned, not leadership positions but similar. Safety, standards, and organizational tasks that were assigned within the group could amplify this influence and set these people apart. How they rose to these challenges—and, more importantly, the character they displayed while executing these tasks—further entrenched their informal influence within the group. Leaders would begin to rely on them for advice outside of the areas over which they had been given responsibility. Good leaders and coaches will assign people roles like these who have informal influence within a group in order to leverage their potential as leaders and place them on a path to leader/coach development.

But the dynamic between informal leaders, especially the power that they can wield within a group, and the formal authority of a leader or coach can have catastrophic consequences if not nurtured and supported in a positive way. This goes back to my dilemma from chapter 1 about people versus mission. I think that recognizing informal leaders and aligning them with formal authority is the first step. Everyone needs to recognize the authority of the coach/leader in making the final call and ultimately directing the team. This includes recognition of the limitations of the group's leader in "changing the world," since every team, in some ways, is a part of a larger organization or of society at large. Next, in order to maintain that alignment with formal authority, the leader or coach is going to have to state and demonstrate the importance of the people in the entire group, both informal leaders and others, their inputs and ideas, thereby recognizing their influence over the conduct of the mission or tasks. Identifying and engaging informal leaders at this point is essential. In doing these things openly and constructively, leaders and coaches are setting the conditions for the highest probability of success. In many teams, merely doing these things, setting the team/workplace culture, accomplishes 90% of the mission. When I was a basketball coach, if we had a team that worked hard and wanted to learn, while listening to the advice and counsel of the coaches… my mission was done. The crucible of sport would take care of the rest of their development.

As a coach, I may have had the official authority of a basketball coach within a club construct, but nothing that came with that flimsy title trumped the moral authority that every adult and parent had to ensure the correct influence and conduct of development of these young people. As a coach, I was always open and transparent with every parent and player. As a leader in the Canadian military, on the other hand, my specific goal or mission could never be more important than the moral authority that I had to take care of the most precious natural resource Canada had, its young people who had volunteered their lives in the service of the nation. When one holds oneself to a standard and principled moral authority and aligns the mission and the influence of informal leaders with that authority, the achievement of whatever objectives are assigned to the group becomes much easier. But do not underestimate how hard this is and how much work it is. Constant attention to detail, scrutiny of conduct, and analysis of performance, followed by regular feedback, is essential. All this will take iterative and constant communication and a mutual understanding not only of the mission and the team's adversities, but also of the various individual and group dynamics at play.

Some leaders will wield the formal authority that they have been bestowed in a manner that is carrot- and stick-like. In the military, the immediate and visible signals of respect for rank and authority can affect a leader's approach to the team. But, in my experience, the fundamental trait of humility within the military construct is what allows these formal traditions to recognize and simultaneously disarm barriers.

Let me explain.

In military organization, it is obvious who is in charge. Highest rank and a hierarchical command structure, along with military traditions of saluting, rising to attention when a superior enters a room, addressing all senior ranks with the monikers "Sir" or "Ma'am"... all of these serve as constant reminders of the formal authority that is bestowed upon individuals in charge. So immediately, this does not need to be established. The good leaders I have seen are profusely thankful for the rendering of these protocols and immediately engage the individuals as just that: individuals. The reason for this is that, during basic training and each phase of advancement after, that leader has been humbled by just how much they do <u>not</u> know that <u>others</u> have a keen grasp on. This, coupled with the understanding that the team will know and wield so much more knowledge than the individual leader ever can, leads to a great sense of humility. The final factor, I believe, in fostering this humility in leaders is the knowledge that even the smallest error could have catastrophic consequences on the lives of subordinates. If this does not make one humble, I do not know what would. Therefore, the leaders who wield formal authority in a "carrot- and stick-like" manner in military organizations stand out significantly. I think it inevitably becomes obvious where they abuse their power. Their subordinates and peers will see it. Some leaders will withdraw into the comfort of the protocols and trappings their positions can afford, thereby shying away from even their formal or informal responsibilities.

There is a significant difference between presenting different points of view, questioning the conduct of a task or mission, using or suggesting a different or innovative approach to an idea...and questioning authority. Leaders and coaches need to foster intellect, questioning, and innovation. Coaches and leaders need to be able to recognize when these items cross the line into questioning their formal or moral authority, or when the intention of the individual at the outset is to question leader authority, even if presented within a guise of perspective and innovation. Leaders and coaches need to set the conditions for this positive environment by:

1. Spending significant time listening and interacting with the team during planning and execution of the task,

2. Ensuring at all times that the team can link the tasks back to the vision (the "why"),

3. Establishing the forums and places where feedback will be provided (privately vs. publicly, where and when),

4. Seeking and openly discussing feedback on the conduct of the tasks (the "how"),

5. Communicating clearly about the timeline on feedback and making it clear where the focus of the team needs to be once a decision is made and execution commences, and

6. Privately engaging and publicly praising informal leaders for their roles in the conduct of the mission.

What creating this positive environment will do is develop a mutual understanding about the vision and associated tasks, juxtaposed against the concerns, inputs, and adversities of the team. For the coach and leader, this creates clear empathy and understanding, which will align people and mission. For the team, it demonstrates that the coach or leader has their best interests at heart and provides ultimate acceptance of the authority of the coach or leader to decide and act.

Informal leaders can hinder or greatly assist. Giving them the ability to directly contribute makes them more likely to assist. They are great sounding boards. Usually, informal leaders also have significant technical/tactical experience. They hold positions of respect within the team. As a coach or leader, seek to enhance that respect, nurture it, and align it with the values and concepts of the team's vision. Culture is what makes it possible to maximize the characteristics of informal leaders to positively influence the team in ways that are already built into them. Good culture breeds good informal leaders. Be careful about informal leaders who challenge the formal authority of the leader or coach, as the position from which they garner their power is an indication of the cultural deficiency of the team. Informal leaders who attempt to undermine the team, the leader, or the coach need to be directly and privately counselled. My advice is to use these sessions to understand and deal with the misalignment between the informal leader's actions or behaviours and the values and goals of the team.

In basketball, I wanted every member of the team—not just the captains—to lead. I would tell my players that all five players on the court are leading. Anyone can rise in a play, a moment, a game, or a practice. When I saw they were all leading, they fed inspiration off each other. When they were down, they relied on each other. This made them stronger. You would see leaders emerge wherever and whenever the team needed them, on the court and on the bench. But be aware that some people are just not comfortable in any position of responsibility or leadership. In the case of my coaching, some players came to basketball just wanting to play. Recognizing this, too, was important. Not everyone is or has the desire to become an informal leader.

In writing this book, I shared this idea with my son Mathew, and he offered this on the role of informal leaders. "They are *the* most important thing on the team. They create new leaders. I see it as having leaders as peers. They enable collaboration. It's like having a 2i/c[29] but without formal authority. There is no friction with informal leaders because without formal authority, people don't feel threatened. Enabling them encourages team performance. They are fundamental to a goal-oriented culture. The good informal leaders are able to take minimal direction and move on and do their jobs."

---

29   "2 i/c" is a military term that means "second in command." I love that Mat uses military terms based upon his lifelong indoctrination at numerous military bases growing up and his close ties to many military things at his work.

CHAPTER 12

Lead by Example

Coaches and leaders need to set the tone for their organization. It is not good enough to "talk the talk." You have to "walk the walk." The hypocritical nature of many business managers or leaders who follow none of the clearly defined work ethics, burden-sharing, or even foundational principles of the organizations they work for is what directly undermines their credibility.

Let me give you a few examples of leading by example, both in coaching and in the military.

I was coaching my son's basketball team. One of the players always had a somewhat cocky edge to him. As we got to know each other, I loved his edge because it was centred in a fun-loving sense of humour and a wonderful, caring personality. And, in the midst of tough games, that edge allowed him to step up and be confident. So, we came to the end of a practice, and he said to me, "Coach, I challenge you to a three-point shooting competition!"

I looked at him. "Okay, for what?"

He thought for a second. "A set of lines." A set of lines was a shuttle run going back and forth between the end line and the ever-expanding court from foul line, half, other foul line, and, finally, end to end.

"Okay," I said.

The entire team and the parents stopped to watch and were cheering him on. (When had I become the bad guy?) I stepped up to the line and asked how many shots. He said best out of 10. I proceeded to hit 11 threes in a row. (I was so surprised that I had to keep going until I missed.) He missed on his third shot.

As he started his set of lines, he had a huge smile on his face, I gave him a high five, and I think Ryan and a couple others even joined in running to support him.

Who was setting the example there, me or him? I think this young man was smiling because *he* had set a challenge and taken his best shot (pun pun) and, within the supportive environment of his team and their parents, was happy to be on that stage. *He* set an example for the rest of the team. There would be other challenges, from him and from the rest of the team. I ran my own fair share of lines. He set an example: work can be fun; play can be hard.

In the aftermath of the devastating earthquake in Haiti in January 2010, I was sent to the country on a moment's notice to command the air component of the Canadian Joint Task Force assisting in the relief effort. I had a few hundred folks deployed to two main bases on the island, living in austere conditions. After a month or so of operations, things settled into a bit of a routine. I knew that my helicopter technicians were one of the hardest-working bunches—they had to work in the hot sun, ensuring a high rate of serviceability with very few pleasures to offset their deprivations. So I asked to assist with a 25-hour inspection on one of the Griffon helicopters. I knew how to execute this and was qualified to assist in the inspection. They had four stations set up for me with four technicians. I got up on the top of the helicopter and was greeted by a master corporal technician. "Sir, start greasing the rotor head." And then the master corporal had his opportunity, with nobody else listening, to tell me exactly what he thought about how things were going and the specific problems or issues he was facing. Funny, they never lacked for material, nor for opinions on how my command was going!

"Am I doing this greasing right?" I would say.

"Don't worry, sir, I will redo it when we are finished. Just listen."

Next, they wedged me up in the hell hole under the helicopter. Once I could barely move, the tech said, "Now that I have your attention..." I came away from that and a hundred other experiences like that with a clearer understanding of the trials and tribulations that the people working for me were facing and with a "to-do list" of some very specific things to address. But, more than anything, more than the opportunity for those people to air grievances, what mattered was that I was willing to get dirty and put myself into uncomfortable positions, sharing in the deprivations of the people I had working with me.

Simon Sinek wrote a fantastic book called *Leaders Eat Last*. Simon Sinek has had a lifelong relationship with some great leaders in the U.S. military. But, even before I read his book, I had my own personal relationship with this exact concept. When I was a young aircraft captain, we were always on the go. When we were in the field, we were often only on the ground long enough to eat and go to the bathroom, and then we were back in the air. On one such occasion, we only had a few minutes before getting back into the air. The unit was on the move, and the field kitchens had just been set up. My friend Colin and I, both young captains, were at the front of the line. The commanding officer, then-Lieutenant Colonel Phil Campbell, called us both out of line to speak to him. He explained that, even though we needed to go fly, he could not accept officers eating before the non-commissioned officers and being first in line. He told us to go grab some hard rations and get back in the air. He needed us to set the example as part of his leadership team. That lesson stayed with me.

Years later as I have previously mentioned, I was in Haiti after the earthquake and now a full colonel. When the Port-au-Prince airport finally started accepting civilian airliners again, a member of my team who had been working on the tarmac came to me with an Air Canada pilot in tow. It seemed that the Air Canada hub in Montreal had gotten together, and they had brought down 300 pizzas, all cooked up and ready to go, from a pizzeria in Montreal for the Canadian troops. We had been on hard rations for over a month by that point.

I got my team together; I had Phil's words ringing in my ears. I told my team, "Folks, we are the air component. The rest of the task force is out on the ground delivering aid in sweltering heat every day. We have the pleasure of being in the air, moving about the country easily and living on airfields. We will focus on those who need this more than us. And... the navy is getting three square hot meals a day on board ship... they get nothing." My team divided up the pizzas between the infantry battalion, the Disaster Assistance Response team (DART), the field hospital, and the JTFHQ, with my troops taking the last and smallest share. I was very proud. I had my helicopters deliver those scrumptious treats right to the front lines. But when it came time to disburse the small amounts to our folks on my camp, I saw two captain pilots at the front of the line. Yup, they had to go fly. Yup, there would be none left if they didn't get theirs quick. But I walked up to them, put my arms around them, and led them gently away from the line. Example, leadership, privilege, responsibility...things had come full circle. (Thanks, Phil.)

This example of leaders eating last (literally!) was not the only thing that I did to lead by example. I wove this principle into almost every practice and daily ritual that I had as part of my personal and professional practices. I visibly washed daily, doing my morning routine not hidden from view in a tent but out where it was visible. I cleaned my uniform and oiled and detailed my personal weapon every day. I would choose a different group to eat with for every meal or would eat at my desk, which was exposed under a section of modular tentage right where my team worked. I was always available to them. I took this even further when I was in command of 1 Wing. I would make it a point to help prepare meals and feed the troops where and when I could. I would eat among them and try to sit and chat with anyone and everyone. I would make sure that I was sharing in the same physical discomforts that they were. When I was working in the NORAD enterprise, I went from running a command centre, being a deputy within a region, to running all operations for NORAD. I would take the toughest shifts to free people up to be with their families on Christmas, Thanksgiving, and New Year's. I would visit crews on duty on a recurrent and continuous basis and ask them how things were going. I would visit not just when it was convenient for me, but also on Saturdays, Sundays, or on long weekends when I did not have to be there.

Lead by Example Summary

1. When you make a mistake, own it publicly. This is essential for coaches as well as leaders. Coaching errors can truly frustrate teams, and coaches tend to put all losses on the players.

2. Make yourself available to subordinates. This is an example that will enable them to provide feedback but will demonstrate to future leaders the benefit of that visibility.

3. Lean into difficult conversations whenever they arise. Be willing to explore other points of view and perspectives. Be willing to challenge long-held traditions and SOPs.

4. Lead the hardest missions personally.

5. Publicly demonstrate trust in subordinate leaders. When I would arrive at a subordinate unit location, my first stop was always to speak with the commanding officer. And my first question was, "What items, support, or guidance do you need me to reinforce to

assist you?" Then I would use the phrases and words that they gave me in my conversations with their people. This reinforced their leader role demonstratively in front of their own people.

6. Share in their adversities and their defeats, and champion their successes.

I am going to insert a young leader's perspective here. Our son Mathew has a different idea about leading by example. "Pragmatically, yes, I want to set an example. But sometimes it's a more basic assessment of 'Should I just do it myself?' This is based upon my assessment of time, the effort it will take me, and the quality that I need to ensure. In the end, when I do some things myself and set a bar, that needs to lead to an increased competence in the team/informal leaders so that I can get out of the 'do' mode and back to supervising." Thanks, Mat. Not sure I totally agree. But, at the same time, we have all been there. There is a cost-benefit analysis to be done regarding doing something yourself and having it done how you need it to be done versus allowing someone else to struggle through it because they need to learn to get better. I think that, either way, by admitting that we are setting an example for either the standard of work ("I will do it myself") or the trust and empowerment in other people ("I will allow them to struggle through this"), we are leading by example.

CHAPTER 13

Balance

In November 2020, after 36 and a half years in the military, I came to a very stark and very sudden realization: I couldn't do it anymore. I had experienced huge success in my career, I had good prospects for the future, and, as a major general at 54, I had at least six more years to serve before I would be forced to retire due to age. I had deep knowledge of the NORAD mission and loved working with our American counterparts. Not to mention that Colorado was a great place to live. But I was exhausted. Done. Nothing left to give. I worked out almost every day. I tried to eat a balanced diet and even enjoyed cooking for Val and I. When I was not at work, I played music, spent lots of time with the love of my life, the Valy girl, met with friends, read books, journalled, listened to podcasts...but none of it could take away my sense of deep spirit fatigue. The leaders I reported to in Canada and the U.S. made it clear that I was doing a great job. I had a great team, and I was surrounded by friends and colleagues I deeply respected and liked. But nope, couldn't do it...*done!*[30]

I am still sorting through how I came to that realization and what was behind it. It hit me like a ton of bricks, and we made the decision within

---

30 It would take another nine months after I signaled my intent to release to the Chief of Defence Staff (CDS, the head of the Canadian military) for my separation from military service to occur. The last few months of working once I had come to my realization were excruciating.

a few days that that would be the end of my career. I had spent my entire career learning how to fly, plan military tactical and operational missions, dismantle countries, fight insurrection and insurgency, and effectively and efficiently hone the skills to take life. Some of the best and most noble elements of the profession of arms still have a rooted conflict against the spirit and divinity of life. That definitely played into my decision. I wanted to make, grow, and build things, not plan to destroy them. I knew that some of my fatigue was due to my own relentless drive to change things and make them right. Sitting back and letting things just "be" was not something I could do. With each new job and the higher and higher responsibilities that came with it, it felt like more and more of myself was being sucked into work. Try as I might to create balance, I could not. So, this chapter is *not* "do as I did." It's "set yourself up better than I did for the long term."

One of my executive assistants in Alaska was Kris Kaehler. Our families have become close friends. Kris and I used to talk about all the heady principled things involved in leadership. When it came to balance, Kris told me that our language needs to change. It should be "life-work balance," not "work-life balance." By putting your priorities in this order, you hold fast to the realization that your life will trump the conduct of your job. I like that. But how can a person find that balance?

This was obviously not just some binary calculation of time spent at work and time spent at home. Well, at least, not completely. At the end of my career, I felt that I had time…but the nature of the problem with the work I was doing was that I was always on call and the phone rang around the clock. When you are watching the world…something is always happening! Being able to disconnect emotionally and intellectually was a skill that I had fostered over the years. Compartmentalization is an important coping skill that makes it possible to be resilient and maintain focus in emotionally charged situations, but it has its downsides if one does not acknowledge the underlying emotions and deal with them. I think that it was this capacity that, ultimately, I ran out of.

When I was the director general of Air Readiness, the position had been a rotating door for general officers for a few years. Through no fault of the RCAF nor of the individuals occupying the position, nobody had remained in that position for longer than 12 months in years. I was committed to providing some continuity there. Within a few months of taking over, I took a couple of weeks of leave to settle into our new house and spend time with family. What I noticed right away was that my team accelerated everything in the days and hours before my departure on leave. I was working until 9 p.m. nightly and was at work by 6 a.m. every day. Once I started my leave, my BlackBerry was constantly blowing up with emergencies that needed my attention. Then, finally, because I had ignored work during the leave period, the days and weeks after I returned were filled with fixing problems that had developed, undoing things that had been poorly done, and trying to catch up on an inbox that overwhelmed me for what seemed like an eternity. At one point, I remarked to a fellow brigadier general that going on leave was not worth it. *Aha!*

I don't know how I fell into this habit, but I started taking days off one at a time instead of taking big vacations where it took me a long time to come down from the stress of work. The intent here was to reduce my daily and weekly stress, to manage a tempo that was conducive to an overall balance. I called this approach "Wednesdays off." (I know, not inspiring.) However, my logic was clear. Every day was a "Monday" or a "Friday." I would come in to work on Monday, and it would be a Monday. But the next day would be a Friday! My team also knew that they could just hold Wednesdays' fires until Thursdays. I could also go out to dinner or plan medical or admin appointments on Wednesdays and enjoy a day off in the middle of the week. I would come back to work on Thursdays refreshed, feeling like Thursday was a Monday. And the next day would be Friday!

I had enough leave to do this a ton. To be clear, I sacrificed any big vacations and never came off that general level of stress. But I found that my ability to balance became much more enjoyable in a job that was one of the craziest, if not *the* craziest, of my career. My boss, the commander of the RCAF, was not too happy about this, and the entire thing started coming apart at the seams when I was needed to replace him at crucial meetings within National Defence Headquarters, many on Wednesdays. But, for about a nine-month period, I held on to this "Wednesdays off" approach, much to the chagrin of many around me. It allowed me to survive. But it taught me an even more valuable lesson about balance and stress.

Fact: Work will occupy the time available, especially in high-end-performance jobs. Choosing a job that is synchronized with the balance you want to achieve is important. Moreover, discussing the balance you wish to achieve with bosses and mentors as your career progresses is important. Finally, setting an example and valuing an honest conversation surrounding balance with the people you lead, mentor, and coach will fundamentally change your organization. Beware the organization that seeks an "all-in" commitment with no limitations from its rising stars. This displays no concern from the organization as to the health and longevity of the individual and fosters no trust. The individuals will tell you what you want to hear while making family and professional plans in direct opposition to those of the organization. You will discover this dichotomy only when they decide it is time to leave with no notice. Indeed, the new generation of workers is looking for this balance first. HR specialists and leaders alike must address portfolio balancing and must spread work to more individuals. This may have pay implications. But I think the research in the coming years will bear out that people are willing to earn less to be more balanced.

Fact: In almost all high-performing jobs, there is an expectation of continuous self-improvement or study on top of work. In some cases, there is an expectation that workers will obtain formal academic certifications. In the military, we were always told that we should be continuously studying. I found this to be hilarious, especially when I was spending 60 to 100 (or more) hours a week working and even more hours than that away from home. (In my first year in command of 1 Wing, I spent 270 days on the road. The second year was worse.) The military also told me that the maintenance of my physical conditioning was a "personal responsibility." Translation: it was to be done on my own time. This theme of "on your own time" was not only applied to physical fitness but to much of our professional development. I watched colleagues of mine struggle with this, especially those who had not had the benefit of a formal university degree or the requisite command of a second language (English and French standards exist for all Canadian service personnel, and those standards increase with rank). The approach of the institution was mostly, "This is on top of your daily job." Unfathomable. With many of my subordinates, I took the approach that achieving these individual education and second language goals was clearly part of their job description, and I assisted them—and disciplined myself—in establishing the priority for them to achieve these goals, even if it meant I needed to temper or reduce their personal performance goals in the short term. If we want our people to grow, we must give them the tools to do so, especially in terms of advice, but more importantly in terms of time and priority, to allow for that growth. This is balance.

When things in the team or workplace or with an individual member of a team start getting out of balance, leaders and coaches need to accept their part in setting the conditions for that imbalance, along with a responsibility to help.

For your own personal balance, you must start with knowing what *you* need.

1. Self-assess.

2. Prioritize, hard! (Make a list and journal the logic so you can come back and check in, and even update.)

3. Be okay with the compromises you have to make! Especially regarding that which you are not going to do/get after and the consequences of this professionally and personally (see chapter 31,

"Prioritization").

4. Don't make it an accident—missing family time (especially with kids) could create resentment. *Choose your family!*

I used to ask myself, "If I had a few extra hours in my week, what would be the *best* area I could spend them on?

→ Leading or connecting with the team,

→ Catching up on personal work,

→ Academic advancement,

→ Exercise and fitness (self-care),

→ Time with family, or

→ Self-study (reading, listening, journalling).

Then I would go straight to my phone or computer, open my schedule, and make sure that it reflected my answer. I would schedule drop-ins with the crew that was holding the watch. I would have an hour on my calendar that was "exec time" that I knew was just for my personal work. I scheduled outings, cooking, and even meditation. I was sending myself, and by extension my team, a message to prioritize balance.

This brings up the idea behind self-care. To be an effective leader or coach for your team, you must be okay first. This is an interesting dichotomy when compared to leaders eating last! But, at the centre, it's rooted in the same premise as our approach to health-care workers. If we don't protect them first, they will not be there when we need them, so we start by having a robust system to enable them. The same is true for coaches and leaders. Next, it is fundamental to understand that if you want your team to practice their own self-care, then you need to be seen doing the same thing. If you don't take the leave days allocated to you but instead sacrifice your family and reward those subordinates who do the same, don't be surprised by the stress and workplace satisfaction that result—not to mention how difficult it will be to find people to step up into new responsibilities.

Obviously, self-care is about taking care of the individual and preventing burnout. But it is also about maximising performance. Although you can make the case that I experienced burnout, I also think that my routines and habits (eating, sleeping, workout) are what allowed me to perform at that level for that long. My advice is to take the long view. Overloading with activities, keeping a high tempo, and pushing the team might look okay now, but over the long term, these things only lead to less longevity, less productivity, and workplace environments focused on binary performance objectives. For me, my warning sign was losing my patience. Or maybe... losing it more than normal?

Stress exists in every workplace and family situation. All the research points to the fact that we should not view all stress as negative. Indeed, positive stress is what pushes us to perform and achieve highly positive things. Removing negative stress from your life is important, but more important still is to identify negative and positive stresses. I also found it better to focus on stress prevention as opposed to stress relief. That being said, every once in a while, my lovely wife Val would tell me to "go to the garage and shoot something." (That is where I had the Xbox set up, *Call of Duty*.) My tips for stress prevention are:

→ Sleep. Program sleep and count hours. Eight to nine is the goal. Six to eight is tenuous. Everything less than that undermines the fabric of your resilience. You will have to catch up, or your health and the floor will hit you... sometimes at the same time.

→ Exercise hard and daily. I always had a personal goal I was trying to achieve and morphed my exercise routines and techniques to push myself.

→ Be mindful of eating and drinking in a healthy way. And be mindful of enjoying that which you eat!

→ Develop skills for self-awareness: meditation, prayer, setting intentions at the beginnings and endings of days, taking a breath when you feel overwhelmed.

→ Hobbies—make time and do them. I played guitar, was in a band, played the drums, and liked cooking.

→ Socialize with friends, but also, most importantly, with your life partner. Spend deep time here and discuss life, and enjoy laughing and living together. Enable your friends and family.

→ Program space before meetings—prepare by reading ahead and laying out what you want achieved and how you want to run the meetings/events.

  • I use cue cards with my main points on them for meetings. This is especially effective for virtual meetings. Doing this allows me to set the right tone and makes me feel better.

→ While doing all of the above, be in the moment and recognize when you are struggling to mentally focus and detach from work. I have stopped working out or playing guitar many times because I could not get my head off something. I have found that it is best to put in some time to resolve that single issue. Then I can relax. Yes, this means I destress by working (on the surface perhaps a bit counterintuitive). The balance will not be defined by your ability to walk away from things, but by your ability to see them for their relative importance. A trick I learned here is "fake it till you make it." Set up a schedule for what you want to do and try to stick to it. After a month or two, this will become a routine. After six months, it will be a habit, and then you will be hooked. But the only real way to approach any of the things listed above is to be in the moment. If you are cooking, turn on the music you like or the TV (I used to cook on Sundays to a myriad of rom-com movies on

TV) and enjoy the moment preparing food for your family or for yourself. *Be in the moment!*

There is an inherent link (for me, at least) between organizational/managerial methods, especially as they pertain to self-care and good leadership. It is why professionalism is one of the tenets of my personal leadership philosophy. As a coach or leader, I am setting the example for future leaders and coaches. They need to see a leader practising the self-care needed to lead and coach well. The opposite example occurs all too often; overworked, over-stressed leaders and coaches reacting poorly to pressure and events results in "I do *not* want that job." This is a doomsday cry for organizations and their culture, as you want to foster a culture that has individuals who desire to advance. It is even worse for organizations that must recruit and promote from within, like the military. If you are not busy deliberately creating high-quality people to take your place, then you will be disappointed with the accidental quality of those who do. Balance is a key element to creating the culture that is needed.

CHAPTER 14

Creativity

How does one create a workplace, an environment, in which creativity is systematically encouraged and supported? Is this just giving people "space" to figure things out for themselves? Do coaches achieve this by empowering the team to decide for themselves? In military terms, is this merely mission command?

No.

It's not as simple as that. I think that coaches and leaders are in a unique position to understand a few things about individuals and teams that are essential for fostering creativity. The first thing is where the team or individual is on their journey toward mastery of skills. In any skill, there are fundamentals that need to be understood to maximize innate creativity while enabling access to the freedom that true creativity needs. There is an interesting balance here between creativity and fundamentals. Fundamentals set up frameworks within which people can create and accomplish, but many coaches and leaders see these as a set of rules—and this influences how they coach. Thinking and coaching like this limit the initiative of the team and especially the individual. An example of this is coaches who set up all their offences around specific plays and describe where the ball is to go, who is to shoot, etc. By dogmatically applying fundamentals as rules, creativity, allowing the team to evolve based upon a deep understanding of the fundamentals, is de facto limited. But merely allowing free-flowing thought without any bounds can have its own drawbacks. If the same basketball team is told to merely scrimmage with no set framework, this will descend into each player trying to take the shot or drive against the entire defence alone. Passing and engaging the remainder of the team only occurs once they enter into difficulty. The fundamentals that underline mastery of a skill also enable progression beyond the boundaries of the "basics." So, for leaders and coaches, first understand where the team is on their mastery of your skill(s). Next, realize that even in free-thinking, innovative teams, setting goals and framing the creativity has benefits. But not all creativity manifests in the same way.

Keith Moon and Neil Peart are my favourite drummers. They couldn't be more different. Keith Moon's style was totally spirited and emotionally charged. He created magic in channelling that energy into wild and exciting rhythms. Neil Peart, on the other hand, was known as "The Professor." He broke down every beat and syncopation and saw them in contrast to the melodies and harmonies of his fellow musicians. He saw tension and release, ebb and flow within the pieces of music just as a professor versed in his craft would. Moon and Peart both accessed creativity in different ways—clinical versus emotional, perhaps—but each still based his creativity upon fundamentals of music, collaboration, and skill.

Gary Benn, one of the most creative people I know—if not *the* most creative person—believes that there is an inherent amount of creativity in each person. In his mind, the job of a leader is to maximize the potential for creativity that is inside of each person. My question to him was whether he believes that a leader or coach can enhance that potential. Is creativity taught or innate?

Now, I have a belief that there are those with inherent talent, whether that's creativity, a mind for numbers, leadership, or something else. But, more importantly, I believe that almost every skill or talent out there can also be taught. I think that leadership is a taught skill. I believe that coaching is much the same. But creativity…I wondered.

Gary is an artist. He paints, draws, and is a phenomenal musician. But I see his innate creativity in the craftsmanship he applies to almost everything. But contrary to my friend's belief, I think it is a learned skill. I am not a do-it-yourself pro. I need directed guidance and exact explanations on all projects. But I have watched Gary draw on various skills in an imaginative way that, to me, is something he learned by being creative in his arts. Val and I used to have a turtle lamp. It glowed orange and was the coolest thing. It broke. Gary and Lisa (his wife) found this rooster lamp (we all call it a chicken, but it really is a rooster, guys) on the local Facebook marketplace. He had to buy the lamp, repair the cracks in the glass, then research how to paint the glass. He poured this mixed paint stuff and glaze into the belly of the rooster and then baked it. The result is beautiful. But I never would have thought to do it that way…I mean, baking a glass lamp?! In another example, I left my 12-string guitar with him for years because we moved so much. It had a crack that he employed several methods to repair, and now it looks awesome. He didn't just use a single idea, but multiple expressions of craftsmanship and creativity to achieve beautiful results. In my mind, Gary has an innate talent to see images, create murals, infuse colour and light, write, and play music. He channels these into almost everything in his life. But he learned and honed that creativity by studying and practicing music, experimenting with painting and drawing, and constantly wanting to improve himself. So how would leaders and coaches have maximized his talents?

We have already discussed how the connection between the coach or leader and the individual or team is key to inspiration. This is not merely the inspiration to get through the workday. To truly elevate our teams, we need to inspire them by connecting their development, enabling their personal advancement to the ultimate achievement of team goals. The highest personification of that inspiration is individual and team creativity. When self-starting teams use individual and collective talents to create innovative and effective solutions, that is the product of this inspiration. Here are a few tips to elevate your team's creativity:

→ Set the stage, bold, big, and inspirational. Only you as the leader and coach can capture the imagination of the individuals on the team. Group settings are also where they can collectively connect to the emotional element of what you need them to create. Do not be afraid to set lofty goals, perhaps beyond achievable. Just be tempered with your expectations once execution commences.

→ Use keywords and open-ended questions. "Imagine if we could create a framework within which domestic emergency response and preparedness were intimately tied to a framework of deterrence and military response in a time of security crisis?" Use words and phrases from your vision but that project to the team. Challenge the team to solve issues that they have railed against. Use your vocabulary to give them the license to explore any and all solutions.

→ Seek team collaboration. Whether the smallest group or a large organization, collaboration will enhance the variety, expose blind spots, explore false boundaries, and spur intellectual innovation.

→ Enable or devolve responsibility to an informal leader. Sometimes leaders in a position of authority are very clearly the largest impediment to creativity. Perhaps comments we have made in the past will prevent team members from putting ideas out there. Recognizing this, removing yourself from the environment, and trusting an informal leader who may be better at inspiring the creativity within the team is a positive way to overcome this.

→ Schedule personal updates with no agenda. The leaders who enabled this best in me were ones who not only issued the challenge but later came down to my level and "checked in," sometimes bypassing multiple links in the chain of command to "just see how it was going." This informal approach allowed me and the rest of the team to ask questions, test theories and boundaries, and oftentimes get re-inspired. It is a great opportunity to show enthusiasm for where things are going and express pride in the team for embracing the process and their individual creativity.

Here is a quick tool to enable collaboration and get involvement from people who are perhaps shy or who get dominated by other, stronger, personalities:

→ For the next two minutes, only ideas, no criticisms. Anyone criticizing must stand up and bow to the group. (I enjoyed "Drop and give me twenty push-ups," but...)

→ Next, for the following two minutes, we will *only* criticize the points or ideas we just made. Anyone who tries to defend a point must stand up and bow to the group. (Again...push-ups...)

→ Finally, for the next two minutes, we will only try to address the issues with each proposal.

By the time you finish this portion, you will most likely have involved most of the people in the room, spurred on by the fact that they cannot be criticized for their comments at any point. The true spirit of creativity in collaboration will be unleashed as people begin to build on the logic of others. Don't be afraid to wander around the room and individually coax people to contribute. Also, watch the body language of the team and make sure that those who are shyer have an opportunity to contribute. And don't be afraid to leave the room and allow the team to go through this on their own devices. This demonstrates trust. Above all, make sure the team knows that only through collaboration between the whole group will true creative maximizations happen.

What inspires each individual will be different. Each will display various degrees of creativity in all aspects of their lives. Some teams and individuals can be spurred to access their creativity by merely connecting better with each other. Team-building opportunities and offsite experiences can assist with this. Exposing the team to experts in the field for their own individual development is another excellent way in which creativity can be developed. Place yourself as the leader and coach in the intersection between what is and what is possible and project your team into the wondrous variety of possibilities.

CHAPTER 15

Service

I want to start this chapter with a quick story. Story: I used to play lunch bucket basketball at RMC. Tuesdays and Thursdays. I was not good. But I could run…okay, not quickly, but I had distance legs. I am the antithesis of a basketball player. Short, not quick, can't jump. One of the cadets who had just graduated as a second lieutenant had been an All-Canadian player. He was a big man who could run the floor. I didn't think he knew me, but I totally knew who he was. I was just another player who showed up and played twice a week.

One day, as we were waiting for the other players to show, he came over and asked me if he could ask me a question. He knew that I was a lieutenant colonel in the Air Force, and he wanted some career advice. I said sure. He told me that he had been given an offer to go play professional basketball in Europe after graduation. He was in the midst of his occupation training, which, when finished, would result in a posting to a line unit. What he was considering was submitting a request to defer his obligatory service so that he could take advantage of the opportunity to play ball in Europe. I told him that that was an amazing opportunity, and he should pursue it.

He looked at me and said, "Really?"

I said, "Sure."

He obviously noticed the perfunctory fashion in which I answered and perhaps the dismissive tone that I had.

He pushed me again. "I really want to know what you think."

"You really want to know?"

"Yeah, I really want to know…"

What followed was a quick burst transmission (Clancy style) on how the government and people of Canada had spent a significant amount of money and time training him to be a soldier and officer. That what I really thought was that the skills and leadership that he had honed as a player-leader and cadet were exactly the skills we needed in the current war in Afghanistan. That the crucible of high-level university basketball had given him unique insights into adrenaline, defeat, grief, victory, controlling emotions, and, above all, leading and creating cohesion through chaos. He needed to pick up a rifle and deploy. His training to this point was not about him, it was about his country and service to the nation.

He thanked me, and then we played basketball. (I think he dunked over me very early on as a statement.) I believe that that young man deployed, performed in an extraordinary fashion in combat, and has gone on to be a coach at the highest levels of his sport in the country. He personifies the word "service" to this day.

Those who answer the call to serve the nation in their military resign to give their lives if required in that service. The same is true of our police forces, who, in many ways, are the ones who are securing our communities. Although we should never diminish the remembrance of those who have given the ultimate sacrifice in the service of our nations, we should also honour the fact that the commitment to make that sacrifice, although cashed in when the last full measure of devotion is given, is actually made when the individual raises their hand and takes an oath. This is why we honour service before self. Our police and military forces provide an example of what service truly means. Despite the obstacles. Despite the adversities. Despite what our populations might think of us on any given day.[31] Rooted in the knowledge that society cannot survive without the security that police and military forces provide. None of this diminishes the need for oversight and improvement in the conduct of police and military operations and education, but it recognizes that the service that is being provided is, at its root, coming from a good place.

Leaders and coaches need to embody the phrase "Service above or before self." More than this, they need to demonstrate that the principal service that they as coaches and leaders provide is to the team that they are leading and coaching. This is where the paradigm of "servant leadership" meets the dilemma from chapter 1 about people versus mission. But perhaps the idea of servant leadership allows us to coalesce the many concepts at play in the debate between people and mission into a singular concept, "purpose." The connection between the coach or leader, the team and the people in it, and the mission can be a connection to a *higher purpose* for all. Even in the most business-oriented teams, the connection to a sense of purpose that the team can rally behind must be rooted in a positive and value-based frame. Once a purpose has been established, both individuals and coaches see the benefit of serving that purpose. Team and individual goals become the same, or, perhaps more often, aligned.

Leaders and coaches could find this sense of "purpose" in the way coaches and leaders support and reward their employees, or perhaps through the work that the organization is doing, but it's also possible to find it in the way the work is being done. Companies that have the stated goals of being the lowest carbon emitters, or that have associated philanthropy and charity campaigns, that contribute to youth sports or provide work placement

31 I refer to the collective instances of the Canadian population's reaction to the Somalia affair and the decade of darkness that pursued, the reaction of the U.S. people during the Vietnam era, and the daily reactions that many populations have shown to our police forces.

for homeless people…all are providing an element of service that connects coaches and teams to a purpose. There is also an inherent link to the concept of connection that we have previously discussed. Rooted in our natural DNA is a need for connection and a desire for purpose in our lives and in what we do while on this earth.

Indeed, it has been my experience that, in discussing the service that leadership is providing to the team, it is rare to find a team that is not already focused on the objectives of the mission. However, their sense of service gets lost when compared to the personal and/or professional sacrifices they are making for it. In addition, they cynically see many leaders and coaches, even if professing good things, as being only "in it" for their own advancement. So, as coaches and leaders, we must see purpose, or a sense of service, beyond the primary delivery of whatever output is in our workplaces and teams, as something to divine. I believe that purpose is a primary antidote to disconnected teams.

Since I have retired, I have been asked to speak with and mentor senior military personnel. In one such encounter where I was explaining the overwhelming nature of a portfolio designed merely to defend the continent, I was asked how I got through it, what motivated me to continue. I surprised even myself when I said, "Service to my country."

How is your team exemplifying service? What is the way you as a leader and coach connect people and mission? What is the team's sense of purpose? How could you elevate the team or organization to enable purposeful engagement? How can the product or output of your team be aligned with a sense of greater service?

There is no silver bullet here. Even in the military, continuously using the overarching mantra of service to the country and its all-encompassing dedication will, at one point, ring hollow or fall on deaf ears. By honouring the service that our teams provide on a continuous basis, specifically their service to the organization and the combined sense of purpose, we place ourselves as coaches and leaders in a mindset of enabling them to continue to serve. This is the true alignment of mission and people. Be cognisant of individual and team sacrifices that are being made to achieve organizational performance goals. Know and understand these sacrifices and the impediments to their continued service in detail. Recognize, publicly and often, their service and the hurdles they face. Do not allow for ever-increasing performance expectations to erode that. Be the champion of those things that your team needs in order to continue to make the sacrifices they do. Advocate for your team incessantly. Be ready to compromise your own individual advancement in any organization to better lead and coach the one you are in. This is what service means to a coach and leader.

CHAPTER 16

Leading with Emotions

What is the role of emotions within a group? What role and responsibility do coaches and leaders have regarding a group's emotions and their own emotions as leaders? These questions are very important to answer, and the answers can be divided into two categories. Category one: emotions allow us to inspire people and teams to our vision and mission. Category two: emotions allow us to interact in a positive, empathetic, and helpful way, to create the conditions for success and health in our teams. These bins bleed over and help each other, as most of the tools are the same.

In chapter 6, "Connection," we discussed connecting with the team as a coach or leader and having each member of the team connect with the mission and vision for the team. This is the nucleus to inspiration and "category one" of our emotions. But inspiring someone is more than connecting with them and connecting them with the vision. "Inspiring" means lighting that fire inside of them that makes them become autonomous. They become self-starters. Emotions need to be engaged to light that fire. These emotions might include a desire or drive to achieve, to better themselves, or to help other members of the team. Maybe the actual mission becomes a "cause" for them. This is especially true of people in the service industries, first responders, and the public service. So, we must engage emotions to progress from connection to inspiration. Okay.

But emotions are not just tools we use to amp people up and get them fired up to "charge that hill." They are also the colours, sounds, and textures that ultimately define our relationship with people at work and our relationship with the work and its environment. This is "category two." So, as leaders, we need to set the correct emotional framework to enable the team to thrive. To thrive, members of the team need to feel valued.

The problem I saw as a leader and coach is that I never made a deliberate connection between the emotions I was feeling and how I was portraying those emotions. To me, they "just happened." When I was being mentored, one of the pieces of feedback that I heard most often from my coaches and mentors was that I needed to work on getting control of my emotions. "Calm down. Don't be so intense." Two errors here. First, there are no tools being suggested to really execute this. That is a mixed responsibility between myself and those I had coaching me. But the most important error was mine and mine alone. I dismissed much of this feedback under the guise of "I am who I am, and I am not going to change who I am." Okay... ummmmmm...wow, Scott. You must think very highly of yourself! So... you're perfect? Far from it. But self-reflection needs a door to open your mind to possibilities. To me, my emotions were, well...me! And if organizations didn't want me, then @#?! 'em!

As I noted in chapter 5, "Self-Awareness," the "door" for me came in the form of reading Mark Divine's book *Unbeatable Mind*. This was my first introduction to the idea of the monkey mind. The idea that you have a voice that is constantly saying things in your head—mostly negative things—was novel. But the idea that thoughts or emotions could be separated from reactions was revolutionary. What helped as well was understanding that these negative things were born out of millions of years of evolution as hunter-gatherers, during which time humans needed to second-guess and question everything. This internal negative dialogue was key to being ready for every threat, to maximizing our chances for obtaining food and water— basically, it was key to our very survival. But it does not necessarily serve us well in the modern world. Recognizing that this monkey mind is not "us" can be empowering.

My study moved on from there to the work of Susan David, who further expanded my understanding of the emotional and mental dynamic. Beyond the kind of mental focus and resilience that Mark Divine explored, Susan David describes the idea of inserting space between experiencing the emotion, driven by that monkey mind, and the behaviour that we exhibit. The space was equal to "choice," and I could choose how I wanted to react.[32] Or, at least for me…theoretically, I could choose. Putting this into practice would prove much more challenging. Welcome to being Scott! Engage mouth on emotions; brain will follow.

Okay, I am being a bit disingenuous. I always engaged my brain. But I would specifically not think through the emotions I was feeling to choose perhaps a better reaction. At a minimum, I needed to be aware of the emotions I was feeling. But I had no baseline for emotions. My experience had told me that when I got upset, that was bad. Okay, so there are bad emotions? But is that it? Just don't get angry or pissed off and you're good? Are there more nuanced emotions? And how was I going to be self-aware enough to actually realise when I was getting emotional?

Susan David's work on emotional agility is very compelling, and, since I am a highly sensitive person and very emotional, I like her idea that there are no negative emotions. In my readings on emotions, the most important thing I discovered was that there was a role for emotions in leading and coaching. But I also agree that we must expand our vocabulary of emotions and get away from labelling positive and negative emotions. This led me to the research of Brené Brown. Brené Brown has worked significantly on enhancing our emotional vocabulary in her awesome book, *Atlas of the Heart*. In that book, she identifies 87 emotions. However, what I

---

32   This is Susan David's premise on emotional agility.

found even more revealing is that, after surveying over 7,000 people, she found that the majority could only identify three emotions while they were feeling them: happiness, sadness, and anger. For leaders and coaches, the vocabulary around emotions is crucial. There is a difference between feeling overwhelmed and feeling fearful. There is a difference between feeling disappointed and feeling guilty. And categorising things into three generic emotions (happy, sad, angry)—or simply not being able to connect to an emotion because we cannot label it—is an area we need to work on.

Imagine a team member who is struggling with a project. Do you understand why? How can you help that team member without understanding the underlying emotion they're experiencing? Being overwhelmed by the tempo of the work is different from being fearful that they are not qualified or experienced enough to actually do it. Being angry at you as the leader for assigning them this work is different than being resentful because you got promoted into that leadership role and they did not.

I don't think that I ever evolved to where I was clearly creating that space—and was self-aware enough of my emotions that I could choose my behaviours—prior to leaving the military. But I was aware enough to put in place mechanisms to enable my awareness of situations and issues that would trigger my emotions (see chapter 19, "Setting Intentions"). I also began to speak much more frankly with my team, especially my senior leaders and friends, about those things that "got me going."

Here is some of my advice for coaches and leaders concerning emotions:

1. Establish a base of emotional vocabulary so that the team has the verbal tools to express themselves.

2. Identify group emotional elements. This will bring the team to a more personalized sense of purpose and ground the team in the "people reality." Introduce this into recurrent meetings. Ask questions using the vocabulary. "How do you feel about the

workload?"

3. Develop trigger/flag phrases that cue into the need to explore the emotional side of things. (Hard to do with young men especially.)

4. Avoid externalizing/pointing fingers; not "you make me…" but rather "this situation makes me feel…"

5. Apply this specifically to tight timelines and managing tempo within teams.

6. Have this as a component of update meetings when dealing with organizational structure upheavals/change.

7. Review/assess trust. This needs to be layered over a foundation of trust, leader/coach-led, and reinforced.

8. Recognize that this is a leadership tool rather than a management tool.

9. There is individual prep work for this, and it can be used for all interactions.

My entire career, I was mentored that I needed to control my emotions, which made me feel that having these emotions was bad. Good leaders, I was told, are even-keeled, sage, and not prone to emotional outbursts. Well, I always thought that these kinds of leaders were boring, not inspirational, and had difficulty connecting with the people who worked for them. When I read Susan David's work, it made me understand my own emotions so much better. There are no good or bad emotions, just good and bad behaviours. Seek the space between emotions and behaviour to connect with your values. Let your behaviours reflect those values. But simultaneously recognize and validate the actual emotions. They are leading you somewhere. Be in control of where they are leading you.

When I was in the field in charge of training an air task force for deployment to Iraq, I was told that my dad had been taken to the hospital and that he had had a stroke. They told me that the time to come and see him was right away, as his situation was deteriorating rapidly. That same day, a member of the air task force was told that his own father had just passed away. In the swirl of emotions I was feeling and the responsibilities that I felt for these people, I insisted that I see this still-grieving person before I left. We met as I rolled out of a jeep beside his tent. He had tears in his eyes, and so did I. We didn't speak. I hugged him, he hugged me. We both cried for our dads. That was an emotional connection. There was no space. It was raw.

I am not sure how to control my emotions, and sometimes I believe that a coach or leader shouldn't always try. I have always known that when family stress gets magnified by work issues or imperatives, I go to my emotional side quickly. It took me years to identify this and see it for what it was. But it was in my work as a coach that I developed more patience with myself and control of my emotions.

I hated close games. Hated them. I am not really that competitive. In games where we were losing handily, I did not feel the stress and I could coach the players the way I wanted to. When they were winning, I coached them even harder and challenged them more specifically. But in close games, I felt the pressure of the score competing with my true underlying goal, which was the development of the players and not the product of a single game. Yet in that moment, I had to enable these young men to rise to the occasion of the moment and succeed. By creating space between the emotions I was feeling and my desire to let an assistant coach the team so that we could just win (or lose) and be done with it, I calmed myself (somewhat) and provided sage coaching (I think) to the players both individually and as a team.

As we come to the end of the "Fundamentals" section, I think we should look over our shoulder for a second. From developing trust to leading with emotions, these fundamentals are at the very core of skills and knowledge required to be a good leader. As I have said, it is not good enough just to read about them. It's not good enough to say, "Yeah I agree with that." What do these fundamentals mean to you? How would you say that your leading and coaching reflect how you think and feel about each fundamental? How do your daily routines, interactions with team members, and organizational processes reflect these fundamentals? How do you want to change or incorporate a fundamental?

Taken as a group, evaluating this might be a tall task, but you need to reflect and internalize, and perhaps even reject these fundamentals. I would tackle them one at a time. Perhaps use them to spur on your own journalling. Take some key words and punch them into your favourite podcast provider and see what comes up. For new leaders and coaches, some of this may be completely new and foundational. To experienced leaders, this might be largely review. I think going back to basics always helps ground us in the practices and values that we hold dearest. It makes our decision-making easier through clarity of mind and purpose.

As we now look forward on our journey, how are these fundamentals applied? How do we deal with difficult crisis situations, team members who defy us regardless of how much effort we put into them, or complex organizations with already-existing structures of human relations meant to alleviate all the workplace frictions? The tactics, techniques, and procedures that we will explore next should magnify the fundamentals we have just covered. Hopefully the linkages begin to be developed through which the tools in TTPs give life to some of the basics. The foundation is set...now let's apply it!

Section 2

TACTICS, TECHNIQUES, AND PROCEDURES

I hope that at this point you have even more questions than you did when you started. I always think that the more we know, the more we realize we don't know. How do these fundamentals apply practically? How do I approach crisis situations with high time and performance pressures without barking at my team and losing their trust? How do I balance the overwhelming organizational demands on me as a coach or leader personally with the needs of my team? What tools are available to help me control my emotions and organize my schedule and mind to accomplish what I think are my fundamentals? How do I approach a team member who is dragging the whole team down?

In this section, we will focus on elements that relate more to the "how" surrounding coaching and leading. To me, the distinction between fundamentals and TTPs is a bit of a blurry line. However, a major part of the distinction is that TTPs are about the implementation or execution, as opposed to the lofty theory ideas contained in fundamentals. Some of these topics will flesh out fundamentals covered so far by showing how we can put them into practice or how a few of the fundamentals work together to form a technique. Others will seem completely new.

Let's keep in mind that this should be a continuation of the journey and that no technique or procedure is going to replace good fundamentals. You can, however, expect to see techniques and procedures that will leverage the fundamentals that you have perhaps already developed or inherently know. The ability to be self-aware needs to be supported by a systemic approach to setting intentions before meetings and at the beginning of each day. This cannot be random and needs to be scheduled. Scheduling and prioritization of work and a systemic approach to organizing all your meetings are key tools for maintaining balance. I want you to see the TTPs in concert with the fundamentals.

Don't be afraid to jump around if a topic interests you. You can even go back to a fundamental to remind yourself of that concept. Make notes in the margin. Or star an idea, flag it, and perhaps even say it's crap! Perhaps you disagree with the connection or premise. On the other hand, perhaps a particular TTP will ring true to you. Maybe it is a subject that you want your team to discuss and delve into. Remember, what I share in this book is all my opinion, so please use it in any way you can to be a better leader and coach.

Let's dig in!

CHAPTER 17

Mentoring/Coaching Techniques

The techniques being used to coach and mentor people and teams are directly related to the type of coaching being done and to the people and situation involved. I would say this is much more evident in coaching than in leading. When we think of the application of a style and varying approaches in the "Fundamentals" section, effective coaches and mentors are much more fluid than perhaps leaders in this respect. Therefore, the techniques used by coaches are similarly more varied than those used by leaders. What works when coaching a team on a basketball court may not work when mentoring a person on career or life choices for them and their families.

The most important technique for a mentor or coach is establishing rapport at the individual level. This is an extension of the concepts of "connection" and "trust" in fundamentals, but not at a group level—*at the individual level.* Many leaders and coaches have expressed to me that they are uncomfortable doing this. Some state that they worry about how they will be perceived by other workers. New leaders, especially those who are being promoted from within organizations, feel that they have no moral authority to ask these questions. Others are fearful of the answers they may get when they try to establish that connection. Even some experienced leaders and coaches have expressed to me that this takes too much time and personal energy, and it is easier to merely coach their teams. In the sphere of coach and leader development, one of the habits we are seeing is leadership via email, text, directive, or any other mechanism that removes that personal one-on-one connection with our people. The further up we go to higher levels of responsibility, the more this becomes the norm. The work-related results of the pandemic, the pervasive use of video conferences and remote work, alongside a desire to create a better balance in our lives, will continue to compete with establishing human connection with our teams. I believe the connection at the personal level distinguishes great leaders from good ones, and, for coaches, I think this connection is even more essential.

To connect with people at that individual level, we need to understand them first. Start by getting to know people at that individual level, employing the skills of good listening, so that you can understand the context within which they are operating. Many coaches will be working right down at the personal level, trying to maximize individuals' performance. That rapport, the intimate knowledge of what drives a person and their connection to the task, is the foundational piece of information from which to begin building a plan for personal development. As a minimum, the rapport is a foundation from which to have an honest conversation. Remember that the person being coached or mentored is going to decide to what extent they will be coached or mentored. The coachee or mentee is in control here. It may take much more than a single engagement to even establish that rapport. But, when you try, the honest conversation will grow to more over time.

My technique for beginning a coaching or mentoring relationship in that first encounter is to get to know each other. For this, you need to prepare well. In many large organizations, there will be some formal business or information file about individual performance and development that is passed on to you as a coach or leader. Okay, but when conducting that first encounter, don't make that file the focus. In preparing, read everything you can about the individual from their personnel file or from your notes. Then seek out past leaders or coaches for their perspectives—just don't be swayed by their biases. Lastly, prepare questions that tease out the key issues for you. If an individual is missing a key developmental piece, then asking them their plan for that piece is important. Lastly, look for overlapping interests and information. Establishing an individual connection because you both enjoy cooking, or fishing, or basketball is good. I always asked a lot of questions pertaining to where people grew up, where they have been in their careers, and how they liked those experiences. Allow that conversation to flow easily to wherever it takes you. This is all done with the purpose of establishing rapport or connection with them at the personal level.

As the coach/mentor relationship evolves, don't be afraid to talk frankly and openly about emotions when having these conversations. I might be slightly leery about emotions in an initial encounter, as it could be overwhelming to you both. You may also be thrust into a mentor situation where you must resolve issues immediately, so slowly developing rapport is not an option. Regardless, even simply acknowledging how situations make you feel—or, even better, have made you feel in the past—can provide a positive environment that will allow for open discussion. For coaches, this is crucial.

Sometimes, perhaps often, people do not wish to convey emotions even though acknowledging them is the only way to have a frank discussion. A couple of good coaching techniques at this point are to:

1. Describe how that situation would make you feel. "Wow, being in that position would make me feel discouraged and I would get down on myself." And/or,

2. (Quickly) describe a similar situation that you were in and how that made you feel. "I think I understand how you feel. When I sat on the bench as part of a team years ago, it made me feel like I

wasn't good enough, so why try?"

The "fundamental" of having a good emotional vocabulary, one that can be shared and mutually understood, is of huge benefit here. As a coach and leader, you may not have the benefit of having that baseline established before you must jump in and establish this rapport. Although it's important, I would advise against using initial engagements as an opportunity to dive deep into emotional agility and vocabulary. This is about your coachee/mentee, so make sure that your pontifications are not the focus. Using small suggestions and/or probing questions that have good emotional vocabulary can help: "Is this anger…or are you frustrated that your hard work is not being recognized?" These tools will help you tease out *in them* the things that are at the root of their motivation. Just remember: these conclusions need to come from them.[33]

To develop an emotional vocabulary, I recommend starting with any of the available images, online or in books, that portray the wide variety of emotions. Print out one that you like and put it in your daily planner or pin it to your wall where you can reference it. When you are setting intentions for the day or dealing with your team, don't be afraid to reference that image as a reminder to think through feelings more deeply. Next, I recommend that, in your practice of journalling and reflecting on your leadership and coaching performance, you try to associate behaviours with the underlying emotions. This should not only be critical in nature but also reinforcing. We learn when we succeed and recognize why, not merely when, we fail or make mistakes. For example, "I am proud that I recognized that this team member was confused, not angry. We aligned quickly on establishing clarity and communicating better, and I saw an immediate shift!"

Rapport will not be meaningfully established unless there is mutual trust. Establishing that two-way street of trust may take more than a single en-

---

33 Using the Socratic approach by asking questions and not providing solutions is an excellent tool here.

counter. In fact, most people are not spring-loaded to trust immediately; they need some proof of trustworthiness first. My advice here is to first, not allow that fact to deter you in taking the first step in establishing rapport, and second, never forget that you are constantly building on that rapport even in group settings. Your actions and words as a coach or leader will reinforce, or undermine, any rapport that you establish. Be cognisant of this. In addition, do not be afraid to use techniques such as body language and non-verbal communication to reinforce individual rapport and connection. When speaking with a group after having established a connection with an individual, a head nod, eye contact, quick handshake, sidebar exchange, or pat on the shoulder can go a long way in demonstrating how you value that individual and the connection. Just remember the balance of not singling someone out too much.

Next, make sure that you follow up. The technique here is to not always make it random. Random engagement of individuals will cause you to default to only engaging them when warning signs, problems, or administration make you engage. This indicates a complete lack of empathy for the individual and is crucially detrimental to trust in coaches and leaders. So, when ending a mentor engagement, don't forget to mention when you will follow up next. This does not mean that the only engagements with individuals will be programmed mentor times. Whenever you are passing by sections, teams, or people, don't forget to drop in and just say hi with no agenda. This informality usually opens the door to honest conversation about what is going on in the moment. People are often disarmed by your impromptu and thoughtful engagement and will speak more freely. Honour this by listening, taking notes, and giving feedback right then and there. Close this loop by following back up on issues or subjects that are raised informally with those who bring them up. It will not take long for a solid rapport to be established, as the trust that these techniques underpin will flourish.

It is important to remember that, even once rapport is established, not all engagements will be positive. As a coach or leader, you will never truly know how that dynamic is changing or evolving. My advice is to always view the *relationship* between you and the individual being coached or mentored as being *more important* than the singular issue that you are trying to resolve. In this manner, even if the news or issue is something extremely uncomfortable and detrimental for them personally, on the balance of things, the person being coached will value the relationship and connection over the specific topic. My technique here is to always strive to look beyond the issue within the coach/mentor relationship. When I was delivering results of merit boards or informing very senior officers that they would not be placed in line for key commands, this was very important. Be frank and straightforward concerning skills, performance, and shortfalls. Clearly state the decision and the rationale. Then state the value of the individual and the way ahead along with their options. Make it about them *because it is about them!* Individuals, in my experience, will default to criticizing the system and the individuals running the system. Remember at this point your fundamentals of trust. Demonstrating empathy for the individual in this tough circumstance cannot lead to compromising the foundations of trust in the system that you are coaching and leading within. If you go down this "we vs. they" road, you will not be helping the individual and you will not address the key issues at play. Most importantly, the trust that the individual has in you as a coach cannot be rooted in a mutual hatred of the system and its leaders. It must at heart be rooted in a belief that, as a coach/mentee team, you and the individual can overcome these issues. To trust that and get beyond the current situation, they must trust that you have some beneficial value in understanding the system and assisting them in overcoming—or at least dealing with—their circumstances. In these tough situations, I employ the practice of listing the facts, followed by having them lead the conversation to possible options.

For example:

"You finished 56 on the merit list. They will promote about 25 people this year. So even if nobody passes you by, you might get picked up next year. However, you were ranked 60 on the merit list the year before and they promoted 30. This means that you were bypassed by 20 or so people this year. Your evaluations are good, but you are missing this one key piece of experience/qualification/ranking. In addition, you are approaching the end of your career. I see a few options for you. (Use suggestion and inquisition here.) How do you envision getting that final piece of experience? Have you discussed with your spouse and family what the next career step looks like for you? Let's talk about the various options that achieve both your work and family goals."

Some of the facts that you present are "pills" that the individual needs to swallow. Being tactful, you still must face the issue head-on. Too many leaders and coaches fail here by skirting the issue, shrugging it off as being out of their control, and casting blame elsewhere, either to the larger organization (this is pandering to the emotions of the person being mentored) or to the individual (this is not helping them).

In carrying on the example from above: "You cannot advance without this key piece of experience/qualification. You have openly stated to me that you don't want to do that. Raging against the system is not going to help this, and we must come to terms with that fact."

It is important at this point to return the individual back to a positive application of their talents. If advancement is the only goal that the individual has and they are not willing to make the sacrifice or do the things required, then mentoring toward movement to new employment, education, or even retirement is a good move. Asking about other goals is important. These can be life-changing moments! Many people working in tough jobs for decades feel they are on a hamster wheel, and the freedom that is experienced when these people no longer feel the need to advance can be liberating. Thereafter, some can find huge solace in the current work, team, and environment they are in without the stress of ever-expanding performance goals. Some can finally decide to put family first, with everything this entails. Even more, once this perception or demand for constant advancement is removed, many actually come into their own and begin to demonstrate the leadership and coaching skills they were lacking before. For you as the coach and leader in these situations, seeing the individual relationship more than the systemic relationship means that this is a starting point for coaching and mentoring, *not* an end point. Far too many organizations cease coaching and mentoring people who are not being groomed for advancement. *Wrong.* Use your own network of contacts to enable these mutually developed goals, even if they mean that a high-quality individual will leave the organization. State categorically that you have a relationship with this individual beyond the formal one that you have been thrust into. Reinforce that some of the best leaders, coaches, and high performers have no desire to advance and are doing the yeoman's work of the organization. (This will fall flat if, as a leader, you have not been expounding these things publicly within your team prior to this.) Finally, reinforce that they will always be able to call on you for advice and mentoring. With people I have mentored, I have even gone so far as to say that I might have to call on them one day for advice—and, on numerous occasions, I have later done so.

It is important here to mention vocabulary. Establishing a mutually understood and accepted vocabulary allows for communication on clearly established lines of accountability. But it also provides a framework of understanding that allows for discourse. You know that the people working for you have bought into the vocabulary when they are using it against you and their logic is infallible. I hate that…but I love it.

I remember a specific conversation with a subordinate squadron commander and personal friend, which took place in front of the rest of my commanding officers: "You purport 'Fly—Shoot—Spend'… but if we are merely drilling holes in the sky without programming that which we are achieving in a more deliberate fashion, we are not going to be able to provide the lethality and integration so key to our mission. It takes a day and a half to plan a tactical mission that might only take one hour of flying time. That same crew could fly six to eight hours in that same timeframe. How do we rationalize that?"

What follows will be a frank discussion on how to achieve that balance. Whatever the outcomes, the vocabulary that frames the discussion forms the foundation for mentoring leaders and teams on achieving goals. I am referring to vocabulary here larger than only emotional vocabulary. The vocabulary sets limits on and channels emotions: "What do we say about officials? Put the ball in the hoop so many times that it doesn't matter what they say." "Wow, what a great game. Now go out and shake hands and honour the competition of that other great team."

The technique here is to deliberately develop a vocabulary that enables you to lean in to coaching and mentoring at the individual level. It resonates with the individual and with the team. You will see examples later on in the book where I use vocabulary and key phrases. But what I want you as coaches and leaders to know is that the vocabulary, tone, and technique are all tied together. Being hard in practices and extremely positive in games was my technique. I only got frustrated with my players in games if I saw unsportsmanlike conduct or lack of effort. With my subordinate commanders, I always wanted to be in a position of offering advice; there was plenty of time for me to give very specific directions, and my tone of delivery was very different in those instances. However, my personal time with my subordinate commanders was all about coaching and mentoring. It was me speaking to them as if I were behind them, talking over their shoulders. I would employ inquisition and suggestion and sometimes have them explain where they were mentally to understand their logic and leadership. I would use soft tones (well, I would try to) and pragmatic discourse, but not direction, as I wanted to let them work things out. But I also wanted them to benefit from my experiences and feel they were in a safe position to question my direction so that they could flesh out their understanding of it. Sometimes I would see that their organization needed a more fulsome look at itself. I would seek out a specific item and task them with it, knowing that passing through that process would make them better overall.

I think it needs to be stated that it took me a long time to develop these skills and I did not always succeed. Here is an example from Colonel Trevor Teller of the RCAF that explains some of this evolution:

I would parcel the mentor relationship with Scott Clancy into three bins:

Early Days

I was a subordinate and the acting commanding officer of a helicopter squadron. I had been tasked by Scott's team to offer comments on a plan that implicated our squadron. My comments questioned the feasibility of execution on the tasks assigned us, and therefore brought into question the logic of the entire plan. Shortly after sending my feedback, I got a phone call from Scott that was relatively direct and felt disciplinary. He pointed out the errors in my observations and the process and considerations that had informed the analysis at their (higher) level. I challenged him by stating, "If I understood any of the logic of what you are explaining now, my comments would have been different, but if you are going to ask for my feedback, that is what you will get. It will be from my perspective."

The tone of the conversation changed immediately. I believe he appreciated that the absence of that context mattered. "Okay" he said, "let me explain. This is how we came at the problem. This is what we understand the risks to be. This is…" The tone of teaching and coaching blended and provided me an understanding of what was being asked of our unit and the risks that had already been considered. It was not the most comfortable conversation in the world! I remember going home and telling my wife that I had either made an important connection or would be fired the next day. It ended up being the most important mentor/protégé relationship of my career, leading to a friendship not just between us, but our families.

COS

Flash forward a few years, and I was now Scott's chief of staff (COS). Scott had become the wing commander, and I was working directly for him (in his old position). By that time, we had developed a rapport that allowed for open and honest conversation without risk to the relationship. Proximity to the commander was essential to the achievement of my function, but also personally formative in grasping how he used multiple perspectives to address known and potential issues. It was almost "coaching by osmosis." So long as I was present for conversations with his subordinates and superiors, I was able to understand his leadership intent and provide those perspectives to both the staff and subordinate units. The relationship was no longer about instilling core skills and understanding; rather, it was about nuance and dealing with complexity amid the day-to-day grind or in crisis. The tenure as COS was characterized by hundreds of personal interactions with Scott.

Commanding Officer

I left my job as COS to become a commanding officer of a tactical helicopter squadron, still working for Scott but now in a command role. As our unit conducted gruelling exercises in preparation for deployment overseas, Scott tasked me with developing a set of information requirements to inform my decision-making. The unit had been training for operations with its affiliated army brigade over a period of many months. I felt the squadron was running well and our decision-making processes were sound. So, this task he assigned me was somewhat confusing.

After several weeks of batting it around with little progress, I went back to Scott and expressed my confusion at what I was being asked to do. I told him that I was comfortable with how we (I) were arriving at decisions. "Yes," was his reply, "the decision-making process is sound, but I question if you are making all the required decisions." Put succinctly, he told me he thought I had an information blind spot that would manifest as risk during actual operations. He took lots of time. He contextualized, provided examples, linked the task he had assigned to work I had done for him as his COS, and reframed my perspective on what was being tasked. We understood each other perfectly and, in the process, I saw very clearly what the deliverable was. After that, it took a day and a half for me to develop the product I needed. The leadership competency that I acquired in being mentored through this thought process is one I would turn to in future command billets and coach my own team on. The nature of our relationship allowed Scott to state the concern frankly. Our relationship did not skip a beat. As the wing commander, he had a responsibility to lead and to set the conditions for mission success. Part of this process was coaching me as a commanding officer through the processes with which I needed assistance.

....

I hope that you can see the elements of learning— attempting to be self-aware to control my emotions, use of tone and vocabulary, and developing and maintaining trust—in this example. I have always believed in the concept of mission command, which is to lead by explaining the mission, intent, where we need to get to at the end, and enough of the "how" that each leader or member of the team knows how things fit together. The remainder of the "how" is left up to the individuals. In leading a wing for the RCAF that was dispersed over the entire country—and, in many cases, around the world—the element of trust here was crucial to mission command. My thought process was that I had to maximize coaching and mentoring to enable this approach. The example above highlights that the "deliberate" mentoring occurring while working at these remote unit locations was focused on shortfalls in individual competencies identified by the coach (me) as the result of an event. Something happened that triggered the coach (me) to engage. I refer you back to the previous notion that an effective coach and mentor will not *only* be deliberate in their presence around those they are coaching. Your mentoring approach should also have an element of being "unplanned." In addition, in the example above I also made the error of defaulting to only mentoring issues. I needed to insert a more relaxed and un-structured mentor engagements, or "let's chat about anything." Because of these two facts, you can see that mentoring can become very transactional and based upon something going awry. Good leaders and coaches understand these dynamics and work to apply continuity, unstructured and spontaneous mentor engagements combined with deliberate, and structured ones.

After retiring, I was asked to be a senior mentor on a course designed to train very senior RCAF officers as air task force commanders. (Funny enough, on one of those courses, Trevor was one of the mentors.) My role not only involved coaching and mentoring, but also mentoring the mentors. For the first time, I had to sit down and explain what I expected from uniformed mentors (colonels) and how they added to the learning experience. Once I wrote down what I wanted to say, I saw that, in many ways, it was what I had been employing in many past mentoring or coaching situations. Here it is:

1. Examples. Provide the individual(s) with tangible use of the knowledge that they are being taught, the applicability of the skills that they have, and the benefit of that knowledge and these skills within the system/organization/team, as well as the benefits of the knowledge they are gaining on their personal development.

2. Linkages. Tie together disparate elements of work, the system, and life. Get them to see a bigger picture beyond their own limited view or roles. Show them how things are put together or how they relate to each other.

3. Why. Make people understand why things are done the way they are. Provide historical or theoretical rationales. Link things back to the larger vision and mission.

4. Tips. Dos and don'ts. Explain relationships that are key. Things that need to be read/understood. Checklists or aide-mémoires that are helpful. Tools or techniques to use. Processes that matter.

5. Perspectives. Yours, or others' perspectives on the individual and the organisation they are coaching or leading. Perspectives from the outside looking into their team/organization, and from the inside. Compare these with opinions that you mirror back from those you are mentoring (e.g., You are confident in the balance you are achieving, yet your team complains about being overworked).

Another technique I used applied when I was conducting career mentoring. In these sessions, one can get hyper-focused on the specifics related to the last merit board results, upcoming positions, advancement, or, especially in the military, the next posting. I always thought it was important to have a framework upon which to analyze the situation together and then ask key questions to give the individual the perspective they needed. I used five "areas" that I would query in:

1. Family. What is your family situation? What does your family want? What are your work, education, living, and lifestyle desires? What are your limitations?

2. Geography. Where is it important for you to be? Why? When? How are moves and advancement tied together for you? How does geography relate to the family concerns above? Are there places that you have not considered? What location excites you? What are "no-go" places for you? Why?

3. Next steps. What is the logical next step in your career advancement? Why? How do the next few steps need to be sequenced? Is there another way? If you had your druthers, how would this play out for you? How is this going to affect family and geography for you? How are these three related?

4. Experience and development. Where are you strong/deficient in experience or training? What jobs, positions, and experiences play to your strengths? Where do you have clearly identified gaps or shortfalls in your experience or professional development? How important to you is staying in your area of expertise? How would you go about filling in these areas of development or experience? Are there areas, functions, positions, or experiences that you have always wanted to explore (working in HR, career management, flight safety, innovation, technology, diplomacy, policy development, equipment acquisition)?

5. End. How do you see your career ending? When? Where? Why? At what point? What do you want to achieve personally? What is beyond your current career? Another career? In what? Doing what? Where? How does this relate to family and all the other pieces above?

Okay. Now, how do we employ some of these techniques of coaching, teaching, and mentoring? Where do we start? How do they morph in the various situations that we will face as leaders and coaches?

Before we jump into where to start, please take a second to recognize how some of the fundamentals from the first section are shining right through in these techniques. The concept of trust in the relationship I have with Trevor was enabled by using solid techniques (or at least evolving my techniques) in mentoring over the years. Connecting at an individual level, connecting the team with the material at hand, and focusing on individual as well as team development should clearly be seen in this TTP. But starting out, this can all be daunting. Where do you begin?

CHAPTER 18

Beginning, Starting —Basic Training

As a coach or a leader starting with a new team, new posting, new leadership position, or a new season, remember that starting out is daunting for everyone involved, no matter the level of experience, size or complexity of the team, or type of job. And you aren't the only one entering new territory. It is new for you as a leader, your team, your supervisor, and all the associated supporting cast in these relationships, including your family. In reality, people and situations are always evolving and changing. It feels like we are always starting over. That's okay. You will pick up things that work for you and those that don't. Don't get discouraged or overwhelmed by things that are uncomfortable or new. Instead, dig in!

Begin by studying, whether you study the team itself and its goals, the people, the organization and its vision or mission, or the skills being acquired. Whatever it is, study hard. Brendon Burchard highlighted that highly performing people are always actively learning. He recognised that these high performers have a detailed approach to constantly improving and learning new skills. Each new beginning will require new learning. Embrace it as the development opportunity that it is, but also realize that it will be hard work. Do the work! Put in the time.

Introduce yourself. Introduce yourself to your team, to the people that the team depends on, to the people that the team's results are important to, and to those who can enable your team. This will be an iterative process that you can use to your advantage in a new role. By asking the team who the key enablers, leaders, and authorities are, you get their input and create buy-in. Be careful about setting up their biases as yours, however.

Tips for introducing yourself: This is not a bio reading, nor is it an ego session. What you have done in the past that relates to your position can be important. However, what is of utmost importance to the team is your belief system, how you operate, what you value, and any personal preferences, ticks, and foibles. Lastly, and most importantly, communicate things about you that are lines that people need to not cross or at least know about.

For example, my boss, when he was a young lieutenant colonel, used to warn us that when he is deep in thought and we interrupt him, although he might respond, he might not have actually broken contact with what he was working on unless we truly got his attention. Once, I went into his office and told him I was about to do something. It was a quick and straightforward thing…in my mind. He looked up from his computer and said, "Okay." So I made the adjustment. It was an issue concerning how to route funding for flying hours for a deployed mission.

A day or so later, I was back in his office.

"I didn't agree to that!" he said.

"Yes, you did," I responded.

"Did you have my attention? Isn't this important?" It was. My bad.

From there, I developed the habit of going into his office when something was important and talking to him about anything but work until he got annoyed. Then I would say, "Okay, now that I have your attention…" What was important is that the vulnerability that he showed to all of us as part of his team was key. It was his introduction that allowed us to work well in harmony.

During my own introductions, I would tell my team that I used the phrase "What's next." When I reach that point in any conversation, I am done and it's time to move on to the next item. The introduction is about you knowing your team and them knowing you. It can be a great lead-in to setting expectations. Don't be afraid to be vulnerable and personal here.

It is important next to watch the team go along for a while with limited or no changes. This is valuing the past. It also allows you to ask questions and get to know people. By getting to know them and asking good questions, you will get a good sense of what is working and what is not working. Sometimes, in sports teams especially, that assessment needs to be done very quickly. Understanding the level of baseline skills and IQ for a team is tough. But showing some patience with a new team and watching them go through their processes and work/practice without your interference will allow you to objectively assess and to demonstrate an immediate trust for their competencies. Many coaches and leaders here can make the mistake of wanting to immediately add value and demonstrate an ability to lead change. This can lead to significant loss of effort as organisations swing from one legacy item to the next, wasting individual and team effort. Recognizing the benefits of your predecessor's vision and continuing it applies a level of stability that can be very reinforcing. In many of my past jobs, my predecessors, most of them friends of mine, had laid out extraordinary visions. Not all of these were completely supported by subordinates. Some would even petition me as a new leader to immediately change things. Seeing through this and making my own determinations often led me to maintain the vision and focus my efforts on the execution. But whether you maintain or adjust a vision, it is key for you to set that vision and tone as a leader or coach.

So, the next thing to do is to set that tone and the vision. Whether you set this for the team or develop it alongside them, establishing the vision and setting the tone for the environment of the team will point everyone on the right vector. This needs to also introduce or reinforce a vocabulary that is specific to the team. Some organizations come with this. The military culture is full of jargon, buzzwords, and phrases meant to frame the culture and enable coherent linkage to the vision and the inspiration so crucial to motivating a team. Most important in this beginning stage as a leader is to link the team—and the team's mission—to their daily tasks in a fashion that enables the team to clearly understand their roles and responsibilities. This will serve as the baseline for accountability and therefore standards to which those tasks must be conducted.

Some of the vocabulary that I used to use:

In basketball: See your man, see the ball. Be the help. Create space. Be moving. Deny the drive.

At work: "Fly—Shoot—Spend." Availability creates serviceability. We have The Watch. Plan fast.

There are those who will say that to establish the framework you must go right back to the basics and establish a completely new foundation. I have watched university-level coaches recruit players for their fundamental abilities but also with consideration as to whether they will be a good "fit" into their systems. In either case, these coaches tend to start a new season by going right back to the fundamentals and affirming how they expect things to be done at that basic level. There is a similarity to basic training in the military. Recruits all know how to walk and can follow basic instructions like "Go over here" or "Run over there." But to be able to do this under fire, in extreme pressure, when every fibre of your body is telling you to run away, is a very different thing. So, the military teaches basic commands and drills recruits to follow orders so that, under pressure, they will respond to their training. And, for the most part, it works. The same is true on the playing field. Practices reinforce basics and evolve them up to complex systems of options, and the players in the crucible of pressure respond by trusting their training. As a leader and coach, your initial assessment needs to ascertain whether this is a wholesale reset, something that does not need to be done, or something in between that can perhaps be done alongside the day-to-day work.

I would, however, caution about complete resets that mirror the basic training ideas that we see in Hollywood. One does not need to "break people down" in order to build them up. When I look back on my military experience, I see very starkly now that the key elements of basic training that allowed for the creation of the high-performance teams that I was a part of did not "break me down." In fact, it was the very opposite. The effective leaders I followed were reinforcing values and objectives that I already held dearly, if only intuitively. I valued friendship and camaraderie. In the military, team cohesion and the team accomplishment of the mission is everything. All a good leader needed to do to direct me was reinforce that idea. I admit that maybe I was not typical, and this was not the case for all recruits. However, it has been my experience that even the most self-serving individuals, when given a mission, a vision, and a cohesive and motivated team surrounding them will mirror/reflect the values or ethos that the leader or coach has espoused and reinforces. The concept of reinforcement is key, regardless of the level of reset undertaken. There are clear carrot-and-stick analogies here. But they are not focused on breaking people down, but rather on reinforcing things that the organizations and teams value. By reinforcing the mission, values, and effort of the team, by valuing them and their work, coaches and leaders create an ethos and culture and the work environment that is a solid foundation for success.

As a basketball coach, I had seen so many games lost over a few points with huge stress at the end of games when double or triple that number of points was missed in free throws. I chose to value work that could be done during the entire game, not merely in the last few minutes of play, therefore valuing free throws. So, at the end of every practice, I would choose two players to shoot free throws. If they both made their shots, the practice was over and the cooldown commenced. If they missed, the cost was a set of lines. I had to be honest with this. If they knew they were going to run regardless and I was just going to keep picking players until one missed, it would be an exercise in futility. Instead, it became a point of pride and cohesion for the team. On more than one occasion, players who rose to the challenge at the end of particularly hard practices were cheered as heroes.

At work, I valued family and family time. I set out work goals for my teams. On every single instance that a member of my team asked for time to do family things, not only would I say yes, but I would be curious as to the nature of the event and what more I could do to enable more family connection in the future. It was part of my vocabulary and our shared values.

The Canadian author and journalist Gwynne Dyer wrote on the experience of basic training in his book and video series *War*. In the episode called "Anybody's Son Will Do," he describes the effect of military basic training as setting out clear standards where "The only right way to do something is the way that we tell you to do it." Those standards cover behaviour, ethics, and integrity. In so doing, there is a team and individual accountability in a very open way. If an individual or team screws up, it is obvious and can be corrected. All of this is done with the key goal of cohesion. Small unit cohesion is at the centre of morale for all military organizations.

This concept of cohesion is one that, as a coach or leader undergoing a new "beginning," I would pay attention to. When doing your initial assessment, try to understand where individual and team affiliations or identity lie. What is the hierarchy of importance in their minds? Do they affiliate mostly with the job and the company that pays them, or with their small team in their specific office space? Or is their affiliation to the mission or objectives of the team?

In the military, the small unit cohesion required for infantry-related combat has historically focused on the platoon or company for individual combat motivation (the person next to you), but the unit or regiment for its historic military traditions. I think that this has evolved over time across the various branches of the military. Air Force personnel affiliate more with squadrons or units. But neither of these examples completely explains where motivation or cohesion is nascent. Many people feel more of a cohesion within their specific occupations (pilot, infantry, logistics etc). Others feel more of an affiliation with the community they work in (tac hel, fighters, etc.). For coaches in sports, sometimes you see players who identify less with being a member of a team than they do with their position (point guard). If you as a coach or leader are going to elevate teams to the very top of their potential, the members of the team will need to place the needs and achievement of the group ahead of their individual needs. This is the personification of service, team, and community. The best players or performers are those who are willing to be selfless in the accomplishment of team goals. In so doing, they actually outperform themselves. It is almost reverse psychology. In the military, this is an obvious goal. The unlimited liability of military service means that the ultimate sacrifice, or what Abraham Lincoln termed as the "last full measure of devotion," could be paid in the service of the nation. By understanding the affiliation hierarchy and seeing what motivates teams in an open and transparent fashion, the leader or coach can create a team that is better than the sum total of its parts. Teams that begin this way believe that they can face any adversity presented to them because of the strength of the team and their belief in each other.

Teams that have a sense of themselves can also self-adjust, even without their coach or leader. While I was coaching a game for Ryan's team, I became frustrated with the team's performance. The fact that we were losing was not what bothered me. What bothered me was that the players were not playing within themselves. I could see that they were not in the moment. I called a time out.

Now, usually in time outs, coaches make adjustments to how the team is playing. My assistants in this case were recommending some changes to our approach on the court. Instead, I moved myself and the other coaches away from the team and told the players that this was their time out and they needed to sort themselves out. I knew that they had to find themselves and that none of that could come from me.

The informal leaders of the team, especially the two co-captains, rallied the team. Not pump-your-chest stuff, but real authentic leadership, vulnerable admissions of what was going wrong and what needed to be done to fix it. We could hear the words we coaches had repeated over and over: "Talk it up on defence, be the help, let's take care of the ball." The team got themselves in the mindset of the game and pulled together. By the end of the time out, they had self-adjusted back to being in the moment, all due to the character of the team. All we did as coaches was set the conditions that made this possible at the beginning of the season.

Great. We have an idea of where to start, and we have a small road map to start with. Now I want to shrink back to you as the individual leader and coach. There is a key technique that I learned *waaaaay* too late in my career that is a key enabler for every interaction that I was planning, or even that would spontaneously occur. If I followed it, I could control my emotions and prepare myself to be the best leader or coach in that moment for my team.

CHAPTER 19

Setting Intentions

This is an important thing for individuals as well as organizations. By setting intentions as individuals, we enhance our self-awareness and get better connected with our emotions. (Or, for me, I find better *control* of my emotions.) It is important to differentiate between establishing a vision and setting intentions. The vision for where a team or organization is going and the objectives that they must achieve are what make up the framework elements, the structure of the house you are building with your team. But the inside of that house, the decorating, layout, and even the colours and textures of the house are what we are talking about. What are the values that we share and wish to have at the forefront in our considerations in the coming meeting, days, or encounters?

There is an intimate link between the vision that we create for an organization and the setting of intentions. Setting intentions is about centring ourselves on what this day or meeting needs to achieve and *how* we want to go about (and feel during) the encounter.

Once I realized this, I began seeing my daily schedule as a tool for setting personal intentions for the day. I would write down my intentions for certain meetings or encounters in my schedule. Once I got better at this, it also allowed me to react to change (inevitable) and enable my team to perform. They could hit me with different things without it cornering me into an emotional reaction. This was the organizational technique that helped me create the space between my emotions and my behaviours or reactions.

I would set intentions by scheduling time to think through my calendar at the beginning of the day, the beginning of the week (though it's sometimes difficult to see beginnings and ends to weeks), and before meetings. Sometimes I would write these intentions down on cue cards I would have in front of me during the meeting. Other times, it was a simple as writing a reminder at the top of the page in my work journal. Still other times, I would write my intention on the read-aheads my team prepared for me. Margins, sticky notes, reminders…whatever it took to bring my mind back to my intentions. You heard earlier how I wrote "Listen, listen, listen!!" on the top of my page during in-briefings.

Expanding beyond single days or specific events, on weekends, I was able to combine setting intentions with my own focused meditation on how I wanted to be. I am aware that this doesn't work for everyone. I continue to struggle with meditation for personal overall physical/spiritual centring and stress control. But meditating on setting intentions seemed a tad easier as a solid concept to hold in my mind. First, though, I had to have the scheduling part done so that the intention was framed.

For an organization, setting intentions means that the method and direction you are leading will drive the outcomes. As a coach or leader, this is the perfect opportunity to link the values and vision of the organization to the specific tasks and especially the manner in which they are being done. Why are we doing this? What if we just stopped doing it? Who would care and why? What is it we really want to achieve? What are the competing values/moral obligations here? How do we want to go about this? How do we want to feel at the end? What pitfalls do we want to avoid?

Going into tough meetings or conversations, I adopted a practice of centring on:

1. That which I desired to achieve,

2. The next best thing or compromise,

3. The outcome I could not accept, and

4. The motivations/perspectives of the other side of the argument. I tried to achieve a middle ground by stating up front what I thought the other sides' perspectives were, as a sign of understanding and a bridge to finding a mutually beneficial solution.

I have found that laying foundational discussions on the front of meetings means that the content is squared away much more easily. For example, in a meeting where leaders will have to rank or merit list individuals for advancement, don't start with "Who is your top performer?" Instead, open with a discussion of the specific values, skills, characteristics, and experiences that define a top performer with high potential. What attributes, behaviours, and performance criteria distinguish a high performer from their peers? Lastly, what are baseline competencies that cannot be overcome by experience that are pre-requisites to be considered?

By collaboratively going through the foundational discussion based upon commonly understood aims, outcomes, and equities, you'll find that the actual ranking is easily decided upon. As leaders, our intentions were set at the beginning. Therefore, seek to have animated discussion on the first principles, underlying rationales, and key policies that drive the decisions you need in each encounter. They will not only serve to keep the organization aligned, but they will also serve to reignite trust that the team is being well served by its leaders as they think deeply about the "why" and can explain how, in the most basic of decisions, it reflects the values of the organization.

CHAPTER 20

Challenge;
Aspirational
Goals

Under-performing teams and individuals personally disconnected with the work or effort they are putting into a team are common complaints, whether in workplaces, organizations, or teams. Striving for better life-work balance and raging against the ever-increasing demands of performance, leaders tend to set easily attainable goals or are at least fearful of setting objectives that are not supported by definable and data-driven HR norms.

I am going to present an alternate idea here. I am going to propose that the setting of aspirational goals, ones that may be clearly beyond a team's current reach, is crucial to the team's development if done in a supportive environment with good leadership and a solid grasp of coaching fundamentals.

Let's start with the impact of setting easy goals.

If you set goals that are easily attainable, this means that three things are *not* done:

1. There is no aspiration to get better.

2. No innovation is necessary in order to meet the goals.

3. Leaders (informal and formal) are not required to inspire their teams to overcome complacency.

For us as leaders and coaches, the words "inspire" and "aspire" are intertwined. We *inspire* so that people and teams will *aspire* to lofty objectives. We push people for innovation, inspire them to dig deep into their courage, and guide them in refining or perfecting their organizational acumen. To do this properly, there needs to be a sense of challenge to the achievements. If goals are mundane and simple, this will lead to complacency and, quite frankly, boredom. Some teams will seek to challenge by setting lofty organizational performance goals. I have led teams that are already achieving lofty goals and are therefore focused more on *how* those goals are being achieved. Lowering safety violations/occurrences, adopting better lessons-learned processes, crafting better risk-management processes, refining workplace culture, or creating a better workplace balance for people and their families are all based upon existing performance objectives while adjusting "how."

Aspirational goals within business can be a slippery slope of ever-increasing performance quotas. If a segment of a company or organization achieved a 10% savings with the same operational output in a year, then this becomes the new baseline and further savings will be either expected or mandated. Funding allocations will be cut based upon these past savings. Aspirational goals need to be tailored and placed in context with the maximum capacity of the team. I would not expect a high school hockey team to defeat an NHL hockey team. I would not demand 10% savings or 10% increased output for multiple years running without expecting something to break. There is a "do more with less" paradigm here that setting aspirational goals needs to be measured against. As coaches and leaders, it is important to welcome this dialogue. Be ready to adjust while perhaps not critically compromising set goals. In addition, be very leery of casting aside huge gains from the past and merely expecting that (ostensibly excellent) performance as a new "normal." This does not recognize the perhaps herculean effort that achieving those once-lofty goals required.

As I have said, it is important to start with solid vocabulary.

Not: "We/I can't" or "That's impossible." Have teams add "right now" to these sentences. Ask what the elements are that are preventing the team from achieving these goals. Then have a discussion on how to establish the path to actually achieving them, no matter how long it might take.

Not: Excuses like "You will do that on the backs of your people." Instead: "What do we have to do to get there? What do I/we have to stop doing/give up to achieve ____?"

In basketball, we had a drill called the "perfect 10." This was a three-man weave the length of the court and back. The ball could not be dribbled, nobody could travel, and once through the hoop, the ball had to be inbounded properly. The team had to put the ball in the hoop ten consecutive times, or they would go back to zero. This drill seemed completely unachievable for the first three months that Ryan's first team tried it. But the way in which they pulled together, coached and encouraged each other, and thought about and planned each other's roles was exactly the point. Team building. Once they hit their first-ever success, they were hooked. What was the next unachievable goal?!

I always wanted a dialogue as to the thing that was limiting my team's ability to produce. This provided focus for me but was also a frank discussion of balance, capacity, and competence with subordinate leaders and the entire team. In a military context, it was always more than that. I knew I had to inspire leaders and teams so that, when faced with unforeseen challenges that were seemingly insurmountable on the battlefield, they would *believe* in themselves and in the power of the team. They needed to understand that the depths of their own spirits were boundless and that the team would always rise to the occasion. If they believed in themselves, then they enabled action. Think = Act. In these situations, that belief is transmitted by leaders. Leaders would lead.

This mindset could easily be abused by leaders demanding more and more in less crucial situations. All this serves to do is water down the faith that the team has in their coach and leader. Watch out for this. It is a managerial approach to ever-increasing performance.

CHAPTER 21

Coaching Wins and Coaching Losses

This is an extension of chapter 10, "Adjusting Approaches." Should you adopt a different approach to winning and losing or take the same approach to both? In a military context, would I lead a unit through crushing defeat in the same way I would lead them in victory? I think the instinctive answer is obviously not. But be careful about such an easy answer. Would President Zelensky of Ukraine have led differently if his country had not been brutally invaded? Perhaps. Or perhaps he would have always wished he had given himself the opportunity for the clarity that such a fight provides. I think that the clarity that President Zelensky has displayed to his nation that is fighting for its very survival is consistent with his approach to leading and coaching that was both personal and humble from the very outset of his term as president.

If your team is losing or facing adversity, focusing on the things that you can change, rather than focusing on the overall score, allows for the insurmountable to become realistic. It also means that you can still win as a team while losing that specific game. You are creating small victories that can lead to bigger things. If you asked the Ukrainian military at the outset of the invasion if they thought they could defeat the Russian forces, their answer might not have been a resounding yes. But they could perhaps deny Russia the capitol while making the Russians pay dearly for their advance and encirclement of it. As a basketball coach, I never felt that I had to define "winning" as getting a certain score on the board—at least, not completely. This was liberating for me as a coach.

Down by 20 or more. One of my youngest and tallest players was struggling to contain the other team's big man. During a time out, my player was visibly upset. The team knew it. I had fresher legs available, but I needed him to see that he was up to the challenge. I said to the team, "This time out is for Lucky."[34]

My pep talk went something like this: "Team, we get back in this one defensive set at a time. Lucky (establish eye contact, smile), are we having fun?! Look, stand tall. Make him do the work. Like we practised. Feel his body and use your own weight. If he leans into you, step back. He will fall over. If he pivots, stay low. He has not hit a shot yet. Defend the drive as a priority. You've got this. Get back out there. 'Team' on three. One...two... three; *team!*"

On the next play, the other centre leaned in, and Lucky stepped back. The other centre fell over, travelling. On the defensive set after that, the opposing centre pivoted to face up. Lucky got low and the other boy tried to shoot. Lucky got the defensive rebound to huge cheers from our parents. The next time he came off the court, that young man was being congratulated by his team and he looked visibly different. Through all this, we were down 20 points. But who cared about the score?! Not me. Not Lucky. Not the team. Not the parents.

Even more difficult can be coaching or leading teams that are experiencing little adversity and having great success. Complacency and cockiness need to be the enemies of the coach and leader here. But I think that the

---

34   Name changed to protect the innocent!

way you combat these things is the same as when you are faced with adversity. No performance is perfect. There is always more development to be done. Using the framework of the vision that you have for your team, as a coach or leader you must find the details, new concepts, and new or next challenges to keep the team improving. I gained great insight into true legacy by reading the book *Legacy*, which is about the New Zealand rugby team the All Blacks. It is my favourite book on leadership. But most telling in the entire book is how it describes the humble way in which members of the team approach the process of winning. The most brutal of after-game reviews from the players themselves can be of wins. This is a dedication to excellence not merely of sport, but of character. The team's mantra, "Better people make better All Blacks" is the exemplification of this.

From my military experience, I have seen leaders use success as a springboard to allow balance. Teams that come off long, hard training exercises that are very successful can be oriented on to their families to make sure that they are mentally and emotionally prepared for the next challenge. Teams that are performing well and meeting business or production goals can be oriented on to safety, environmental, social, and family balance goals while sustaining (not increasing) production. For us as coaches and leaders, if we put these things as true objectives, can demonstrate how they fit and enable the vision, and are willing to work on them, our teams will respond with the same vigour they apply to performance goals.

So, I approach winning and losing, adversity and success, the same way. What are we focused on? What's the next step? How can we improve? How did we perform on the details? Finally, I hope that it comes through that we as coaches and leaders need to focus not merely on how we lead the team through adversity and success, but how we lead *individuals* through those things. Not everyone reacts the same way. My son Mathew had arguably his best game in club basketball when his team was losing a heart-breaking game that would end their entire season. Although the rest of the team was totally down, I was elated about his personal performance. And his performance did not go unnoticed by the rest of the team. Most of them, though not all, shared in his success. Taking time to coach individually, one on one, allows you to understand the individual perspective on whatever adversity—or success—the team faces. To me, focusing on small victories can be infectious. They provide focus. For coaches, focusing on individual development can have a truly beneficial impact on the larger team.

I was invited to coach an elite team for the Ontario Summer Games. Our region was dispersed over a hundred kilometres or so. Practices were going to be…difficult. It was obvious that we could not match the talent that the big cities could muster. But it was an experience that the boys would never forget. I went into this endeavour with the goal of showing these young men that the difference in the score between them and any other team was not equal to the difference between the teams in individual talent. This was about convincing them that the sum total of their talent was more a function of how they played together than of how good they were as individual players. We lost every game, but every single coach we played against (and some of the parents of the opposing teams) told me that they were very impressed with the class, competitive spirit, determination, and team spirit that our young men displayed.

The final component to coaching wins and losses is to recognize the emotional component for the team—and for the individual. Like I have stated above, that will vary widely. For a military leader, the extreme grief, guilt, helplessness, and anger associated with personnel casualties, even if tactical victory is achieved, can be debilitating. Empathy first is key. Recognize emotions in yourself and connect them to the team. Coach and lead in this space. Recognize individual emotions and value them for what they are. This is empathy. Recognize where emotions are making individuals unproductive or completely ineffective. Take gentle but direct action to deal with this and remove these individuals from the situation until they can recover. Carefully ensure that they know they are valued and must return to the team. Do *not* seek to assign blame in the short term. The priority here is to refocus the team on the task at hand and orient them on to the next challenge. Being present, connecting with as many individuals on the team as possible, and allowing for the emotions to be expressed without judgment is your mission. Communicating your personal vulnerability and emotions in these moments is the personification of leadership by example.

When coaching winning teams, it is important to recognize that the team is still making errors. Even though things are going well now, there will come a time—in the next game, in the next year, or in life—where the opposition or the test of our character will force us to dig even deeper and challenge us in ways we could not have imagined. Facing these challenges is the test of both losing and winning.

CHAPTER 22

Role of Recognition

Recognition is key for helping individuals maintain morale and purpose. Assuming they are focused on the mission, they must also have an ongoing belief that the organization truly values their effort. Recognition is part of the trust relationship of leading and coaching. Recognition is especially key in modern-day workplaces where people are changing jobs, roles, and careers in a never-ending revolving door of advancement.

As I mentioned in chapter 6, I personally, I took up the mantra, "Reward in public, criticize in private." I'm not sure that I always followed through on that, but I sure tried. By doing this, we as coaches and leaders place the relationship above the specific situation we are in, the problem we are trying to solve, or even the behaviour that needs to be corrected.

Now I draw a line between criticizing and correcting. Maybe this is bad semantics. Work needs to be corrected, and there is no problem with having frank discussions as to the standards of work and correcting deficiencies in them. But these need to stop short of criticizing the individual. In fact, I would go as far as to state that an active self-assessment function within any organization is key to its success. Having the ability to go over work, identify shortfalls, deduce root causes, and propose solutions is a hallmark of learning organizations.

When there are team failures, I would indeed conduct correction in public. I remember when I had directed that an air operations directive be projected out 60 days instead of only 30 to reduce staff churn during the Christmas holiday season. I had issued this direction a month in advance. When the time came to conduct the approval briefings, however, I was presented a 30-day plan. I stopped the team. I gave them the choice of coming back during the holidays or conducting the next 30 days of planning overnight and briefing me the next day. This was merely correcting the work. It was not emotional or judgmental. Once the team decided to plan hard for a day, I took them through the number of errors that had been made to arrive at this mistake. The instant that I had identified the issue, everyone remembered the direction from the previous month. Team issue. Readback issue. Leadership issue, at multiple levels.

Immediately after the meeting, I took aside the commander responsible for that planning, and we had a chat. Note: not in public. His team had seen enough stern looks in his direction from me during the (very brief) meeting. He just needed to hear from me, "It's okay. Learn from it. It will be a tough pill for them for the next 24 hours. Lead them through it." But I also followed up by saying, "You okay?"

I had established enough of a rapport to not get a rote "Yes, sir." Instead, he said, "Yes…sir. I am just disappointed in myself and sorry that we wasted your time."

My response: "You had no intent to do that. So, no worries. Live and learn. As long as you are okay and the team rises to the occasion, we will be good."

"Thanks, sir."

Done.

The next day, the team came through in stellar fashion. I not only praised the team and some of the individuals for high-quality work on a very tight timeline, but I also praised that commander's leadership in leading them through it. To his credit, he took full responsibility for the error. Needless to say, he set a strong example for the team by assuming all fault. Every situation is an opportunity, especially those that present us with adversity.

Use the recognition and critique mechanisms and develop an understanding for when correction is bridging into criticism. Sometimes individual errors need not be corrected in public. That focuses too much on the individual. Develop a feeling for the team and the individuals within it as to what their comfort level is with discussing corrections publicly. I used to ask, "Thin skin, or thick skin?" If they wanted a lengthy and detailed debrief, they would get it, and it would be very frank. The opportunity to learn fast and develop fast is great.

I remember when I was teaching at the Army Staff College and had a syndicate that did not like that. They wanted only a couple of points in each debrief. Okay. Come to the end of the course, many were disappointed in their marks. It was clear to me that they had set limits on the amount of development that they were prepared to undertake. They were content to learn less in their fixed amount of time on the course—and their marks reflected that. This wasn't emotional, just factual. Funny enough, the amount of recognition that I delivered to them was equally lacking. Why? They just didn't perform (or learn) well.

Carefully monitor the recognition you dole out to individuals. In most teams, everyone is working well. In some instances, the experience or raw capabilities of a specific individual mean that they can easily and without effort outperform their peers. Recognizing this is no problem. But there is equally no problem recognizing that someone else is putting everything they have into what they are doing, even if the result is simply achieving the norm. Use individualized private recognition and public recognition to very different ends here. Be cognisant of the effects that this might create within group dynamics. Talk this out with your other leaders and coaches.

While I was teaching at the Army Staff College at Fort Frontenac in Kingston, the standard grade was a C. On each course, there would be a small number of students who would achieve a C+. And, finally, there would be a very extra special few who were clearly head and shoulders above all their peers who would achieve Bs. There were no As. I adopted a phrase that I used for years when someone would do something great, finish an excellent briefing, or even be recognized by the organization: "Solid C+!" In my mind, the symbol of excellence in all that we did in preparing for and defending the nation was a pride in our work, equally matched with the humility to know that we can always get better. My team put this quote on the flag box they gave me when I left Alaska. My use of this phrase had to be explained, however, or else it could be misinterpreted as downplaying individual or team accomplishments. Nothing could be further from the truth. However, I needed to get to know my teams and adjust my language before I could use this term, even though in my mind it was a laudatory phrase.

Recognition also, when done right, reinforces that focus on the mission. In almost every team or organization, merely achieving normal performance takes a lot of effort. Yes, it is important to recognize outstanding achievements. But publicly recognizing the daily work, the behind-the-scenes and not usually highlighted work, is also key to group morale and inspiration. I spent much of my career watching the skies and controlling teams that spent endless hours on alert, watching and waiting for bad things to happen. Anyone who has held the watch, served in command centres, and held short-notice alerts will tell you that there is significant effort from individuals, organizations, and their families just to get to that first second of holding the alert. Recognizing the sacrifices and efforts in these areas ties the team back to the mission and vision upon which their effort is focused. It is meaningful. As a leader and coach, never give up an opportunity to say those things publicly or privately. "It is not lost on me that while everyone else is enjoying Christmas morning, you all are here at work. It is also not lost on me that you will be here tomorrow, and the day after, and the day after that. It is your dedication, and the sacrifice of you and your families, that allows our nations to sleep soundly at night knowing 'We have the watch.' Well done."

There was a time in the Canadian military where there was very little formal recognition. "Commendations" did not exist, and there was no visible insignia surrounding recognition, other than medals for tours overseas. The bar for any other medals seemed unattainable to most if not all the rank and file of the Forces. The rationale used here, in my opinion, was to preserve the honour and distinction of the symbol that each of these medals represented.

Now, there is a definite benefit to not watering down the specific symbols of recognition. But visible and tangible awards have a lasting personal effect on people. I watched the revamp and implementation of a system of recognition within the Canadian Armed Forces, which I feel is more in line with what is needed from such an institution: formal commendations with visible insignia on uniforms for recipients, a focus on transparency and attainability of service medals and other formal awards. In maintaining an increased level of transparency, there has also been a more frank and open conversation as to the bar that is set for the conferring of these symbols of recognition. I believe that this has imbued these commendations with a greater sense of honour while protecting the distinction reserved for such formal honours.

Recognition provides lasting emotional and substantive linkage between the organization and the individual. It can and does extend to families, especially if the formal events surrounding this recognition involve them. This recognition reinforces the "self-actualisation" tier on Maslow's hierarchy of needs.

It also reinforces that the organization and the leaders/coaches deeply value not only the work completed, but, more importantly, the people doing that work.

CHAPTER 23

Assessing Leaders

What we need to discuss here is not just assessing leaders for what they are doing right correctly at this time, but also assessing their potential in the next sphere. Coaching includes giving people the opportunity to lead even while developing their skills. Seek out these opportunities. "Ryan, lead the team in warm-up," or "Colonel Bloggins, conduct the priorities meeting and back brief me on the results."

The first stage in setting up assessment for leaders is to set mutually agreed-upon objectives for performance *in the function of leading or coaching*. Since the assessment is really an individual thing, make sure that the goals you agree to are focused on the individual's leadership or coaching development, within the context of their current employment. For unit commanding officers, I focused them on four functional areas:

1. Effectively lead their squadrons,

2. Be able to advise an army or SOF formation commander on the effective tactical use of aviation on the battlespace in combat,

3. Be an effective member of the peer group containing the other unit

commanding officers and lieutenant colonels within my staff, and[35]

4. Develop as an individual to be able to replace me as the wing commander.

It is important to note that none of this would have been effective if I had not gotten to know these people, their career aspirations, and their individual shortfalls and strengths. The categories above are generic, but when I used my detailed knowledge of these individuals, my guidance to them within these categories would get very specific pertaining to their personal flying qualifications, what engagements I expected them to value, what unit outputs they needed to lead through, and any other elements that needed to be tailored to them as individuals commanding their units at that time. Some of them needed to focus more on their tactical expertise. Others lacked specific language or professional education qualifications for the jump to the next rank. These would be highlighted and discussed. This formed the foundation for our feedback sessions later. More importantly, it laid the foundation for trust. Whether a leader does well or not needs to be based upon the parameters you set out here. This does not mean that if they do these things they will be the best, as every system is about comparative analysis to others. But your specific role with them is not to have them compete and win, but rather to maximize their personal development. Doing this right keeps you both accountable. Trust is a two-way street. This was the framework I used for coaching.

Once the framework was set, I employed a model for continuous assessment that was centred on my presence around leaders who were working for me and their subordinates. I wanted to get an up-close feel for how they were leading and how people were responding to their leadership. It is not always comfortable to have your boss in and around your section/unit/

---

35 Important to note that all leaders are members of a team. How they interact within that team, how they show up for their other team members, and how they follow direction as part of that team are very telling indicators of how they are as leaders.

team. As a matter of fact, the reality of the RCAF wing I commanded was that its units were dispersed around the entire country. I therefore spent precious little practical time in and around the units, as even when I was on the road upward of 250 days a year, I still could not match a wing commander who could drop in on a unit for 10 minutes on his way to work, be present in the lines of multiple units in a single day, or have weekly in-person meetings with his unit commanders. Other wings could socialize on a weekly basis at the mess. I had none of this. But when I was present at these units, it was not pomp and ceremony. It was discussion, discourse, and problem-solving. I would see them in action and try to be there when they were going through their most rewarding (and most challenging) tasks. By being there, I showed my confidence and pride in their accomplishments and those of their teams. I was also able to see them—and, more importantly, their leaders—in action.

The analogy I like to use was one of positioning myself behind those leaders while things were unfolding. I would ask questions like, "Was it difficult to rationalize the competing demands of Op Tempo over the past two months, knowing you needed to surge to meet this exercise demand?" or, "How is your new Flight OC working out? I always found them to be a great tactician and pilot but wondered if they had the organizational skills to leap to the next level." We would chat, deep chats on people management, tactics, organization, C2, and often frustrations (sometimes with my policies). When having these discussions, while I was watching over their shoulders, I would listen and offer advice. I would coach. "Have you thought of this? Did you reach out to this other CO? They are dealing with this as well. Let's talk to the wing chief, Jake. He will have great insights into how to approach that delicate issue."

In doing this, I would get a very frank view into not just what the leaders working for me were doing, but how they were doing it and the thought processes behind it. I was assessing them in their current roles but with a vision as to whether they had the skills and attributes to be able to replace me.

It was also reaffirming to them that I was not being directive (I had plenty of other venues for that); rather, I was trying to understand their perspectives so that I could set the conditions for their success, clarify guidance for them if necessary, and, most importantly, coach them on their leadership path. I would highlight tools to them, offer unique insights, and affirm that they were advancing in the right direction and doing all the right things.

This approach to continuous assessment of leaders had another key element to it, and that was my relationship with my wing chief warrant officer (CWO), CWO Jacques "Jake" Boucher. In the RCAF, all unit and higher formation commands are a paired command team between the senior officer, who holds all the official authorities, and a CWO, who is the senior non-commissioned member (NCM, or NCO in U.S. vernacular). That CWO is the voice of the non-commissioned members of the unit or formation. But, more importantly, at least from my perspective, they are an expert on people and leadership. When I was told that I was going to be given the privilege of commanding 1 Wing, the first question I asked was who my CWO was going to be. Jake was not only the best choice, but he had also been a personal friend and colleague of mine ever since our days in 430 ETAH ("*Vive les Faucons!*").[36] Jake's role was instrumental in the assessment of leaders throughout the wing, at all levels. He had a unique perspective and could obtain even more insights based upon his access to all the rank and file of the wing. The barriers that my rank, position, or even my personal character created resulted in reticence or complete refusal of some people within my teams to communicate frankly with me. Although every leader struggles to break down these barriers, we must also accept that they exist. Jake was another story. He inspired the trust of everyone, officer and NCM alike. To demonstrate that I valued that trust, I immediately shared everything with him—and I mean everything—concerning my

---

36 430 is a helicopter squadron. "ETAH" is the French acronym for "tactical helicopter squadron." 430's mascot is a falcon, and the French word for falcon is "faucon." 430 is a squadron richly steeped in history. It dates back to WWII as a spitfire and mustang squadron.

subordinate leaders and their teams. We had no secrets. We discussed, and argued at length, about everything. Being on the road for hundreds of days a year helped. Long flights, days and weeks in the field, long car rides, and many meals taken far from our families meant that we had the opportunity to share and analyze, assess, and finally develop coaching strategies for all our subordinate leaders. I think that leaders and coaches need confidants. Someone to discuss things with and bounce things off, someone who will challenge your biases. Find your Jake.

So, I discussed what I saw with my chief, Jake. We made it a point to see leaders, COs, junior and senior officers, other CWOs, and NCMs in multiple situations and circumstances. We would talk to the people they were leading. But, most importantly, we talked to them! We discussed how *they* thought things were going. We discussed their main challenges. We asked them about their successes, and we asked about what we could do to assist. This last question is key. You will learn a lot from what leaders or coaches ask for and why. Do they want you to solve their problems? How well do they understand your level and the challenges you are facing, and, by extension, their place in the team? Are there specific authorities or policies that could help them? Are there tactics, ways of doing business, or rules (written or unwritten) that are keeping them from getting their teams to the success you are searching for? How much responsibility do they bear in their destiny/problems versus how much do they deflect to you or to their (the) team?

The next part of my approach to assessing leaders was to engage their peers. Peers will be excellent champions of good leaders and coaches. At the outset of every reporting cycle on performance, I would set clear leadership expectations for how I expected leaders to perform as part of their peer groups, and I would challenge them as a group to solve problems. In fact, there were occasions where they were invited to my headquarters to meet, and I was told not to be present as they worked through problems and solutions as a peer group. I always had the final say, but my presence was not required unless there was a key issue or they were ready to present their solutions. By having a feel for the honest respect—or lack thereof—a peer leader has for another, you will get a sense of that leader's skills and character.

Finally, and most crucially, you must give honest and forthright feedback. Plan to provide that formal feedback at least every couple of months. However, this depends on the team size, the level of leadership, and the amount of daily contact. The framework that you have already laid out will set goals that are measurable, and the feedback needs to centre on that. "You did everything I asked and more. But what I saw while you were achieving these objectives was you compromising the balance of tempo with your people and for you personally with your family. And although I am satisfied with the outputs and results, I do not think that you set up a sustainable situation here." As this example illustrates, your comments do not have to be limited to the achievement of objectives; they can also cover "how" they were achieved. Being frank does not translate into being tactless. This is especially true when individuals are competing with their peers for advancement. In the end, everyone is going to know or have a sense of how people shake out in comparison to each other. These things will be obvious when promotions or advancements are announced. A fundamental error is to avoid any element of comparison in debriefing. This is essential for a few reasons. I have led teams where even the highest-performing individual in my team had no chance of advancement in the larger organization beyond their current position. I have led other teams where the comparatively lowest-performing individual had a real opportunity for early advancement, which demonstrated the strength of the entire group being assessed. Although all merit listing is comparative, your debriefs, coaching, and mentoring need to focus on the individual, including their attributes and their deficiencies. Here is where you must be careful not to compare to other individuals. Instead, keep your comments generic enough not to point out individuals. Attempt to compare to an ideal standard, or at least to the standard that will garner advancement. The conversation needs to elevate away from "Why them and not me?" and toward "Without these two key certifications, or this key experience, you will not be competitive." Finally, your feedback cannot be merely a report card—ever! Looking back is fine, but just don't stare too long. The real juice is achieved by squeezing out a plan from the assessment, one that advances the individual's development. This is where the majority of the time must be spent. As a leader, preoccupation with results and consequences will have to be discussed. But you need to turn the corner, talk about the future, and enable development. Finally, how an individual reacts to and adjusts based upon the feedback that is given will tell you much about their potential.

There is a sidebar issue to be discussed here, and that is the propagation of knowledge and understanding for how advancement and development opportunities are chosen. I was an operator all my career. But when I became a senior officer, I involved myself deeply in the intricate system of mentoring and career management within the RCAF. I studied various systems at play within the highly technical world of the aeronautical engineers (AEREs), the reserves, and the other operational and support occupations of the Air Force. I also studied some of our allies, especially the U.S. military. I took all their best practices and blatantly plagiarized and implemented them for the tac hel community. Then I systematically explained all of this to everyone in the community who was leading, who wanted to listen, or who did not have a choice but to listen.

When I became a wing commander, I led training sessions with my lieutenant colonels to bring them up to my level of understanding of the system. I wanted everyone to understand and for us as an organization to be transparent about exactly how things were done. Most importantly, I wanted every leader to be able to understand and, from there, to work within the system for the betterment of those people that they were in turn mentoring. This was always key to the trust that was developed between myself and those I was leading and coaching.

Over time as you work within the same system, the way things are done can be taken for granted. What I realized when I began mentoring individuals beyond my tac hel community was that this understanding of the system—the intricate relationships between career management, the chain of command, and the key elements that can influence results at merit boards—was not a common one. Propagating that understanding enabled me, and many within my community, to be able to provide insights and context to anyone in the RCAF as they progressed throughout their careers. When matched with frank feedback oriented around developing a plan for the future, it is a very powerful thing.

CHAPTER 24

You Can't Teach Height

The role of innate skills versus learned skills is a raging debate I have with Mathew. Mat was 6'3" at 14. Yup, piss me off. I am 5'9" fully grown, and those additional six inches would have made me so much more effective as a ball player.

What does this have to do with coaching?

Well, Mathew saw first-hand that in many basketball situations it did not matter how much I coached a team; the inherent talent of the team facing us was going to drive us into defeat no matter what. As he moved into his professional career after university and had to lead a team of his own in the workplace, he saw this exemplified in the raw talents of the people around him. Some had the personality and the intellectual, emotional, and physical skills to perform. It came naturally to them. But I would say that, as a young leader, Mat undervalued the ability of any organization to foster and teach those skills. Now, admittedly, he was thrust post-graduation into the high-stakes reality of federal-level politics, along with its instantaneous news cycle and the polarisation of the political debate in the Western world.[37] This fast-paced, sink-or-swim environment can create the idea that "you either have it or you don't." I just don't agree with that model.

I think that the most effective leaders and coaches are the ones who have been through the adversity of failing and have *learned* how to improve and operate in that environment. They provide better advice, and they see pitfalls in a more tangible fashion. Finally, they relate with the people on their teams better. The best leaders and coaches are ones who were coached in their leadership. They didn't just "have it."

Therefore, I do not subscribe to the "great man theory" of leadership or coaching being an innate quality. I also think that the study of attributes in leaders can be problematic as well. For instance, many leadership sessions I have been a part of would start with an exercise along the lines of "Name all the attributes that great leaders have in common." The next logical step would be to see if you embodied those traits. But what if a coach or leader saw none of these traits as innate to their character? Were they to assume that they could not coach or lead well? Conversely, if an individual saw themselves as clearly possessing these traits, then did that mean that they were a natural leader? Did this not lead to the deduction that "Whatever I am doing must be right because I have the gift of great leadership"? I do not believe that a focus on traits and characteristics is an effective tool for teaching leadership or coaching. I think the focus should be on knowledge and skills, both of which can be learned and developed. Every single leadership course I have taken falls short of demonstrating a method for developing leadership or coaching knowledge and skills. If it was a basketball coaching class, they spoke about ethical norms, then dove right into the Xs and Os of practice planning, etc. If it was a military leadership class, they used academic theories describing types of leadership approaches. There was never

---

37   When the Clancy boys get together, it can be a tad overwhelming to anyone around, especially Val, as we tend to argue and debate and talk—well, yell—very fast, with high emotion, all on very politically charged issues. And Mathew thrives in this arena. I now regret fostering that innate sense of curiosity and answering the question "Why?" a million times when he was young. Why couldn't he just read quietly and not ask questions?! (Kidding, of course.)

a description of how one developed their own knowledge and skills in leading. In fact, almost all my military professional development on leadership would start with phrases like, "We know you all know how to lead…" Do you?! Did we?! I mean, trial and error is not a great method. It works, but the cost to subordinates is outrageous.

I think that we assume at a certain level of any organization that the individuals who have gotten to that level know how to lead. But I submit that most systems do not deliberately get leaders there, but rather rely on the experience of climbing the ladder for years to teach leadership. This is ad hoc at best and does not ensure the character of your leaders and coaches in a deliberate and thought-out fashion. Not to mention the related ad hoc nature of developing workplace culture that goes along with this. Organisations, both large and small, need to see the development of leaders as a deliberate process. Note, I'm not talking about their technical/tactical prowess, but their leading and coaching skills. Professional development systems and formal 360-degree assessment frameworks need to harmonise these two together with clearly established organisational norms. Finally, these systems need to provide crucibles to train, test, and validate these leadership and coaching skills or else the result will again be ad hoc.

Getting back to what Mat was referring to, is the best leader on a sports team necessarily the best player? Really? Similarly, how do you lead/coach highly technical teams without the requisite technical background?

How do you develop the credibility to lead, especially highly technical teams/organizations/units, without being highly skilled yourself? Is there a crossover point as we climb an organization vertically where technical or tactical expertise and ability wanes in its importance? For me as a basketball coach, how much about the game is about my ability to "do" the things that I am coaching my team to do? How many NBA coaches can dunk?

In my military experience, there is clearly a relationship between tactical or technical proficiency and leadership. This is the role of professionalism. But I have seen and worked for highly proficient tacticians, pilots, or managers who were horrible leaders and even worse coaches. Similarly, I have worked for superb leaders who specifically lacked in certain tactical or technical experience areas. Why were the latter successful where the former was not? I believe this has to do with *credibility*. As leaders and coaches, we must know *enough* about the subject, organization, skill, or technical knowledge of the people we are coaching or leading to establish credibility in their minds. That credibility will be inherently linked to our ability to positively influence the outcomes of their performance. So, one might have huge technical or tactical skills, as much if not more than the subordinates on their team. But if those skills are not going to be used for the betterment of the performance, then no credibility is established. Credibility, it would seem, is based upon trust (it's a two-way street). In addition, if the leader or coach clearly demonstrated superior technical knowledge but could not manage and lead the organization to maximize the entire team's outputs, then again, no credibility would be established.

Establishing that credibility in a military context was always crucial. The consequences of tactical errors could be life and death. I always saw the skills of the leader in terms of technical (piloting) and tactical (fighting) abilities as being the "ticket to the dance." It was a baseline standard. You had to know enough to allow the people around you to lead. In my career, I got sick of seeing "wedding planners" advance instead of those leaders whose expertise was clearly in the delivery of the mission. These "wedding planners" were good at all the surrounding skills, but, when it came to actually flying and fighting, they were mediocre. Be careful about what your organization is prioritising when it comes to promotion and advancement. It speaks volumes to that which the organisation values. When those who are core to mission accomplishment are not at the core of advancement, what message does that send? What expertise is resident in the leadership of your organization? What expertise do you desire to have in your organization's leadership? Now go out and teach those individuals to develop the knowledge and skills requisite for them to lead and coach in the future.

As one is elevated within an organization, the technical/tactical skills and knowledge seem to wane in their importance as compared to other skills. Indeed, the Canadian Armed Forces' leadership and evaluation model does not even gauge tactical job knowledge as a skill required by general officers. There are other skills that replace these job knowledge skills as one climbs the ladder. This is usually countered by the fact that we all wish we were back down at that first job so close to—or even on the line of—delivery. It is where the action is, and it's where we saw the biggest return on the investment of our personal coaching and leadership. I think this is a good balance to have.

Technique Advice Summary

1. Deeply study, and continue to study, the tactical and technical knowledge of your profession.

2. Where able, lead technical/tactical missions yourself as an example.

3. Where able, teach technical/tactical skills and knowledge to your team and within the profession.

4. Know that good coaches and leaders can overcome shortfalls in technical/tactical proficiency. (See item 1 above.)

5. Seek out technical/tactical experts whose opinions you trust and engage them.

6. Ensure that your efforts in leading and coaching will directly benefit the team, entrenching that credibility.

7. As a leader or coach, always be studying and learning the craft of leading and coaching alongside whatever skill your team is focused on.

Mat's right. You can't teach height. But I can still rebound, shoot, pass, and be an effective member of the team. In fact, I might outperform a taller individual on any given day. The sum total of my developed skills, multiplied by the work ethic and determination that I have grown in order to overcome my lack of height, may be enough.

I have found that those who inspired and coached me the best were coaches and leaders who fell into the group that worked hard at developing the knowledge and skills to have technical credibility with their teams, but, beyond that, to have excellence in leading and coaching.

CHAPTER 25

Feedback Loops

Developing a solid network of feedback is essential for understanding yourself, your team, and the performance of both. Your feedback loops must have the following characteristics:

1. Rooted in your vision. Reflective of the things in your vision that matter to the organization and the people in it. Know what you are measuring (performance vs. effectiveness) and why! Know how you define success.

2. Multiple input vectors. Think of this as a 360-degree approach. These vectors might include superiors, customers, employees, team members, peers, outsiders, academics, and friends. You must filter some feedback based upon the relative value of the source. However, ensuring that you have multiple sources is essential.

3. Both subjective and objective. Both measurable performance objectives *and* subjective impressions and reflections are important. You want feedback that tells you honestly what you *need* to hear, not just what you *want* to hear. Set an environment that fosters this honesty and be open to it publicly. Be prepared to have to filter, but be cognisant of the effects of doing so.

4. Revisited. Not one-time inputs, but a routine feedback loop. Not

points of light, but patterns and behaviours. Don't get hung up on beginnings and ends.

The most effective feedback loop concerning execution is entrenched in sport and military training. In sports, after each game the coaches and players go over the salient points of the game. This occurs at all levels of sports. Even the youngest and most inexperienced teams take a few minutes to review what just happened. The more complex and higher the competitive status, the more intense the debrief. As tapes of games are reviewed and then practice and future game plans are formed, they reflect the deficiencies identified in these debriefs.

I watched this first-hand when I had the distinct pleasure of being invited by the owner to go into the Toronto Raptors' dressing room after one of their annual military appreciation games. Watching one of my basketball coach idols, Nick Nurse, conduct the debrief was incredible. But it was so very similar to the AARs) that I had experienced in the military. (From here forward in the book, I am going to call all post-event debriefs AARs because, well, that's what I know!)

AARs left egos at the door and outlined in stark terms those elements where the team and leader fell short and those areas where performance was good and needed to be sustained. I always enjoyed the categorization of "improves" and "sustains." For leaders and coaches, conducting post-event debriefs is a skill that must be developed as part of your feedback loops. In the U.S. Air Force, they are called a "hot wash" and colloquially have become known as a place to air all the dirty laundry and be brutally honest about performance. There is a leader/coach influence on the *tone* that needs to be set, and I think it has much to do with the makeup and character of the team and the situation they are in. AARs while dealing with the grief and loss of a tactical defeat on the battlefield are delicate things. The same can be said for AARs dealing with key losses by children in sports events.

Here are some key techniques for AARs:

1. Plan for them. You know in advance that you are going to conduct an AAR. Throughout the event, you should have notes that focus you on the key items that need to be discussed.

2. Do them as soon as possible, if not immediately, after the completion of an event.

3. Have the members of the team highlight the areas for improvement and the practices they wish to sustain. This is the fundamental principle of the AAR process. Use inquisition and suggestion here to draw out answers. Telling an individual that you will call on them to speak about a specific element will also allow for them to prepare. I cannot say enough about this. Everyone has a different perspective. For leaders and coaches, bringing this out to engender understanding from the entire team so that they can work together on the solutions is essential. Merely stating the shortfall gets limited buy-in. Perfection will be demonstrated by the team moving through this entire cycle of learning without direct input from the coach or leader, through their own discussion. Allow informal leaders lots of latitude here.

4. Use a timeline for the event to anchor your discussions. The temporal framework that a timeline presents allows people to anchor their logic and emotions, which enable understanding and learning.

5. Use other tools that you may have available to you. Professional and elite sports teams will review tapes of games and key plays. Military organizations use battlefield monitoring systems, HUDs, and cameras and then replay their recordings to demonstrate how and when plans came undone or enemies overcame their forces and where mistakes seem to have been made. Again, during the debrief, do not allow these tools to do all the review. Get into

the individuals' heads. "What was going through your mind here?" "Did you see this happening?" "How could we have better recognized this as a team?"

6. Keep a rolling summary of "improves" and "sustains" where everyone can see them. Bring them up at the next debrief/review/ hot wash. Continuity of approach here will be key. The team cannot merely see that they always have more work to do. Crossing things off that they have learned and placing those things into the "sustain" column is highly affirming.

As a leader, I was always taking notes. Always have your pen and notebook (or phone, I guess, for young folks) with you. If someone asks you to do something, has a conflict or complaint, or even just suggests a good idea, acknowledge it, record it, and follow up with them. Keep this point as an open item in your notebook and check it off when you close the loop with this individual. (Accountability works both ways.) For coaches, this is so very important, as the keys to success for the team lie in each member of the team's personal performance. This is very important while practising that age-old technique of "leadership by walking about." Lieutenant General Rick Findlay taught me this. He told me that he learned more, got better feedback, and understood the organization and its people best by merely being out and about with them. This demonstrates presence and approachability and assists greatly in establishing trust. Combining this technique with taking notes and giving feedback on items that people identify to you can be very powerful.

When you are getting feedback, it is important not to defend the vision, policy, position, performance, or individual being discussed to the point of stifling the feedback. Accepting the feedback and the source it comes from must be the primary goal. This was an area I struggled with personally. I heard other leaders say that I should just accept the input at face value, make no comments, and move on. However, I have found it more genuine to make these feedback loops two-way discussions. I want the feedback and do not want to resist it. But I also don't want the people delivering the feedback to walk away thinking that their perspective is the only one if mine or that of the organization differs. This needs to be discussed. The key to this is to always focus on listening. (Listen, analyze, transmit, listen, decide... loop.)

I always loved the idea of breakdown drills. Breakdown drills are so important because they allow for questions, clarification, development of muscle memory, and questioning of whether there is a better way. Breaking down complex situations and operations into their component parts allows for team members to recognize them for what they are. In the cacophony that can be the sports field or battlefield, breakdown drills are useful tools to see through the "fog of war" and act with clarity and judgment. In one basketball game, I remember that we had a real problem getting to the hoop. In the debrief right after the game, the team expressed the isolation they felt when the ball was passed to the wing. In the next practice, I implemented a breakdown drill that walked through the pass, movement, and screen associated with the small portion of the wing on our offence. There were multiple questions from players, we discussed options, and we addressed how to deliver help in the form of the screen. The AAR at the end of the next game moved that issue into our "sustain" column.

The breakdown drill is also my favourite technique to use to attempt to close the feedback loop, bridging the gap between identifying the "improve" and watching it move to the "sustain" column. So, when I see complex concepts and ideas at work and I am struggling to get the right perspective on them, I will break down the component parts, tackle each of them individually, and look for feedback on those items. Doing so keeps me aligned with the first principles upon which all plans are based and it not only allows me as a leader and coach to see and seize on the critical issues, but, more importantly, it gives me a common frame to bring the understanding of the team along with me. Breakdown drills, when done well, can be teaching and correcting methods if they are linked back into the feedback loop of "sustains" and "improves."

Finally, as a leader, you must also have both an anonymous and an official complaint/harassment system. These systems must protect the individual making the complaint from not only those subordinate to you, but also from your own interference. The focus of these systems must be on the transmission of complaints without repercussion, alongside a well-oiled and independently overseen system of investigation and regulation, all with a focus on the potential victim. As a coach and leader, your main role will be to foster the culture and enforce stringent standards to create the best environment. But you also must be very knowledgeable and proficient with these systems. My advice to coaches and leaders is to always have the well-being of the potential victims in your mind and to not be afraid to act to do the right thing.

CHAPTER 26

So... Lost Causes (a.k.a. How Many Second Chances?)

W hen I was speaking in post-retirement at the RCAF's Air Warfare Centre (the RAWC, pronounced "ROCK"), a seasoned leader, a warrant officer, asked me how I would deal with someone who, even after multiple tries at bridging the gap, remains un-receptive to coaching and mentoring. He wanted to know how to deal with someone who is ultimately dragging the whole team down.

I think many of you can relate to this situation. I tried to answer his question by using my "over the shoulder" mentor example. I extrapolated the example, stating that, over time, being the person behind that individual, coaching them in their ear and making suggestions, would turn into me walking around in front of them if they were unreceptive. I went on to elaborate that my approach would change from one focused on "why" to one focused on unequivocally reiterating the task, my authority, and their role in the team and being much more descriptive as to "how" this requirement was to be done. Finally, I stated that there are some people who just will not get it, and it is better to identify those people early and have them leave the organization.

Unfortunately, though, I fear I gave this warrant officer no more tools than he already had. And his question vexed me.

I have already stated that usually, by the time you get into a crisis or confrontation, there are many "set the stage" opportunities that have already failed. I believe that by taking advantage of all of the instances you have to communicate vision, establish trust and connection, etc., you will limit the number of "unreceptive" people to a very small number. I am also pretty sure that the advice I gave in answering the question above—that when all else fails, one should be highly directive—is not the only option either.

Obviously, getting to the root of why an individual will not follow direction is key. However, that individual must be willing to share that rationale. It is important to note that in a military or sport coaching context, the high degree of familiarity that most coaches and leaders have with the technical and tactical requirements of the job helps. Being able to connect and see the perspective of the individual at their level may be enough for them to share what the principal issue is. Be open to the idea that the issue may not be the team or the tasks, or anything else, but rather you as the leader and coach. As humbling as this may be, sometimes there is a clear personality conflict. Also be open to the idea that it might have nothing to do with the team, the organization, the tasks, or you. Finally, when a single individual refuses to cooperate, often it is the informal leaders and the rest of the team that convince them of the correct behaviour. Engaging those informal leaders to determine the root cause is therefore also a good tool.

Above all, demonstrate patience! Patience is not always something we as coaches or leaders can afford, especially in a crisis. But taking the time to display personal and professional empathy in a crisis can be all that it takes to bridge that gap between you and the person who is being unreceptive. Remember to continue to place the relationship above whatever needs to get done. This will enable you to be as patient as you can and see the bigger picture. However, if the behaviour is detrimentally affecting the team or the workplace culture or is in any way compromising established moral, ethical, or value standards, my recommendation is that you take swift action to remove this individual.

I have had a lot of experience in the formal mentoring role, almost all of it focused on the mentoring of senior officers in their professional development in the Canadian Armed Forces. This can lead to a very transactional approach to mentoring. "We are talking now because the merit board sits in a couple of weeks and blah, blah, blah." Relying only on these specific events, the transactional ones, places the needs and demands of the organization first. Some of the most beneficial and rewarding coaching and mentoring I have done, though, has been with people who are truly disenfranchised with the military, or certain leaders or agencies in it, and are on the precipice of making a major life change by leaving. If one were only employing a transactional approach to mentoring in this type of situation, they might say that there is no purpose in continuing discussions once it is obviously impossible to convince such an individual to remain in the service. Two things are wrong with this.

First, long before we get to this point as a mentor and coach, we should have already had a frank conversation about how the person wants to leave the organization. Yes, *leave the organization* (at some point in the future). Having this discussion as a matter of course in early stages of mentoring or coaching demystifies the fact that the individual may make decisions that are not aligned with what the organization wants, while demonstrating that there is more to life than this team and this organization and that you want to help them with all that. In the end, remember, everyone leaves.

Secondly, once the individual is getting to the point of desiring to leave, this is where true mentoring needs to kick in hard. The transition is going to be difficult. Help them! "Do you need letters of recommendation? Is there some preparatory education that we can assist with in the transition?"

My results from interactions like these, even with people who, at the outset, I might have characterized as "unreceptive," have been that many have become friends and remain in contact long after my—and their—departure from the team. What might look to someone else like a lost cause may be a perfect opportunity to help. Leaders and coaches must be the help. Show the patience needed and take the time; it will make all the difference in the world.

Finally, and never to be forgotten, know that the rest of the team—their morale and the example set by being around someone not willing to pitch in—will directly affect the team's ability to accomplish the mission. Acting decisively in moving those who do not believe in the mission and are not receptive to any guidance is crucial. Perhaps they are not a good fit for the team. Perhaps they are not well suited or perhaps they have some fundamental shortcomings that are incongruous with the team or organization. Do not be afraid to be decisive. *However,* from a coaching perspective, what I learned was that having tools to find the individual's personal motivation within the team is key. If a young man I was coaching did not care about winning but did not wish to let his team down, then knowing that and framing my guidance to him in terms of how he could contribute to the team was the best way to coach him towards his best possible performance. An individual might not care at all about the organization or its mission, but they might need and be highly motivated by the paycheck. I could work with that too.

Now, this is a two-way street that you should traverse with care. Team morale can be a powerful enabler to good leaders. However, as I mentioned above, it can also be a toxin to individuals if it is not carefully monitored. Unethical or inappropriate behaviour is the single most detrimental thing to any team. Be aware that an individual's unreceptiveness may only be the symptom of a larger problem, either with them or with the team that they are a part of. Be patient, again, as getting to the root cause of the unreceptiveness is key.

CHAPTER 27

Crisis Coaching/Leading

Combat, or combat-like operations, require specific leadership techniques. These techniques are usually highly directive, describe clearly "how" a task is to be completed, and are enabled by foundational training and cultural development that take years to foster. Much is the same in the crucible of sport, especially in the intense final few minutes of close games with "do or lose" consequences.

There is an emotionally charged element to both these leading and coaching examples. Therefore, as leaders and coaches, our approach needs to take this into account. But let's be clear: in the direst combat situations, good leaders are coaching.

A section commander touches a soldier's arm after the IED blew up the LAV: "You got this! Breathe. Suppressing fire on that mud hut!"

Aircraft commander to crew after RPG impacts the Chinook: "Well, this is going to hurt. Get the MAYDAY out, straight ahead, let's keep her level. Evac immediately upon impact!"

As for coaches, those time outs in the final pressure-driven minutes of any close game are often about settling, inspiring confidence, focusing energy, and being extremely directive as to exactly how things need to unfold for success. They are leading their teams to victory... or leading them to defeat. Either way, they are not backing down from the challenge at that moment. I used to break the tension in close games by starting a time out with, "Are we having fun?! Isn't this exactly where we wanted to be?! Didn't all our practices lead us here? Let's get it done."

In all the examples above, establishing eye contact, or touching the arm of an individual to let them know you are there, humanizing the interaction in these most crucial moments, are key techniques.[38] In the direst of combat situations, good leaders are moving from individual to individual, asking them how they are doing and focusing them on the task at hand. Eyes, hands, ears…all senses working to lead them to the best of results.

Sometimes, in a crisis, all the knowledge about "how" things should be done, all the experience you have garnered by technically understanding the tasks, and all the lead-up mentoring is not enough. Sometimes we need to be *inspired* in a crisis. When I was an assistant coach for the RMC Paladins, I knew that I was there more as window dressing and as a military mentor than for my proficiency at basketball. We played in arguably the toughest division in Canadian University basketball. One evening, we were playing against the reigning National Champion Carleton Ravens. We were down by 30 at the half. The Carleton Ravens were, at the time, the best team in Canadian basketball. They had multiple National Championships. Their head coach, Coach Smart, is one of the best coaches in all Canadian basketball. Theirs is a renowned program. RMC, on the other hand, could not dress more than seven to eight players. Obviously, RMC was focused on military skills, not university basketball, and recruiting players with the very specific physical features required to excel at basketball was difficult.

We went into the locker room at halftime, down 30. The head coach, whom I admired as a coach and as an individual, received advice from the

---

38   I know that I need to be very careful in advocating touching someone, especially in emotionally charged situations. Obviously, I advocate for common sense and good judgment and appropriately conveying to the other person that things are going to be okay.

other assistants on what to focus on. He then spoke to the team about the Xs and Os, or pertinent tactical points that they needed to focus upon. He attempted to have the team focus on the little goals. I notice the defeated body language of the players. The Coach then turned things over to his primary assistant. More Xs and Os were discussed—take care of the ball, better defence. Another assistant pointed out some of the positive things the team had been doing. He made links between those small wins and expanded on them while demonstrating how the team must work together. Finally, and with only a few minutes left, the coach asked if I had any comments. I said I did.

Now, usually, in the locker room and on the court, I had a relatively restricted role. Again, I was brought in not for my coaching skills or knowledge of the game but rather due to my role as a senior officer and mentor to these future leaders. But I have never refused an offer to speak frankly.

"*Waaaaaaaaah waaaaaaaaaah waaaaaaaah!*" I loudly feigned crying like a baby.

"Stop looking at your shoes!" I yelled in my largest lieutenant colonel voice. "Look at me!"

"*Waaaaaaaah...* you're going to lose your little basketball game! *Waaaaaaaaaaah!*" I fake cried some more.

"Do you think I give a shit about this game, that team out there, or anything that has to do with basketball?!"

"I care about one thing, and that is your ability to rise to the occasion and deal with defeat, your emotions, and all the chaos you are feeling! The *only* thing that matters right now is how you *decide* to act! Because to me, this court, this team, this situation…this is only setting the stage for the real life-and-death situation that you *will* be placed into soon enough! So, you decide *right now*…who do you want to be?! Do you want to shrink into a corner, defeated and broken? The IED just went off. Three dead, five wounded. More *will* die if *you* don't act! The firefight is raging, and people will look to you for leadership. *Decide.* Shrink and wait? Or… win the firefight, pass the nine-liners, secure the LZ, and get the medevac in now. What you do *right now* will define who you want to be in the future. *So, decide!*"

I turned and left the room.

Midway through the second half, the opposing coach was losing his mind. We held his team to 25 points total in the second half. Sure, we lost, but I watched those young men fight for every single point like their lives depended on it. Walking into that locker room at halftime, they had had no respect for themselves, and the other team had had even less respect for them. They earned everyone's respect in the second half. I could not have been prouder.

To prove that the team had actually made an impression via their grit and determination, we went into the Ravens' Nest (Carleton's hometown gym) for another game a week or so later. One of the assistants to the Carleton team was an old high school friend of mine. He took me aside prior to the game and told me to get ready. The other team's coach had told his team to pummel us. His team was going into the playoffs, and he could not have the doubt of an underrated team like ours challenging their authority on the court lingering in the minds of their players. Hearing the impact that my team's effort and grit had made on one of the best teams in Canadian basketball made me even more proud. Stand tall against the largest of foes. Never back down from a fight if the cause is right. It's not over till it's over. Never, ever give up. And through it all, lead.

Maybe I should have been more empathetic toward those young men. Perhaps they responded more to the other coaches and their approaches than they did to mine. Maybe it was a mix. Who knows? I could have taken more time to figure out what was at the root of the issues preventing the team from rising to the occasion. But, at that moment, I thought I had a strong idea of what the problem was, and it was clearly their lack of belief in themselves. The first thing they needed to do was get out of their own way and focus on the larger goal of giving their all, regardless of what the result was going to be. They needed to see that, although this was a basketball game, the character that they were developing as a team— and as individuals—was so much more important than the moment itself. So, as a leader, I acted. As a coach, I acted.

There have been hundreds of times in my military career where I have decisively acted in the face of adversity, delivering pointed and specific direction in the execution of operations. Good leaders and coaches usually see clearly that which needs to be done and how to inspire performance in the team. Acting decisively in that moment, being even overly directive, is not a shortfall. Just don't see every situation as a crisis. When not in a crisis, keep adjusting your style and work to understand those situations where you will have no choice but to be very direct and inspiring, focus on the "how," and, most likely, lead by example. Preparing teams in advance for these situations is the pinnacle of training.

CHAPTER 28

Fear

My personal journey to self-awareness did not start with fear. If you had asked me what I was afraid of, I would have had stock answers like "something happening to the kids or Val." Either the persona I had created for myself or my compartmentalization of the serious risks and threats I dealt with on a sometimes-daily basis did not allow the concept of fear to enter my lexicon. I accepted that I was afraid, but I would never allow that fear to come between me and the conduct of my duty.

But the more I studied and the more I read, I came to realize that I was always fighting an inner voice. That inner voice, the monkey mind, was always saying, "I can't do this. If I try and fail, I am no good. In fact, I am already no good, and now everyone will know that I am no good." This voice is the product of millions of years of evolution where thinking critically and mulling over each and every single error in the hunt or in life was crucial to our very survival. Indeed, the need for socialization in surviving (groups survive where individuals perish) is the nucleus to the modern obsession with social media, along with the magnification of every single fault we perceive in ourselves as a comparison to others. So…I guess I was always more afraid than I would let on. I was afraid people would see through the veil of confidence and energy and discover me to be a charlatan masquerading as a leader. I was—and am—afraid of failing as a husband

and a father and a friend.

Compartmentalization is and was my go-to tool for combating my fears. But its effects can be short-lived or can cause long-term issues that the suppression of those fears can later bring up. Recognizing this is important. Always dealing with fears can be counterproductive, especially in crises or where there is no real respite to allow for the requisite decrease in performance while those fears are being dealt with. In my opinion, iteratively talking about the things that I am afraid of, using myself as an example to my team, was a good tool. Not many would open up and share their fears. But, in the instances where I and other leaders showed this vulnerability to fear and demonstrated that our own vulnerability was welcome and okay, the impacts of those moments reached well beyond the individuals who were sharing and positively affected the entire team. By opening up iteratively and establishing a vocabulary that you can revisit with people, you give them permission to deal with some of their fears and emotions. More than anything, these discussions can allow us to recognize our fears and take the first step in removing their power.

We are the most fearful of the things we don't understand—death, for example. It is easier to think of 100 reasons why you *shouldn't* try something that is hard than it is to think of one reason *to* do it. That is why you as a coach and leader must focus on the reasons *for* doing things. Don't let "hard" be the enemy of good or right. Being okay with living with regret is the easiest thing to do in the moment, but regrets last a lifetime. Having open and frank conversations with our teams about what we are the most fearful of or what things are too hard for us to tackle will demystify the very things we are afraid of. These are the moments of true inspiration, when individuals see their fears and see a path to overcoming them.

A very fun movie, *We Bought a Zoo*, says that it only takes 20 seconds of courage to do something great. Ask yourself, what could you do if you could muster up 20 seconds of insane courage? Then jump in and commit.

Have faith that you will surpass any obstacle—human faith, human spirit. Be comfortable with even 20 seconds of discomfort. It can change your life. And the consequences are never as large as what we imagine them to be in our monkey minds.

Finally, surround yourself with friends and family who will not let you off the hook. They are your champions and your safe place. But they need to encourage you to follow through on pursuing that which you aspire, desire, and commit to. This is a tough place for those around you to be in. Having honest conversations with them about achieving the balance between pushing you and emotionally supporting your fears will assist in this. It has been my experience that when we as coaches and leaders open up to our loved ones, we see just how much they love and cherish us. Every single time I have turned to Val wondering whether I can do this next job, face this next challenge, take on this next life adversity, she has been there with loving support and understanding of exactly who I am and who she knows that I can be. In times of adversity, we look to those around us for the inspiration that, in turn, we will provide to our teams.

I loved reading *Wolfpack* by Abby Wambach. What a superb and inspiring individual, and what a great and easy book to read. The ideas that resonated with me in her book explain a lot about how I feel concerning fear. She says, "Level up. Put yourself in those situations that are overwhelming, scary, uncomfortable." "Level up" means that when a team member shows outstanding performance, use that as the new bar for you to aspire to. This is exactly like the aspirational goals that we have already spoken about. But she uses this "level up" function to also fight fear, or perhaps even embrace it.

There is a radical self-awareness that people who embody this spirit of facing incredible obstacles have. It is admirable. We see it in high-level athletes, snowboarders and skiers, adventurers, and explorers. But those same skills are demonstrated in our front-line health workers every day, magnified by the reality of the COVID-19 pandemic. Our first responders, and, from my perspective, our police forces in particular, truly embody the embracing of the scary and uncomfortable as a daily ritual of dealing with fear. Wow! Powerful.

Even more powerful is Abby's idea that "This never ends—in life." We are all facing fear all the time. Some of us (me) ignore or compartmentalize it. But if we can see our way through to being vulnerable and admitting our fears, then we take the first step in disarming them.

Abby's concepts about the wolf pack are so very true. She says that by surrounding ourselves with people, our wolf pack, who will challenge us to be better, we "level up" with them. They raise the bar, they inspire us, and we reach alongside them. But where Abby and I are totally the most in sync is in saying that "*How* you face fear is defining for your character." This is not about anyone else, but about you. Your fears are yours. They're not the product of social psychological theory that enables a categorization and solution to them. They are personal, complicated, simple, tough…whatever…but they are yours. *How* you deal with them will define your character. It has mine. Thanks, Abby!

CHAPTER 29

Humour

Humour can bridge into the inappropriate in seconds. What is funny to one person may be demeaning to another. Cultural, situational, and personal factors make humour a very fickle thing. Used improperly, or perceived that way, it can be seen as ridicule or as demeaning. What is too bad is that we shy away from the fact that humour, laughing, or even just accepting that we did something stupid are all amazing bonds of cohesion that lighten our workplaces and show our personal vulnerability. We just need to tread lightly.

I always felt that a major indicator of how things were going was how—and how much—humour and laughter were part of our work environment. I always thought that even with how heavy and crucial our military work was, without humour, the environment could be wrought with *waaay* to much seriousness.

So, my advice is to see humour and laughter as good indicators of a positive environment. I often exposed some of my vulnerabilities to lighten what were sometimes very heavy conversations. I might open a meeting by highlighting something that I did outside of work that demonstrated my goofy nature at home. Sometimes, I would tell a quick story about a past failure of mine that was truly funny but was related to that which we were about to tackle. Next, I worked very hard to establish relationships with the people around me where I knew them and had their trust, which allowed for levity in both directions. Sometimes in the middle of one of my "sermons" on a topic, I would catch someone rolling their eyes or expressing some other type of judgmental body language. I would call them out in a funny tone: "Don't roll your eyes at me! Am I missing something?" But then I would pause and allow them to respond. This allowed for us to get back on track instead of focusing on my endless stories. Sometimes the people I called out would have funny remarks sarcastically stating how they would never roll their eyes, or things to that effect. I would thereafter gauge everyone else's responses to see how this was taken and to make sure everyone knew this was okay. It allowed them to use humour to let us all know that the relationship we had was more important than the topic we were discussing. And it allowed them to get me back on track. More than anything, I felt it made me approachable and human, while allowing people to communicate frankly with me.

But humour can definitely be a double-edged sword. I was not always smart about its use. When I was in the U.S., I worked with a young USAF lieutenant colonel. During a meeting, I made fun of his new moustache, and I knew immediately after doing so that I had obviously crossed a line. I sat down with him right away and apologized. But it didn't stop there. At his request, we spent some time together reflecting on the relationship we wanted to have professionally. He was so very mature about it (I was a general officer at the time). We coached each other, and we both learned (me most of all). It became a very rewarding relationship. I found that the process of me being vulnerable created space where he believed that he could tell me exactly what needed to be said. In addition, since he was my chief of current operations, this relationship was crucial to mission success. He went on to tell me that he felt supported personally and professionally. It was by going through this exchange of thoughts that I learned that, by understanding the role of trust, we can understand the boundaries of appropriate humour.

Humour is much more easily used in one-on-one encounters. I would make time to ask personal questions and get to know my people. During one-on-one encounters and when asking about things, the opportunity to discover mutually challenging and funny situations multiplies. From the trials of parenting teenagers, to the misdeeds of preadolescents, to my never-ending poor attempts at DIY projects, we could share humour. When we understand the people on our teams, humour becomes a reflection of us all. I had a friend of mine who had a lot of kids, like three times more than the rest of us did. We used to joke about his honed organizational and leadership skills being a result of his not having a choice with that many kids! Because we all knew that his large family was a source of pride for him, we were laughing together. Similarly, when colleagues of mine openly poked fun at some of my personal quirks, I knew we were in a good place.

Finally, as a point of supporting individuals who are dealing with large burdens of life-and-death responsibility, levity lets everyone know, "Hey, you are doing well, and it's going to be okay." In such cases, we are not using humour to make light of anything; we are using it as a tool to make connections and show our humanity.

Using humour well to be who you are, respectfully and appropriately, takes a great deal of both self-awareness and external awareness. More importantly, if and when we make mistakes, having the humility enabled by that self-awareness to admit that we were wrong and work to repair any damage can be so very rewarding, both personally and professionally. In the end, we need to know when we are creating problems. *Aha!*

CHAPTER 30

The Problem Is Me

A result of not having the right perspective is confounding already-complex situations with your own personal biases. You become the main problem. Sometimes we are too close to a problem or are overly wed to a solution. Other times, by trying to direct too much in the wrong situation, or because we know what we want, we micromanage. When we don't see the issues clearly, when we can't juxtapose them with related context, when we cannot judge issues for their relative importance, our biases fog our judgment.

Sometimes, especially in crises, we see immediate "default" solutions and end up rejecting new thoughts. This came home to me in stark reality during the ice storms of 1998. A series of storms dropped a blanket of upwards of 18 inches of freezing rain on Quebec and Ontario. The area of the island of Montreal and the associated South Shore were the worst hit. Millions were without power, and the electrical grid was devastated by the rain that crumpled transportation and distribution lines like so much cardboard.

I was working as the operations officer in 430 ETAH Valcartier, a helicopter squadron just north of Quebec City on the base at Valcartier. Our unit got the order to deploy to Montreal and provide helicopter support to the Joint Forces working to assist the local, provincial, and municipal authorities. We had a sister squadron located just south of Montreal, but their unit was deemed out of combat as they were all dealing with the support needed for their own families affected by the storms.

I immediately gave direction to my team to begin preparations for a deployment to our sister squadron's airfield. There was only one problem: there were about 18 inches of ice on the tarmac. Engineers estimated that nothing short of C4 explosives would get rid of the ice. I proceeded to get wrapped up in finding a way to clear the ice.

One of the people I worked with, a newly arrived captain, a SAR guy, was visibly frustrated with my preoccupation with this plan. He said to me, "Scott, hold on. Let me make a call. I know someone." It turned out that he knew someone who worked at one of the aviation companies that serviced the Dorval airport. The Dorval airport and its ramp were fully operational. In addition, they had an instructional building that we could use to quarter our people. They offered up hangar space where we could set up feeding and loaned us an office space that we could use as an ops centre. Done. But…it would not have gotten done if I had kept being hung up on my predetermined solution.

Recognizing that you are the problem is tough. Surround yourself with people you trust to tell you what you need to hear, not just what you *want* to hear. Many times, we call these truth-tellers "devil's advocates" or "contrarians." They are there in your teams. Many of them might be jaded. Bring them out of their shells by showing the team the value of their perspectives. Reward their feedback publicly when they give it. I have told the story of the ice storms incessantly to my teams since it happened as an indicator of how I value when people express points of view in opposition to my own. It makes the team stronger to know that I value them telling me when I mess up.

Techniques that work in recognizing you are the problem are not easy to develop. But here is my hack:

1. The first will seem repetitive: Try to be self-aware. If possible, when you are setting intentions for engagements, meetings, or your daily schedule, look to those things that might trigger a rote response from you. Emotions tend to blind us more than anything else. These are precursors to being the problem.

2. Next, read others and their body language when you speak. Listening, it seems, is also about watching!

3. Next, when you get any indication that you are at issue in the situation, ask people directly, and with a tone that reinforces your trust in them, "Am I the problem here? What is another point of view or approach to this?" I have found that taking people aside at breaks in meetings or after events are over and asking them open-ended questions like this can be very, very helpful.

4. Don't forget to reinforce that you welcome your team to bring this up in any forum and that the team and you personally can benefit from their perspective, especially if it is contrary to the norm, the accepted position, or your perspective as the leader or coach.

Recognizing when you are pushing a solution well past its utility based upon your personal biases will take some serious self-reflection. Don't be afraid to develop a routine spot or mechanism at the end of meetings or just before decisions are made where you can step back and allow for that one-step-removed perspective. If people come to expect that, then, if all else fails, they know they can address it at that time.

CHAPTER 31

Prioritization

W hen I was a young major, I started using a tool I read about in Stephen Covey's book *The 7 Habits of Highly Effective People*[39] to capture and discuss how to prioritize the work we were doing. Covey grouped things into four quadrants: Urgent/Important, Not Urgent/Important, Urgent/Not Important, Not Urgent/Not Important. The model he created looked like this:

	URGENT	NOT URGENT
IMPORTANT	Quadrant I: *Urgent and Important* **DO**	Quadrant II: *Not Urgent but Important* **PLAN**
NOT IMPORTANT	Quadrant III: *Urgent but Not Important* **DELEGATE**	Quadrant IV: *Not Urgent and Not Important* **ELIMINATE**

---

39   Stephen Covey, *The 7 Habits of Highly Effective People* (Free Press, 1989).

The first thing I would do when starting to prioritize is group work items into quadrants. This is a helpful "binning" process. Next, however, was to have frank conversations about the ranking of the items within each bin. This would always lead to a fruitful understanding of the leaders' thoughts and, ultimately, their guidance.

I never paid much attention to the "Do, Plan, Delegate, and Eliminate" part of the quadrants.[40] And I always felt that the bottom right quadrant (Not Urgent/Not Important) was not helpful. In my earliest stages, I did not think spending time debating the value of a task was beneficial. But more importantly, I thought there was more value in assessing the work that was *not* getting done due to sheer capacity. It was usually a lack of time or personnel resources that was keeping us from getting to the bottom right quadrant, not a lack of importance. I renamed this quadrant "Below the Capability Line." I was spurred on to this as my boss and one of my co-workers got into quite an argument when my boss found out that my co-worker was not working on the things he was directed to complete, but rather on items that a subordinate wing had deemed important. By specifically identifying that which was "Below the Capability Line," my boss was better able to manage the meek planning resources he had to achieve specific effects and not be undercut by subordinates. So, my interim success in prioritization looked something like this:

URGENT/IMPORTANT	NOT URGENT/IMPORTANT
Thing 1	Thing 2
That Other Thing	That Other Other Thing
Meeting A	Meeting B

URGENT/NOT IMPORTANT	BELOW THE CAPABILITY LINE
Thing 3	All That
That Hard Thing	The Thing We All Hate
That Harder Thing	That Hardest Thing

---

40 Sorry, Stephen.

The next challenge with this system was the tyranny of the upper left quadrant (Urgent/Important). Stephen Covey's brilliance in my mind was also revealed in his deduction that if you spend all your time in this quadrant, everything will ultimately migrate there, and your entire existence will feel like a time-crunched panic. Spending time and resources on the upper right quadrant, on things that were important but not *yet* urgent, was beneficial for getting in front of issues. Prioritizing in this way was key to effective organizations. Mastering this skill seemed to make me much more effective as a leader.

But merely listing priorities did not seem to be giving me all the guidance needed to effectively manage workloads. I came to the realisation that if you do not attach a timeline to something, it will never get done. "I want to lose 10 pounds." Without a time limit, this is almost meaningless. It is intent with no plan. However, "I want to lose 10 pounds before my son's wedding" is the beginning of a plan. Now we must plan the time, set intermediate goals, and be frank about progress. We will have to have an exercise and eating plan that supports this goal. Applying this concept, the table morphed to look like this:

URGENT/IMPORTANT	NOT URGENT/IMPORTANT
Thing 1, Mid Jul	Thing 2, Early Aug
That Other Thing, End Jul	That Other Other Thing, Mid Aug
Meeting A, 22 Jul	Meeting B, 12 Aug
URGENT/NOT IMPORTANT	**BELOW THE CAPABILITY LINE**
Thing 3, End Jul	All That
That Hard Thing, Early Sept	The Thing We All Hate
That Harder Thing, Mid Sept	That Hardest Thing

What I found next on my journey of discovery on prioritization is that I was mixing specific events and larger project names in the quadrants. Where the work was easily definable, I would be listing the next milestone. But on subjects where the work was vague and nebulous, we were merely prioritizing the "large project" and kept on pushing timelines to the right. In most cases, the large project was too daunting and, by not being specific, we were allowing for easy outs like "We can't get to this."

In thinking about this, I was reminded of the ancient adage that the journey of a thousand miles starts with the first step. So… for each item, I began asking, "What is the next step?" This served to level the playing field so that simple and complex work items were broken down the same way, and, most importantly, it gave us a system to tackle the toughest problems. We didn't have to fix the whole problem all at once. We just had to start the journey.

So, I would ask my team, "What is the next step?"

"Well, the first thing to do would be a two-day analysis of the current order to highlight what we need to fix."

"When can you do that?"

"We can get it done by the beginning of next month."

"Okay, we have a plan."

In this way, the team was accountable for the specific work, and I knew I needed to give them the resources and time to execute on it. We did not have to eat the elephant whole, just one bite at a time! The table morphed to look like this:

URGENT/IMPORTANT	NOT URGENT/IMPORTANT
Thing 1, Mission Analysis, Mid Jul	Thing 2, Options Developed, Early Aug
That Other Thing, Op Order Issued, End Jul	That Other Other Thing, Order Issued, Mid Aug
• Meeting A, Agenda Issued, 22 Jul	Meeting B, Invites Sent, 12 Aug

URGENT/NOT IMPORTANT	BELOW THE CAPABILITY LINE
Thing 3, Back Brief Commander, End Jul	All That
That Hard Thing, Mission Analysis, Early Sept	The Thing We All Hate
That Harder Thing, Brainstorming, Mid Sept	That Hardest Thing

This system was further refined while I was working in NORAD, both as the deputy commander in Alaska and as director of operations in Colorado Springs. Prioritization had become a true tool for us in Alaska, but I was not sure how closely we were moving the strategic yardsticks of the command. The commander NORAD's strategy had three enduring conditions. I had tasked my then-executive assistant in Alaska, Kris, to look at how we could morph our prioritization system to better align with the commander's strategy. Kris looked at the enduring conditions (a.k.a. pillars) of the strategy and then decided on a framework for us to scope our efforts while intuitively assessing whether we were balanced or focused on the right areas. He assigned each of the enduring conditions a colour (red, green, and blue). Each of the items we were working on was also then colour-coded as it pertained to a specific pillar of the strategy.[41] In this way, we could immediately see which of the enduring conditions we were focused on the most, and, as leaders, we could use this tool to assess whether we were moving the yardsticks of the commander's strategy and achieving what he needed us to.

What became immediately evident to the team via the large amount of red text on the priorities was that we were *waaaaaay* too focused on one specific enduring condition, which was basically "Deter Aggression and Defeat Attacks." Now, nobody can underestimate how much it takes to gain and maintain real readiness. But this commenced a more detailed conversation about deterrence and whether *alllllll* of the activities that we were undertaking in that area were having any true deterrent effect on our adversary. From there, we could see that by better balancing efforts (a.k.a. balancing the colours), we could perhaps achieve better deterrent effects. To do so, we would have to divert resources from this enduring condition and spend more time on "Outpace Our Adversaries and Maintain a Competi-

---

41 Kris actually did a complete analysis about how to integrate innovation and branding into our overall understanding about the "whys" behind the work and the strategy and how to link it to our priorities. But he needs to write his own book!

tive Military Advantage."[42]

We also realized we were being way too insular with our approach. The third enduring condition was "Build and Maintain Joint/Allied/Government Agency Relationships" and there were precious few blue-coloured items in our priorities. The table morphed again into something like this:

In this figure and subsequent ones, "Red" is indicated with a square, "Blue" with a circle, and "Green" with a diamond. The full colour figures are available at www.scottclancy.ca/figures

URGENT/IMPORTANT	NOT URGENT/IMPORTANT
■ Thing 1, Mission Analysis, Mid Jul	■ Thing 2, Options Developed, Early Aug
■ That Other Thing, Op Order, End Jul	■ That Other Other Thing, Order Issued, Mid Aug
● Meeting A, Agenda Issued, 22 Jul	▲ Meeting B, Invites Sent, 12 Aug
URGENT/NOT IMPORTANT	**BELOW THE CAPABILITY LINE**
■ Thing 3, Back Brief Commander, End Jul	▲ All That
■ That Hard Thing, Mission Analysis, Early Sept	▲ The Thing We All Hate
● That Harder Thing, Brainstorming, Mid Sept	▲ That Hardest Thing

■ EC1—Deter Aggression and Defeat Attacks
▲ EC3—Build and Maintain Relationships
● EC2—Maintain Military Advantage

Also, in NORAD, it became obvious that the management of workloads depended intimately on the tempo of operations that were in execution or were immediately imminent. Daily operations were monitored by the command centre. But, as things got busy, depending on the size, scope, and magnitude of the operation, more and more resources would get drawn into supporting current execution. Most leaders understand that when a crisis occurs, it is "all hands on deck" until that crisis clears. The nature of global military operations is that oftentimes, long before a crisis is recognized, we would be well into crisis mode. Our system was not flexible enough to account for the need to confront crisis without losing sight of those things that could directly impact execution. In addition, my teams

42 We adjusted the "Enduring Condition" language on the slide to reflect what we needed to do in the Operations Directorate—and to fit the slide!

directly involved in the delivery of operations and especially in maintaining operations centres did not see their huge efforts reflected in our prioritization system. Simultaneously, other leaders stated that they were doing many more things than appeared on our single slide but that those things were merely enabling or adjunct to our priorities. Uh-oh.

I had spent decades refining my system by this time, but I could clearly see where it was not working for us. Especially as the director of operations for NORAD, I needed to be able to capture and work through priorities in crisis operations. I also needed to be able to deal with the hundred mundane tasks that my large staff were dealing with that did not "fit" or rise to the level of an item on our priorities list. I engaged my two battle buddies, Major-General Dave "Oscar" Meyer and Major-General Pete "Coach" Fesler. I often just got the three of us together to brainstorm stuff. It kept us fresh and forward-thinking. They always challenged me even more than I could challenge myself.

I felt like the time had come to find another way to organize work, but Oscar and Coach both immediately told me *no*. The system worked. The amount of heavy feedback we were getting was because our subordinate leaders believed in and liked the system. Now that they were using it, we had to "work it." We had two problems: crisis operations and preparedness for them and dealing with the myriad of mundane tasks. To my friends' credit, they advised me that the first one was a prioritization issue, while the other was a leadership issue.

To resolve the issue of crisis operations, capture the ongoing effort required to maintain the operations centre, and ensure that the entire team understood that when we ramp up to crisis, everything else will be of a lower priority, we created a new box on the priorities sheet called "Essential Tasks." This box contained the obvious things that needed to get done regardless of the rest of the work and that would always take precedence over all other tasks: the command and control of operations and the maintenance of the watch. I made it clear to my entire team that 100% of our capacity in crisis and conflict might be consumed by the essential tasks. These were the non-negotiable priorities.

Next, we needed to resolve the issue of the things that were being done by my team but that did not rise to the level of the priorities sheet. As Coach and Oscar advised me, this was a leadership issue, and, to resolve it, I delegated authority pertaining to all these smaller tasks to my division chiefs. They had the authority to refuse all tasks or even not do a lower-priority item if a higher-priority one was consuming more resources. The only person who could override their refusal was me personally.

Note that they could say yes. I trusted them to know their tasks and their team. They knew what right looked like and clearly understood my priorities. If another division needed help on a high-priority item, I trusted their judgment. If a completely different element of the staff outside of my purview tasked them or needed their help, I trusted their judgment. All I asked was that, if something impacted our priorities, we discussed it. This empowered the division chiefs to be masters of their domains while being accountable for the work they were doing. The table morphed into this:

ESSENTIAL TASKS
- ■ Maintain the Watch
- ■ Command and Control NORAD Ops
- ■ Train and Maintain the Watch

URGENT/IMPORTANT
- ■ Thing 1, Mission Analysis, Mid Jul
- ■ That Other Thing, Op Order, End Jul
- ● Meeting A, Agenda Issued, 22 Jul

NOT URGENT/IMPORTANT
- ■ Thing 2, Options Developed, Early Aug
- ■ That Other Other Thing, Order Issued, Mid Aug
- ▲ Meeting B, Invites Sent, 12 Aug

URGENT/NOT IMPORTANT
- ■ Thing 3, Back Brief Commander, End Jul
- ■ That Hard Thing, Mission Analysis, Early Sept
- ● That Harder Thing, Brainstorming, Mid Sept

BELOW THE CAPABILITY LINE
- ▲ All That
- ▲ The Thing We All Hate
- ▲ That Hardest Thing

- ■ EC1—Deter Aggression and Defeat Attacks
- ▲ EC3—Build and Maintain Relationships
- ● EC2—Maintain Military Advantage

It became apparent that these last two things were about operationalizing our prioritization process.

My teams and their leaders began using these tools to explain and manage workloads amongst their teams, subordinate leaders, and other members of the larger staff. Subordinate and flanking (peer) commands began requesting to use this process to gain insights for their commanders and asking how they could leverage or influence our work. I had to be able to explain not just how our prioritization system worked, but how we as leaders needed to use it to inform our daily work decisions, including where my subordinate leaders had authority to change things and where they did not.

The next evolution had to be about how I communicated this system so that I could get direction from my boss, work out the issues with my team, and keep subordinate commands informed in order to synchronize efforts. This had to be linked to a detailed governance or battle rhythm. The easy stuff was to begin sending my priorities to my Canadian boss (Canadian three-star general deputy commander NORAD) on a bi-weekly basis. We would talk almost daily, but I would lay out my priorities bi-weekly for him in an email. This allowed him to see where I was with everything that was meaningful to him, and if he wished, he could track things that had popped up or that he wanted me to get after. Thereafter, monthly, I would meet with him specifically on the priorities.

What this allowed was for him, on behalf of the commander, to verify quickly that I had the right current set of priorities. I felt that this allowed him to be reassured about operations and to focus on the trickier and more politically charged elements of the funding, acquisition, and future strategic planning of the command and Canada's role in it. I also think that this system allowed him to relax his mind and think extemporaneously about where we were strategically and perhaps how I could assist in shaping things. These chats allowed me to put my priorities in context with the larger geo-strategic issues at play. Finally, these discussions verified that I was indeed moving the strategy forward and influenced conversations I would have with my senior leader team.

Next, I had to root this system into a schedule. Most organizations would call this "governance," but, in the military, it is called "battle rhythm." Until that point, I had always used a weekly or bi-weekly meeting to prioritize work. But the operational commands of NORAD made me much more aware of the tempo that I was maintaining, both my personal tempo and the tempo that I was forcing out of my subordinates. Additionally, these prioritization meetings could be somewhat lengthy. In Alaska, I started out by having a weekly meeting with the key team members and subordinates, and then, once a month, having them bring in their subordinate leaders so that they could watch the process and we could harmonize across a larger swath of the organization. In Colorado, mostly due to the pandemic, we were forced into a virtual setting, and, between that and the fact that my team was so much larger than any team I had led before, I found no need to invite a larger audience to attend since almost anyone was allowed to attend every virtual prioritization meeting. This helped with tempo.

While I was struggling with the periodicity, or how often to have these meetings, I also struggled in their conduct with how to balance between the need to focus on the specific elements we were trying to prioritize while at the same time wanting to hear from each of the subordinate elements of my team. I landed on a meeting where I led the conversation for the first 30 minutes, walking the dog around the sheet asking for updates on the items I considered critical to the vision, and then, for the second half hour, heard from each subordinate division. Because we handled many of the key priorities up front, the divisions had less to speak to. Even with this structure, though, I struggled to complete the meeting in an hour. To assist with this, I varied the order of speaking for the second half of the meeting from week to week to ensure I got around to all the divisions.

As if it were a full-circle moment, as soon as the team was very happy with the system and the authorities that they had been given, I began to doubt the entire thing. I began to see that the major flaw in the system was that it was inherently reactive. I struggled to get out in front of our adversaries. I knew that we needed to do a better job at forward-looking analysis regarding what we "should" be accomplishing, rather than merely executing on the priorities of the "right now." Even with my monthly meetings with my boss, I found that we remained entrenched in the quagmire of the "right now" priorities. We already had a campaign order and associated planning process that programmed a year of effects we were attempting to achieve to advance the commander's strategy on all fronts. But there was no inherent link between that and the remainder of the work, some of which did not fit nicely into the campaign order framework. I knew that I had to spend more time just thinking through the issues.

I went back to my brain trust, Oscar and Coach. We mulled over a ton of ideas, but what we kept coming back to was not our prioritization system but rather another routine event, the calendar meetings. We were not doing an effective job of getting further out in front of "right now" and programming the work in advance. We needed to make decisions on the concepts *waaaay* out in front, then set the milestones for them in the calendar meeting, while the priorities meetings made the real yardsticks move. We also agreed that we needed the three of us to schedule brainstorming sessions to inform these calendar/milestone meetings. If not, we would be wasting the team's valuable time while we discussed, evaluated, and rejected or accepted ideas.

The result was a planned schedule for brainstorming (monthly), calendar/milestone (bi-weekly) and prioritization (weekly) meetings. The event that needed to be fleshed out the most was the calendar/milestone meeting. Everyone (except me) wanted to run it sequentially from that point out to 12 months in the future. I wanted to run it the other way, from the 12-month point backward by month. In this way, we would discuss and set the long-term goals and effects first, then plan backward. We never came to an agreement on this issue, so I leave it to you. One is intuitive (start close and work out). The other makes better planning sense, at least to me.

In practice, everything became iterative. Thinking about a single milestone would make us move back and forth over the calendar months, setting milestones that would inform our priorities of the day. The brainstorming sessions identified the ideas and concepts out to five years (aspirational, as I left before we really got to that), while confirming our concepts closer in. We did the brainstorming sessions in a very free format, once per month. I wanted to do them once every two weeks, but our personal schedules were too jammed. The calendar/milestone meetings would walk major milestones back from the major concepts that we discussed in brainstorming. The priorities meetings were then focused solely on what we were doing (or not) in the moment.

As I look back while writing this, I can hear my friends asking, "What does this have to do with coaching or leading?" In fact, one can make the case that this is clearly an organizational management tool. True, it is. However, effective prioritization, and the decision-making behind it, although structurally a management tool, is only there to support good leadership. It needs to be driven by leaders who are willing to see the benefits of doing lower-priority work early, sequestering assets, timing decisions, and accepting feedback on key decisions. It also empowered my subordinates to get on with their business while keeping themselves, their teams, and me accountable to what we agreed upon.

Prioritization Summary

1. Effectively prioritizing allows frank conversations about the amount of work people are truly capable of in specific, measurable times. Subordinate leaders or team members will be setting clear expectations and will have a framework with which to discuss organizational management with superiors and subordinates alike. This engenders mutual trust in a pragmatic fashion.

2. The hidden gem in the process is in seeing a "Not Urgent but Important" item and making the hard decision to sequester resources (people and time) to get after it. During my time as the director of ops for NORAD, we had to get after rewriting the standing NORAD Operations Order (hundreds of pages) that formed the operational framework within which NORAD responded to threats and conducted operations across the continent. But the only way in which the team could get after it was to plan it in advance, cease doing a bunch of other things for a time, and accept some risk on everything other than the essential tasks. This was a tough decision, but, once it was made, I had to stick to it, even when things got dicey, and protect the resources that we had sequestered. Without the system in place, I would never have had the framework to be able to make such a decision.

3. This process allows a frank conversation with the team and subordinate leaders concerning the impacts that tempo and workload have on them personally and on their teams. Each division could gauge their workload at any given point in time, and we could have a discussion, influenced by the work priorities, about where we had to make adjustments to achieve better tempo. This allowed all team leaders to be able to move about and discuss the work with anyone on our teams.

4. Your organization can make "leave" or downtime a priority. I consciously made summer leave an "Urgent and Important" priority. This was reflected in the subsequent decisions to slow down, push off deadlines, or not start projects until after the summer leave period. This was signalled well in advance, allowing us to plan the "how" in pushing certain items to the fall or accelerating others in order to achieve it.

5. The system set the stage with the team. The team buys in to the priorities. They must be able to use your priority system against you

when you inevitably push tough timelines on deliverables. That is when you know it's working: when they are quoting your words back to you and showing you how your demands are incongruent with your system. Love it!

6. What your priorities look like at your level is different from how it translates to your subordinates. There are differences in tempo between teams. Mutually understood priorities provide opportunity to shift personnel resources, even temporarily. You can truly manage your team from the point of common goals. Everyone does not have to fight a "set piece" battle with the resources assigned to them. This common understanding of priorities can free up subordinates for innovation and, at the same time, it ties the whole team together.

7. I mentioned before that you must also deal with those things that do not—or should not—appear on the list. Many organizations have people other than direct supervisors making demands on their people. Some of this enables collaborative flat organizations, so you must allow subordinates to manage this at their level. This does not mean to turn a blind eye. I would do deep dives with division chiefs individually, and I would ask those kinds of probing questions while reinforcing that the division chiefs had the authority to deal with these relatively minor items and that I would back them up no matter what. As leaders, remember that there are standing or routine tasks that end up eating many resources as well.

8. This system also allowed for the development of a matrixed team able to augment essential tasks in crisis or conflict. Since I knew what the essential tasks were, and I knew that in a time of crisis 100% of our resources would be focused on fighting the crisis or (God help us) would be used in a conflict of survival, I could assign team members matrixed tasks that they would train and prepare

for, then pick up and execute in times of crisis at predetermined decision points or phases. This allowed for my subordinate leaders to plan and schedule the training and experience required for these people to execute these matrixed tasks, which cycled back to affecting the tempo and priorities that these leaders could handle at any given time.

CHAPTER 32

Scheduling

When I arrived at NORAD as a colonel on my first day, my administrative assistant handed me my schedule. I had meetings programmed back-to-back from 0620 until 1730 that day. No lunch. No bathroom breaks. No time to even walk from one meeting to the next. And sometimes it would take five to ten minutes to go through the four or five levels of security to get in and out of the command centre, up three floors, and across the building to a meeting.

To add insult to injury, I walked into meetings in the afternoon and had supervisors ask me what I had done about items they had mentioned to me that morning. *What?!* I had not relieved myself, let alone been back to my office. How was my team to know that they had raised an issue—telepathically?

Right then and there, I did a brutal analysis of what meetings I was *required* to attend, what was *nice to have*, and what was fluff or repetitive. Moreover, I asked myself, "If I don't go for like... a month, and nobody notices, isn't that an indication of the value of my attendance?"

I had naysayers tell me that it was essential that I attend this or that meeting, or that we had always done things a certain way. Yup...didn't care. I needed to set the right tone. If information was important, then leaders would choose the correct reporting method and I would have a frank conversation with my boss on what was achievable and what was not. I would not get bullied into death by meeting.

This is where I started my personal journey into effective scheduling.

The skill of scheduling may seem like a binary management tool and not a leadership or coaching tool, but I disagree. As a good coach and leader, you will always feel like there is not enough time to practise, plan, meet, execute, or do any one of a thousand functions. Scheduling, linked to the prioritization skill just covered, is a crucial part of this. And I'm not just talking about your personal schedule, but also the schedule of your team.

Let me explain this through a basketball metaphor. As a basketball coach for youth, I was always under a time crunch to develop players while preparing them for their next games. These can be two very different, and at times competing, obligations. I needed to:

1. see the amount of time available (weekly practice schedules, how many weeks),

2. be able to break it down before the next milestone (next game or tournament),

3. put it in context with the overall year (assess team performance and player development), and, finally,

4. produce individual practice plans, filled with the associated drills and exercises matched to the two outcomes of player development and preparation for the next event.

This same skill in coaching is required by leaders. Organizing work, breaking down the objectives into manageable chunks, and then moving the team through the required motions in the most efficient manner takes planning. Not to mention the effort it takes to adjust plans and execution along the way. It doesn't just "happen." As a leader, don't be fooled by the idea that you can merely set things up well and they will go off without a hitch. Oversight and coaching are required to hit objectives and to garner feedback to keep focused on efficiently meeting those objectives or adjusting the objectives to meet the realities of your team's capacity. One of the key techniques you can use to do this well is scheduling.

My first piece of advice is to master prioritization. Priorities stem from our vision and our "why," and scheduling is birthed from that. My next piece of advice is to break down your vision into manageable milestones. This can be hard. To assist, I recommend using three filters to break down major problems:

1. Time,
2. Function/organization, and
3. Project/plan phase.

For example, a basketball season can be broken into pre-season, season, and playoffs (time). The revamp of an operational design would move from the strategic plans division to the combat plans division to the combat ops division for final execution (function/organization). An operational deployment usually has five phases: warning, preparation, deployment, employment, and redeployment (project/plan phases). Throughout this, however, the coach or leader needs to be focused on the performance that is required. Although these filters allow for a cognitive breakdown of the task or project, it is the *performance* that links this process back to the objectives/milestones and the vision. Alignment here is key. I recommend asking tough questions like:

1. What would we need to be accomplishing in May to ensure that success in September is guaranteed?
2. When does (insert organization or functional area) need to receive fiscal guidance to purchase goods for production?

3. What teams do we need to be competing against well as the season starts to get us into the playoffs seated in one of the top three positions?

4. If we needed to clearly establish that we were having a deterrent effect on Vladimir Putin and Russia, what would that look like in six months? One year?

Once we have these milestones, it is important to understand how to frame scheduling from first principles. I will revert back to my military roots here. The foundation of all military operational planning is Boyd's OODA loop (observe, orient, decide, act). Most civilian organizations know this as "governance." The reason why I prefer "battle rhythm" is that the military focuses its operational planning on outputs that achieve results. My experience with institutional governance is that it is inherently based upon providing oversight and control, linked to liabilities and responsibilities; it's not necessarily focused on getting things done. When I was analysing recurring meetings, I always wanted to understand what decisions were being made. Where was this meeting on the cycle leading us to act? If I felt as a leader or senior staff member that we were not getting the guidance we needed or supporting decision-making effectively, I looked to our battle rhythm, our governance, to see where the shortfalls lay. I asked two fundamental questions: "Do we have to modify current events/meetings to enable better decision-making?" and "Do I need to create a new event/meeting to fill this gap?"

In keeping with this first question, I recommend starting with an analysis of any recurring meetings that you are currently having with your team. My simple analysis always focused on five things: frequency/length, purpose, attendees, agenda, inputs/outputs. Write these things out on a cue card, one card for each meeting. If you prefer, put them on a slide so that you can visualize a month, week, or year for you and your team. An aide-mémoire for this is:

1. Frequency/length. How often do we conduct this event/meeting? How long is it scheduled for? Does it often go long? Is it a meeting that always seems to have an overflowing agenda? Do people complain about having to attend this meeting due to its length or frequency? I would also add in here an analysis of when in a workweek, workday, month, or year this event or meeting is held. Meetings need to match the energy and focus of the team. Heady thinking meetings reflecting deeply on work outputs and the link to complicated elements are not well programmed at the beginning of a week or at the end of a workday. Much the same, gauge the interest of the attendees at meetings that are scheduled late in the day or week and that tend to go long.

2. Purpose. I highly recommend *Momentum*,[43] which is an excellent, easy to read book on organizing meetings. I personally don't categorize meetings too extensively. However, trying to state the purpose of a meeting is a great way to illuminate its value. Beware meetings focused on merely passing information and providing updates. To me, if meetings do not have an element of decisional capability to them, then I question their value.

3. Attendees. Start with who heads up the meeting and why they are responsible for it. Who else attends, why do they attend, and how do they attend? Think through the position, function, and specific individuals while analysing here.

4. Agenda. Is there a standard agenda? Who develops the agenda? How is it developed? What is it focused on? Look at the last five meetings. How was the agenda linked to the purpose of each meeting? How did it reflect the frequency/length? Was it relevant to all the attendees? Was the agenda helpful to the person/position

---

43   Mamie Kanfer Stewart and Tai Tsao, *Momentum: Creating Effective, Engaging and Enjoyable Meetings* (Lioncrest Publishing, 2017).

that is chairing each meeting? How did the agenda reflect the inputs/outputs related to the milestones of the team?

5. Inputs/outputs. Most organizations are not simple single echelon flat organizations. Most have deliverables associated with their performance, and the governance covers how they report and control the performance to meet objectives and milestones. But there is a time delay involved, and there are decisions associated with the information. If the decision is to place ordinance on a specific target, then, with enough time prior to execution, the aircraft must be ordered to load the correct munitions and the pilot must be given enough information to plan and follow complex control mechanisms to the target area, to know where to get gas from a tanker, and to be aware of the rules of engagement for the target. The time necessary for these preparations will drive how far in advance the order must be delivered, which will drive when the decision must be made, which will drive when the nominated targets must be provided, and so on and so forth. This complex dance between decisions and actions, linked in time and space, is the fundamental premise behind governance and battle rhythm. It drives subordinate actions, but it also drives information needed from subordinate elements or disparate divisions in order to understand the situation and therefore make informed decisions. Meetings must have inputs and outputs. This will drive how information is passed and why. In many meetings, attendees are there specifically to provide the inputs in order to frame decisions that turn into the meeting outputs. Is a review of the decisions part of the agenda? How is the production of outputs tasked?

Now remember that we will always be hard-pressed for time. Therefore, asking the question of value added for these meetings is important. By walking through this aide-mémoire above, the value added by each meeting, and indeed the inherent linkages from one meeting purpose and conduct to the next will be understood. Moreover, it can be explained easily. Once understood, the team can not only adjust and feed the decision cycle, but they can also recommend how to adjust the various elements of these events (frequency, agenda, outputs, etc.) to enhance decision-making.

The next technique I use is to extrapolate that team scheduling down to my personal schedule. Employing a different mindset here is important. I struggled with personal scheduling as I moved higher within the Canadian Armed Forces. I had the benefit of some excellent executive and adminis-trative assistants who were stellar at helping me with this. To be honest, I also had a few who did not perform so well, and the strain that that caused on me personally only served to exemplify how essential administrative and executive assistants are and how important the scheduling function is. But I struggled not just because of the quality of the people working to help me, but because of the inherent balance between the demands of an organization that I did not control and the desire not to be a victim of my own schedule!

Personal scheduling took a lot more communication to get right than even the team battle rhythms did! But by taking personal ownership of my schedule and having daily meetings with my executive/administrative assistant on it, I achieved a good balance. The first thing to do is extrap-olate the team event/meeting governance or battle rhythm to your own schedule. Clearly identify to your personal staff (if you have this luxury—if not, then make it clear to yourself) which meetings/events you must take, which can be delegated, and to whom. Next, program time to prepare for these events/meetings. This needs to be related to the meeting and reflected in how you wish to receive preparatory information prior to the meeting. Military leaders rarely walk into meetings having had the time to reflect on the specific material in advance. This is true even when most protocols insist on "read-aheads" more than 24 hours prior to each event/meeting. However, in my experience, the most successful meetings are those where everyone has had the opportunity to review the material, do additional analysis, and come prepared to focus on the key "sticky" points. If you require read-aheads from your team, you must program the time to do those readings and come to these events prepared. In addition, this is the point in a daily or weekly schedule when you want to specifically schedule time to "set intentions." Sometimes this can be layered into the same time that you are reviewing the material for the meeting. In any case, make the time to link what the meeting is focused on to how you wish to *be* in the meeting and what your desired personal outcomes are.

A quick side note on read-aheads. In many of the organizations I have been in and affiliated with, the people in these meetings are seeing the information for the first time and are required to make a value judgment on that information on the spot. This needs to be followed up by expressing that decision in a rational way, which in turn will most likely influence the decision's success or failure. When the team, and especially the decision-maker(s), are not prepared in advance for these meetings, the results are no better than a coin toss. Value judgments that are instantaneous are emotionally based instead of being based upon a deliberate governance structure, even if an excellent one is in place. Even the best scheduling mechanisms cannot overcome this. Sending material in advance as a read-ahead package is the best way to overcome this and set the conditions for a good outcome.

If you are not chairing a meeting but rather presenting information for decision or to a group at the meeting, use the same process. Schedule time to prepare the inputs, provide them in advance if possible, and schedule time to set intentions prior to the event/meeting commencing. Finally, and this applies to everyone, schedule time after the meeting to address meeting outputs. Too many excellent events or meetings have clear and defined outputs that are lost because we move on to the next thing and do not either capture the direction or execute the actual outputs. Set aside time in your schedule to produce the desired outputs.

In "Fundamentals," I discussed the issue of balance. I think that using your personal schedule to reflect the balance that you desire to achieve in your life is crucial. The same way that you program time to prepare and set intentions, you must schedule family events, family time, rest, eating, exercise, and relaxation. I add to this idea of scheduling balance the imperative to also schedule your personal development. In the Canadian Forces, officer development included professional military education and self-development, with standards associated with both. Many leaders saw these as things "you do on your own time." I disagreed with this perspective. As I mentioned earlier, I had many people whom I was leading or mentoring who needed to hit qualification standards for things like education and second languages. I would tell these people to treat those development goals as part of their jobs. I would insist that they blend them into their personal schedules, and I would make myself accountable for their work tempo to ensure that I was enabling them to do so.

Sharing your electronic calendar can be an interesting process of trial and error in both public humility and invasion of privacy. I liked to control my entire schedule, and I did not have separate home and work schedules because time and detail required me to integrate these two calendars together. As I moved into the realm of being a general officer, I was requested to have my schedule shared with…well, it seemed like the entire world! This included dozens of other senior officers, admin and executive assistants, and people I had never even met! My initial reaction was "No way!" But the staff of an organization like the RCAF could not function efficiently if it could not have a system of coordinators working in the background to make the most of every single minute in a daily routine, so I had no choice but to acquiesce.

I was not ready for this, for hundreds of people to be analysing my schedule to try to second-guess what I was doing to figure out what was important. I never resolved this. On more than a few occasions, I had people embarrass me by making comments about what I had been up to all weekend, as I programmed my time down to the 30-minute blocks to get through everything I needed done. On other occasions, I had people critiquing why I was or was not attending certain events or meetings. This felt bad, especially when it was none of their business, but I had to just accept it. I needed the schedule, and key people needed to harmonize my schedule with that of other key leaders. My advice is to think through this and make sure that you personally know how you want to deal with having your schedule shared if that is something that is a possibility.

The last thing I would like to discuss in the realm of scheduling is the aspect of "creating space." I evolved to think about scheduling as a more creative way to arrive at key outputs. I was not only creating space for setting my own intentions, brainstorming with my team, or maintaining the personal balance I needed. I was also creating space for others to move the organization forward in transformative ways. Here is what I am talking about.

While the director of operations for NORAD, I remember having a specifically rough time working through a complex approach to aligning future development concepts, operational plans, training and exercise development, and current operations. My team had highlighted to me this "gap," or need for alignment, across the various elements of the command. My two deputies (Oscar and Coach) and I had discussed this at length in a brainstorming session. We knew we had exhausted all avenues of alignment at our level. We had to get the various executives in a room with the commander, unfettered by subordinates and prying eyes, where the commander and the other executive leaders could speak and engage frankly. I needed to present an idea but allow the space for the other executives to present their opinions without feeling railroaded by our ideas. We had to create space for dialogue, compromise, disagreement, and, ultimately, reasoned decisions.

I asked one of my brightest minds his opinion and gave him space to think and respond. I studied his response and then Coach, Oscar, and I analyzed it in a meeting with him. The brilliance of my team was that they knew where all the other points of opposition would be. Instead of just baking our responses into our presentation of the ideas, I programmed the specific space for those other executives to articulate their perspectives. We had a framework for alignment and an authentic process to make that alignment happen.

I used the format of a whiteboard session, which turned out to be highly beneficial, and I think the format inspired straightforward conversations, real discourse, and sound decision-making. Sure, there is an inherent struggle with the "on-the-spot" discussion without a "team of experts" (and their predetermined outcomes) shepherding along the way. They have answers for every counterargument. In my experience, there is a time for that expert advice, and there is a time for leaders to speak freely. Create the space needed for leaders to speak freely and discuss.

It is one thing to have good technique and process surrounding meetings or practices. It is something else to put in the right variety, predictability, value, energy, and preparation to ensure that the human interaction is enabled. Going through the motions of a boring meeting will not inspire creativity, performance…or anything, for that matter (except perhaps taking an early retirement). What do we have to do to avoid this? Schedule well.

CHAPTER 33

It's Always More Than a Meeting

It's an opportunity! **Make it so!** Grab the moment! Have the conversations you wished you were having. Not all the time, but sometimes, just ignore the "work" and talk about the real things going on; how we perceive each other, what is working, and what is not.

I once told my staff (I was a chief of staff at the time) to tear out a piece of paper and answer a few questions about what was going well and what we should stop. They all thought I would read their answers. Then I told them to pass their papers to the left, and they read each other's responses out loud. Not only was this a test in the character of the individuals to read aloud criticisms of their peers, but sometimes those criticisms pointed fingers straight at the people or sections who were reading the page! By the end of that meeting, we had frankly shared more about our weaknesses and strengths and increased our productivity more than we had in any other meeting we held. Seize the day! Just not every day.

Read people during meetings. Watch their body language and their tone. This is obviously much harder in virtual meetings. After you do this, then try to ask probing but not "single you out" questions to get after those items where body language indicated discomfort...like, "I am not sure I completely agree with this. I feel there might be a different approach. Does anyone else disagree? Why?"

Sit at the side of the table. Mix things up. If you are a leader, then don't always place yourself at the head of the table. Sit beside different people. This is the balance between humility and effectiveness. Don't let your ego, your sense of authority, or any of the "trappings" of "position" or proper protocol get between you and good leadership/connection with your people. Go into a meeting and make everyone's position at the table important. Recognize attendees who are new and welcome them. I learned this from my sister Ann when she was the director for HR at the Canadian Red Cross, as she would go into a meeting and sit at the side of the table, bringing herself (figuratively) down to the attendees' level. It would surprise people that she hadn't sat at the head of the table. She set the tone. I found this practice even more meaningful in military settings. I used to have a round table in my office (like King Arthur's) that was very effective in taking away any uncomfortable hierarchy.

Do not, however, outright dismiss tradition and protocol. I know that I risk contradicting myself here, but I also think that there is a danger of fostering a level of cynicism for position and authority if organizations do not hold to certain traditions and protocols. In the Canadian military, I watched this wane over the years I was serving. When I joined and was on my first squadron, when the commanding officer (CO) of the unit entered the briefing room in the morning, the room was called to attention, and we all stood. The CO would bellow out "Good morning," and we would all answer. He respected each and every pilot and flight engineer. He listened to us and accepted our suggestions and criticisms about flying operations in his squadron. But make no mistake, he was in command. In the 20 years that followed, though, I watched this practice erode until I experienced a room full of Canadian service people, when called to attention at the arrival of a three-star general, barely shift from their slouched positions in their chairs.

Traditions and protocol hold us to a set of standards for respect and honour that should only be compromised if proven improper. Without those standards, very low bars for respect will be set, and the teams and leaders involved will all wear the impacts of an overall lack of mutual respect. I don't believe that any sound traditions or protocols ever prevented a leader from leading or connecting with their people.

Share the limelight. Celebrate your team. During meetings, don't let it go unnoticed that the team is working hard. But, at the same time, make sure that you don't laud your team into apathy. When I took over as the chief of staff to 1 Wing HQ, within three months we had our annual training session that reset the team for the year and provided onboarding for the newly arrived folks. As the COS, I opened the meeting. During this opening presentation, I gave the staff an F for its performance, but I did so on purpose. We were in the midst of the war in Afghanistan. We had already taken combat losses and were expected to take more. The teams coming out of theatre were adamant about what they needed to fight effectively there. We as a staff were not firing on all cylinders to get those things to them. A year later, I gave that same staff a B. (In my old Fort Frontenac Directing Staff or "DS" style, there are no As.) They had impressed me in the intervening year.

Create the balance between recognizing effort and gauging what that effort is delivering in terms of results. Your feedback and your meetings will reflect this balance.

Meetings, beyond the purposeful outputs they are designed for (see chapter 32, "Scheduling"), are opportunities to reiterate vision, recognize performance, and, most importantly, lead, teach, coach, and mentor. Recognize the opportunity, think about your leadership style, and have the meetings you hold personify that style. When you set intentions for your meetings, keep these things in your mind alongside the business of each meeting.

I like the spirit of the phrase "It's always more than a meeting." It inspires us to strive beyond that which is already laid out, to be different from the "norm," and to embrace new things alongside tested and true ones. The balance between new and old, innovation and proven truths, is a path that most leaders and coaches, especially those in dynamic roles with fast-paced organizations, tread constantly as part of change management cycles.

Innovation has not always been my strong suit. I guess as a student of history, especially military history, I am a staunch believer that history teaches us solid lessons for the future. But the pace of change in our world today, driven by accelerating data and technological innovation, provides a new dynamic for leaders and coaches. A modern approach to innovation and change is clearly required by leaders and coaches.

CHAPTER 34

Innovation versus Plagiarism

I was introduced to the concepts surrounding innovation very late in my career by the commander of the RCAF. The commander took all his general officers to the Innovation Hub in Waterloo, invited by the president of Open Text, who was also a member of the RCAF Advisory Council. I saw first-hand the partnership of the business community with Waterloo University. I learned how the "idea accelerator" between the academic world (ideas are not bound by economics), industry (money can assist in solving problems), and multi-party innovation (someone may already have a solution to your problems) can enable growth, scaling, profit, public service, and, ultimately, *everyone* in such a fantastic way.

The innovation bumper sticker was "fail fast," and it was all about speed, scaling, collaborating, and getting ideas into implementation. It was all very exciting. But for me, it was hard to envision and implement innovation within the dogmatic military bureaucracy, or, more importantly, within the government of Canada's bureaucratic system. And, although I tried, I still felt that, at its core, there were some better ways to approach innovation than "failing fast."

I always encouraged innovative ideas. But before—and since—that time seeing the Innovation Hub, I felt that I was merely plagiarizing the good ideas of others. (It sounds *sooooo* much more boring.) Yup, I blatantly plagiarized other people's ideas, practices, and processes and adopted them/manipulated them for my purposes.

→   I took templated policy directives/operation orders and used past orders/documents to speed up my production of the next policy or order.

→   I stole leadership ideas and fun experiences and used them with my teams.

→   My prioritization framework comes from Stephen Covey.

→   I stole the Canadian Armed Forces risk-management framework for flying operations (MALA) and had Alaska develop a risk-assessment framework based upon it.

→   I forced myself to study military history, tactics, and lessons learned incessantly so I could explain *why* something was done in a certain way and therefore had a bank of options that history had already attempted.

So, while I encouraged an innovative spirit and ideas, "reuse, repurpose, and recycle" seemed to be more in tune with how I was operating. But the bureaucracy of the military and government and my tendency to plagiarize were not the only reasons I was sceptical about innovation. There is an inherent resistance to innovation in a military context. The tactical cost of failure in military terms is lives and equipment. The strategic costs are security, sovereignty, and national survival. In routine business and government, the cost of failure is time and money. Does the military cost warrant the advantages of a "fail fast" culture for military organizations? The tenets of manoeuvre warfare underpin all our modern military processes on the battlefield. Fundamental to manoeuvre warfare is an understanding that the fight is on both the physical and cognitive planes, but that, while victory on the physical plane may result in a specific objective being met, victory on the cognitive plane will have a cascading effect on multiple objectives, both physical and cognitive. Overwhelming the enemy with tempo is not necessarily about speed, but rather about presenting a series of events to an adversary that they cannot cognitively deal with. This leads to always having the initiative, which will ultimately result in victory.

There is an inherent similarity between the "fail fast" spirit of innovation and the cognitive victories of manoeuvre warfare. However, at the tactical level, trialling new ideas at a time where the cost may be in lives or countries lost has a risk calculus that needs to be better examined. As a minimum, it leads to reticence in the implementation of new ideas without being trialled.

Where do I stand, then? I am a fan of both the new innovation and the old plagiarizing approaches. There must be innovation and innovative spirit in vibrant organizations. This is the same spirit that tactical leaders show to achieve results in ways nobody else had imagined. Innovation and leaving "how" things are done to those doing them is at the essence of mission command in a military context and empowerment in all workplaces. SWIPE (Steal with Integrity, Pride, and Energy) is an interesting business practice but one I champion from a military perspective. As a leader and coach, make sure your team is doing both—and that they understand the consequences of both. Moreover, always try to engender that innovative spirit in whichever approach you are taking.

I always thought that innovation started as an intellectual process about being able to shift one's perspective. Let me explain. Innovation, at its core, rooted in no context, framework, or foundation, is ultimately unimplementable. But, by only setting our roots in that which has been tested and trialled and is based upon historical analysis and best practices, we limit our ability to free our minds from preconceived notions. The best jazz musicians are the ones who know the rudiments and fundamentals but can still embody spirit, playfulness, and vulnerability by experimenting and trying new things, even if those things fail. At the core of all of these processes is being able to ignore some first principles because we understand them intimately, being able to not follow heretofore unquestionable "rules" because they constrain our thinking. This is shifting the mental paradigm or lens through which we see a problem. It opens us up to other solutions, and some of those solutions may be repurposing already-established practices in other fields or areas of expertise.

As a coach and leader, it is important for you to understand innovation and set the conditions that foster it while celebrating those who achieve based upon tried and tested practices that they appropriated or adjusted to suit their needs. There is a common element of creativity in both of these approaches. My experience has been that the most effective teams are able to fuse these qualities together and foster both.

CHAPTER 35

Don't Be Templated

When I started teaching at the Canadian Army's Staff College at Fort Frontenac, I watched the group dynamic of the students carefully. They were very supportive of each other. Military values have always focused on the team and its cohesion, with training specifically designed to reinforce these behaviours. When I would ask students to critique other students' plans, they would instead agree with those plans. In fine "Scott Clancy" style, I would tell them, "I did not ask you to agree. If as a military planner you cannot get your mind around the other side of this problem and present the opposing point of view, then we are doomed to all be defeated in short order by those who have the intellectual capacity to do just that." It was an intellectual drill, not a team-building challenge.

This is the essence of diversity of thought. I always strove to get more perspectives, more approaches, more ideas, than could be held within my teams, which were a non-diverse group of predominantly white males.

To make this point, I would tell my students about the power of the opposing point of view. Those people who founded our great nation knew the power in this perspective. After the governor general (GG) had invited the party with the most votes to form a government, they would invite the party with the second most votes to be "Her/His Majesty's *Loyal* Opposition." *Loyal!* The GG would then charge the leader and their party to present the opposing point of view to government policy. Having a group set to counter the government would force the entire team of elected officials to at once critique, defend, and possibly modify government policy. This made us stronger as a nation. And this was all done publicly, which made us stronger still.

As coaches and leaders, it is important for us to develop minds and spirits that are open to this intellectual process, that encourage the challenge function, and that know its place. It is especially important to distinguish between your personal beliefs on an item and the process of articulating the opposing point of view to it. This change of paradigm or perspective, this challenge function, combats nepotism and weeds out conformists or yes-men. Demographics can also help this. Having a diverse group of people in a team brings a diverse set of perspectives and opinions. This allows for a better consideration process and, ultimately, better decision-making. It's not merely about innovation, but about thinking around a problem. This will set the stage for informed innovation.

There is another phenomenon that is closely related to this called "narrowcasting." Narrowcasting focuses on a single element of an issue or group, ignoring the surrounding information or perspectives. The term was initially developed to differentiate between media "broadcasting," which was dispensing information to everyone, and narrowing down the target audience to those of a specific nature. It has subsequently been used to describe reactions to emotionally charged issues that are centred on the reactions to the emotions. To me, this is related to groupthink, where the perspectives of the people involved are so homogeneous that the solutions seem self-evident and there is little dissension. The example that I gave in "The Problem Is Me" concerning my channelized attention on deploying to an ineffective heliport during the ice storms is a classic example of this. Challenging teams by forcing them to present other points of view is key. This technique will assist in developing a team that thinks through different points of view, as the demographics and experiences of the team are widely varied. Diversity of team makeup will inspire diversity of opinion and thought. But do *not* allow this to be at the discretion of the team. Again, groupthink or narrowcasting will creep into any team that remains together for any significant period of time. It is a social reality. The role of the coach and leader is to keep the team open by demanding other points of view, giving them insights into differing perspectives, and even challenging them to go find those differing perspectives. While challenging the team, be careful in your language:

"Does anyone disagree? Does anyone have a different perspective?" (Note: this is lame and will elicit a groupthink response like *"Nope,"* or just silence.)

vs.

"Arnold, can you give me another option that would work here, please?"

"Steve, is there not a way in which our competitors could do this differently or perhaps better?"

"Jane, what other options need to be considered, or have you considered and dismissed, and why?"

And my favourite: *"What is the opposing point of view to this?"*

By fighting off the inherent risk of being cast into a single mould, group-thinking our way to mediocrity or, even worse, failure, we set in motion the means by which diversity of thought is fostered and sustained. This fosters innovation, and, if entrenched systemically, will also foster diversity culturally in the organization. This is how we keep from being templated.

In military terms, we used to use red and black teams during planning. Now, red team planning was pretty much standard. It involved the intelligence community trying to figure out our plan and would have teams dedicated to hacking into our systems during planning and execution. However, the most interesting thing I ever saw was a black team. This team showed up for the initial encounter that presented the situation for which we were to conduct a planning cycle. After this they had no contact with the Red Team nor our Blue Force planning team. They went back into their cave, and we did not see them, nor did they have any contact with any portion of our team, either physically or electronically, for the next few days. Immediately prior to the decision brief to the commander, the black team presented their results, which were their assessment of what course of actions and recommendations we (Blue Force) would present for a decision. They also presented what they believed our intelligence community (Red Team) had offered as the adversary courses of action. They were usually 100% on the mark. We had been completely templated. Someone operating in complete obscurity, only knowing how we usually reacted and thought, had not only discerned what we would want to do, but also exactly how we thought of the enemy and their actions. We were templated right down to our thought process and were completely predictable. The *only* way to combat templating is through diversity of thought and innovative thinking and behaviour.

The phrase "don't be templated" is also a warning. All too often, I see young leaders and coaches imitating that which they think they need to be, say, or do when they are coaching and leading. Now, this is a delicate balance. There are many leaders and coaches whose practices and techniques are indeed worthy of imitation. One of the best ways in which to learn how to coach and lead is to imitate those whom you have seen being effective. What I am referring to is not this but rather imitating behaviours or ideas about what coaching or leading is from books or movies. Even good coaching techniques are not prescriptions (or at least, they should not be) for your personal character. Your coaching or leadership style needs to reflect *you!* Don't be templated.

When I finally sat down and figured out what my leadership philosophy was, I got great advice from a host of mentors and senior general officers in the U.S. and Canadian militaries. They listened to my rants and advised me to look internally at what I valued most from good leaders and why those things resonated with me. I did indeed take on best practices and imitate some of the behaviours of leaders and coaches I admired, but I did so thoughtfully. There needs to be an intimate connection between you and your style. It is purposeful, and it is who you are. Don't be templated into a style of imitation, yelling because that's what's done in the movies (I know, hilarious coming from me!). Those templates are Hollywood ideas. Be authentic. Be professional and personable. Be respectful and straightforward. But above all, be yourself.

Finally, don't be templated even by your own style or by your success in how you operate. I established very specific ways of doing business in various organizations and within a wide variety of governance or battle rhythms. But, once these were established, I would divert from them, spice things up so that the team was always thinking. I would get through info quickly in meetings, and, with the freed-up time, I would ask questions about the things we were not getting after, those things that were below the capability line. Or I would ask the open-ended questions that were scary: "What if the attack that we never want occurs tonight?" Or… "What if our governments give us all the resources we need?" The reflections from the teams answering these questions during these moments shaped future work and our priorities significantly. Don't be templated.

CHAPTER 36

Zoom Perspective

Zoom perspective is the ability to change focus in or out as the situation warrants but also to ensure harmony of vision across strategic (macro) and tactical (micro) elements. In this way, coaches or leaders are "zooming" in or out like you would while looking at a map on a computer. Many people are happy with a certain level of "zoom" in their work life, or in life in general. Some people are comfortable with the big picture, not the messy middle or details. Others love the highly technical and sometimes predictable details and outcomes. Indeed, as I left the world of global military security and defending nations and continents, I gained huge comfort from reverting back to a level of "zoom" where my focus was on my family, my home, my close friends, and the immediate community I was living in.

Highly effective leaders and coaches will need the ability to zoom in and out to see the varying perspectives. They need to develop the judgment and ability to decide how to transmit and employ those varying perspectives to best enable their teams. It's not easy.

Let me dive a little deeper into the ways that zoom perspective can work. I will use a coaching example first.

If I am harping on the inability of a single basketball player to "box out" effectively, I have zoomed right into that individual level. If I then zoom out, perhaps in that moment, in that game, we are holding the other team to a small number of points. Zooming out gives me a different perspective. That perspective gives me the opportunity to choose and use my judgment. Am I focused on the right things? In addition, this perspective allows me to choose the best approach for the situation. I can adjust my style and relay to the players and the team that, although we are leading, now is exactly the time when we should be working on those things that need developing, without the pressure of winning the game. I can zoom out to see the entire season and give the team the perspective that, later in the playoffs, we will have needed the experience of game situations to hone these skills. I can also zoom right in on the individual again and personalize this and their role within the team and this game, and even how it relates to their lifelong development. Being able to zoom in and out quickly allows connection at that micro level with the work being done and gives me the ability to explain how it is directly linked to the overall vision. In general, it also enables coaches and leaders to decide whether adjustments in the macro or micro elements are warranted, and, most importantly, how they should be made.

For leaders, the work applications of this are easy to see. Firstly, it is a skill that ultimately enables the ability to explain how each cog in a complex system or organization contributes to the vision. Secondly, it allows for leaders to get out of their lofty and somewhat disconnected ivory towers and immerse themselves in the highly technical and tactical business of their teams. As we have learned in twentieth and twenty-first-century warfare and business, the smallest of details can make the most strategic effects, both dire and positive. Leaders who can zoom in to understand this, zoom out to see the implications, and then apply their reasoned and experienced judgment for the benefit of the mission are mastering the skill. Lastly, and perhaps even more important than the rest, zoom perspective enables a coach or leader to connect with, sympathizing and empathizing with, the people on their team. Too often, I have seen coaches or leaders who get stuck at a level of zoom, and their preoccupation or focus on that level taints all the communication with their teams, preventing them from connecting with them.

Okay, a few techniques related to zoom perspective now. The first is to be aware of what level of zoom you are at. This is related to being situationally aware. As a wing commander in the RCAF, I would go and visit the various squadrons often. Physically, I was now down at least one level from that of my command. While meeting people on these visits, my zoom was often down even further, often right at the level of the individuals. But that is a physical thing. I was also wary regarding my mental space. Although I might be visiting unit A, my thoughts and preoccupation on that day might have been set by an early morning correspondence with my boss two full levels of command above the unit and perhaps five or six above the individuals I was going to be spending the day with. Applying some rigour to setting my intentions and compartmentalizing my emotions surrounding other issues helped me in being able to zoom in during my visit. When you do the same, use the key phrase "be present" to help you set these intentions.

Almost every visit to a unit involved some sort of town hall or event that enabled the people of the unit to ask and get first-hand answers to the questions that vexed them. Here, too, being cognisant of the level of zoom I was at was important. Some questions would focus on policies and directives that I was responsible for. The level of zoom here was easy, as I was at my level but trying to relate it to the unit's More difficult questions asked of me challenged national-level policies for which I was not responsible but that were having direct impacts on those with whom I was speaking and their families (military housing, posting allowances and procedures, childcare, family medical care, etc.). As a leader, being able to zoom in and empathize with the specific consequences of a policy, often showing my personal frustration as I challenged those policies through the chain of command, while also being able to zoom out and explain the details of those policies and their rationale, went a long way in connecting at that individual level (at least, I believe it did).

On at least a couple of occasions, my ability to zoom in and out and see conversations for what level they were at was crucial. On one occasion, my boss happened to have been visiting one of my units while I was there. On occasions such as these, I tended to try to blend into the background (I know, tough to imagine) and place the spotlight on my boss. I obviously ceded the town hall that was scheduled that day to him. However, during the town hall, the members of the unit began to ask questions that were clearly about policies and directives, or interpretations of them, that I had made at my level. This could easily be compromising and embarrassing for my boss. He had given me a lot of latitude while I was running the wing, and I had a good deal of respect for him. Although I kept him aware of all decisions and directives made within the wing, he had multiple wings and 13,000 people working for him. He was running the entire operational portion of the RCAF and working directly for the commander RCAF, with all that goes alongside that operational- to strategic-level interface. Therefore, in this instance, I interjected and asked my boss if I could take those questions first from my level. In so doing, I would be able to reinforce to the individuals asking them the rationales and vision pertaining to the questions at hand. My boss would not be put in a compromising position of either not being aware or issuing opposing guidance publicly (at least, not first). When he waded in, it would demonstrate the alignment that we shared on these issues.

There was more than one occasion where he supported my directives as an extension of his. There was also the odd occasion where he acknowledged the friction between the policy, the individual concern raised, and my interpretation of it. He would turn to me and ask me to revisit the situation. No probs! The team saw him actively leading and me being responsive not only to my boss, but also to the team. But, in every engagement, the team had a connection with the leaders. They saw my boss as leading me and challenging me to align with and further his vision, an alignment that they could now see applied right down to their level. If I hadn't been able to zoom in and out, this would not have been possible.

I also saw the opposite side of this. On a couple of occasions during public town halls, I would be asked questions about policies on which I had clearly given guidance and direction but that the unit leader had not acted upon. Again, in most situations, that unit leader would rise and clearly state that this was a unit-level issue and that they would tackle that issue themselves. But there was the odd time where a unit leader would leave those questions for me to answer. I am not one to shrug off my responsibilities, ever. I answered questions clearly and directly, always. (One of the reasons many of my leaders always advised keeping me clear of the press.) When I answered some of those questions, it would become clear that unit leaders had had everything that they needed to resolve the issues, but that they had not taken action or issued clear direction.

This only occurred a couple of times. I had highly effective and seasoned leaders. But I highlight these instances because it is my ability to zoom in and out that allowed me to know what level I was at. Debriefs after these uncomfortable times would sound like me asking, "Do you want me to issue unit-level guidance? I can. I know what right looks like. I can easily do this. But, if I do so, that would lead me to question the value of having you lead at this level. You need to take ownership and responsibility for your role in this issue, which is why I insisted that you issue unit-level guidance on it."

The other reason to be conscious of your level of zoom as a coach or leader is that it will assist in fighting a tendency to micromanage. In many of the discussions that I had in preparing to write this book, micromanagement showed up again and again as one of the key negative tendencies in leaders. I believe that two things directly contribute to micromanagement: the inability to trust subordinates with responsibilities and the ego of knowing about tactical/technical aspects of our teams. We have already discussed trust at length, but zoom perspective allows us to embody that trust. It enables us to connect with what it is like to operate down at that level. But, by being aware and zooming back out, we are able to apply self-discipline, which is the antidote to micromanagement. We recognize the importance of the technical/tactical knowledge of the individuals and can put it in context with the big picture, connecting the dots.

Finally, zoom perspective and our communications skills enable us as coaches and leaders to ask questions and make suggestions to tease out any issues that we see without being overly directive with subordinates or teams that can clearly resolve the problems themselves. Use your zoom perspective to give others the insights they can't see because they are deep in it—in the fight, in the technical job, in the game. When zoom perspective is matched with your seasoned judgment as a coach and leader, great things can happen. Once you divide up responsibilities, then apply self-discipline and stick to this approach. Discipline yourself to live with the errors or mistakes associated with allowing the team or your subordinates to execute, while staying at your level of zoom to help them. When I was coaching basketball, this manifested in my approach during games: coach the concept, the technique, the bench…but don't over-control the floor.

Okay. Time to zoom right back out to the macro level and look at all of our coaching and leading concepts that we have covered. I know that standard conclusions might wrap up by summarizing what was said. Like a good presentation:

Tell them what you are going to tell them,

Tell them, and

Tell them what you told them.

But I think there is some more analysis of the material to be done. You deserve some more perspectives, not on each individual fundamental or

TTP, but on the overall approach, themes, and how you as a coach see your personal development and that of your teams in some or all of these concepts. While you move through the last section, "Prove It!", keep those issues and questions that come up for you at the forefront of your mind. Try to analytically see whether the material presented in the previous chapters, as well as the following analysis, assists you in solving some of the problems you and your teams are facing. Finally, I recommend making some judgment calls on how the knowledge and skills apply to you as a coach and leader in your personal development.

Section 3
PROVE IT!

When I was teaching tactics and planning, I used a description of cutting an orange in different ways to describe comparison. Comparison needs to be done in more than one way to get a complete sense of a subject. If you cut an orange in half along its north-south axis (or top to bottom), open it up, and look at it, you get a perspective on the orange. But if you cut open that same orange along its east-west axis (or side to side), you get a completely different viewpoint. By then comparing these two perspectives, you create a more fulsome comparison.

At an even more simple level, merely rotating the orange and looking at it from a different viewpoint aids in the comparison. If the orange is the problem that you are trying to solve or the issue that you are dealing with, then the more ways you can gain a different perspective on the orange, the more complete your comparison will be.

For us, the subject is not an orange but rather leadership and coaching. Therefore, in this final chapter, I am going to use some different views of the amalgam of information that has been presented so far.

The first perspective on leadership and coaching will be initial thoughts on some specific themes or even single fundamentals and TTPs that seemed to resonate larger or be applicable in more places throughout the book. Writing this was quite the journey for me on my study of leadership and coaching. In the beginning, the various ideas that I had collected and then organized into fundamentals and TTPs were a somewhat nebulous group. I knew inherently that some were more important than others, but I did not necessarily appreciate the impact of some overarching concepts.

At the outset of our journey, I wanted to show how leaders are made better by adding coaching skills to their repertoires. But I also knew that leadership skills were applicable to coaches as well. I also knew that some of the topic areas would be more applicable to one role or the other, coaching or leading. Throughout the previous chapters, the applicability of the item has been self-evident (I hope). In wanting a perspective for comparison, I decided not to merely summarize those that are more applicable to one or the other. Instead, I wanted to explore my own approach to leading and coaching, as well as the proximity of these two roles in my mind and in my life. It is the duality of these two roles that will enlighten our understanding of the relationship between coaching and leading.

I have said that comparison is all about perspective *waaay* too many times. However, as I looked at the topics that were covered in the previous chapters and took a step back from the actual content of each (zoom perspective... see what I did there?), I saw that I could bin the topics into ones that were focused on team development and ones that were focused on the personal development of the coach or leader. I think that looking at the list of topics through the lens of this paradigm provides some unique insights into the ubiquitous value of a few specific topics while demonstrating that we are always developing in more than one way.

My favourite analysis in this "Prove It!" section links some of the concepts or chapters together. As I approached the end of writing the previous chapters, it was apparent that separate "streams of logic" emerged. I could draw lines between specific elements from conceptual fundamentals, through self-development and into implementation. I had the most fun with this, and it was the most revealing to me personally. In some ways, it reinforced ways that I had been doing things. In other ways, it brought out stark new synergies that I had never truly grasped before.

Lastly, there needs to be a section where, in fine Scott Clancy form, I rant and "ramble on" a bit. So that is where we will end the section and the book. Grab your orange and start cutting!

CHAPTER 37

Initial Thoughts

L et's start by looking collectively at the amount of detail, skills, knowledge, and complexity this topic of coaching and leading involves. I continue to be humbled by the importance and scope of both of these roles. As professionals, the more we know, the more we know how much we don't know or understand. Thinking about poor workplace cultures, underperforming teams, and disconnected members of teams, the solutions begin with solid fundamentals, but ones that we can see through explanations and examples to be implementable in our teams, in whatever roles we have. The task now is to take the aide-mémoires, hacks, lists, and suggestions here and identify where they work for you in a practical and pragmatic way. You can change and adapt by weaving them into your practice as a leader and coach.

The definitive phrase we used at the beginning of the book was "**Leadership and coaching are emotional trust relationships**." There is no way that one can achieve anything without first setting the foundations of trust, putting a system in place to monitor and evaluate that trust, and planning modifications to rebuild or sustain trust. You must listen, be self-aware, recognize when you are the problem, and empower the people on your teams to develop trust. There was an element of trust in every section, and I found myself going back and reviewing what I had written on trust to make sure it was right. Trust paired well ("foodie" term) with all of the other fundamentals and TTPs. If we are going to solve those wicked leadership problems, we will have to start by recognizing the role of trust and how we develop and maintain it.

The theme of creating space between emotions and behaviours as part of the overarching goal of being self-aware and recognizing your emotions for their inherent value weaves throughout the book. It is easy to see why. This is an area that I struggled with throughout all my career and life. My reactions and the authenticity that I believed I was applying to my roles often got in the way of my ability to coach and lead (or be a good dad or husband). They also figured heavily in my self-study and research from a personal growth perspective, especially later in my career. So what? I think that there is wisdom that comes with age, simply because there is a humility associated with being okay *not* knowing things.[44] But for the longest time, in my professional and personal life, that was not an acceptable answer in my mind. This approach made me hugely defensive, or, more pertinently, over-defensive. It is true that if you know you are right, defending your position either through discourse or behaviour is akin to standing up for what you believe in. But it can also be the enemy of seeing different perspectives and opinions. Most importantly, understanding this led to me realizing that recognizing others' opinions is as important as believing in your own. In fact, detaching from your own opinion, then listening and accepting others' opinions, has the effect of de-emotionalising reactions. Doing so allows access to even more authentic emotions and values, not merely reactive ones. I wish I had tapped into this earlier and trained myself to set intentions and practise skills that centred on this. Learning from my errors here can hopefully enable you to be a better leader and coach. This is a key skill upon which many of the fundamentals and TTPs will be implemented.

---

44   Val has taught me that the answer "I don't know" is not just okay, but much better than reaching to create something from circumspect.

Creating space led to me seeing my personal deficiency in listening. Yes, *the* most critical part of communication... and I don't do it particularly well. I guess that's why I leaned heavily on the perspectives of those who had worked around me in writing this section of the book. I think that they provide, through their ever-honest and appreciated feedback, a window into what "right" should look like. These insights show how barriers like rank and position prevented me from having the most rewarding exchanges possible. Moreover, I think that they provided a window into the fact that even well-intentioned leaders and coaches might not have mastered all the techniques of communication and that anyone in the chain can use their personal tools to enhance the whole team. The analogy of the bridge was one that I thought of while trying to rationalize my shortcomings into a metaphor that I could hold in my mind and set intentions with before a meeting. I have had some success in doing so, but it is still an arena where I must practise more. I think it is a fundamental enabler and catalyst to all the TTPs. Moreover, I think it is a crucial skill required to resolve disconnected team members and underperforming teams. Look into your communication toolbox and reflect on how you want to be a better communicator as a leader and coach. Focus on the bridge, and it will enable many of the other skills.

As you read through the chapters, I hope that you saw that all the fundamentals and TTPs are learned skills, not innate traits. As I mentioned earlier, I used to hate the "great man theory" that was taught at most leadership institutions for many years. Here are the key leadership traits; emulate them. BS. I always believed that good leadership was a learned behaviour. My reading of Major "Pappy" Boyington, commanding officer of *The Black Sheep*, who was one of my teen heroes as the most decorated Marine aviator in WWII, rooted me in the humility of one of his favourite quotes: "Just show me a hero, and I'll prove he's a bum." Humility in never ever knowing enough not only drives innovation and pushes people to meet aspirational goals, but it also means that self-development is essential for leaders and coaches. The fundamentals and TTPs discussed in the previous chapters bring out very starkly that these are all learned behaviours and skills and, even if there are those who can pick them up easily or even seem to have an innate ability to do them without effort, this does not mean that they are not, at their essence, learned skills.

I worked really hard and fought against some of my most compelling urges to be a more refined and controlled leader. And I truly trust those who admit vulnerability and yet strive to be better every day. Coaching and leading are learned skills. You will need to be uncomfortable in practicing what you know to be right. Use the tips and hacks, stay rooted in the fundamentals, and use this clarity of mind to develop new muscle memory.

I also challenge you to be more reflective on your personal journey as a coach and leader. Take time to write down and think about your actions and behaviours alongside those of your teams. When I looked back on what I was doing during my time in the military and as a coach, it became obvious to me that I spent most of my coaching and leading career merely "doing" and not reflecting on how to do things better. The work on yourself as a coach or leader cannot start at the end of your career. If we are to accept that, then we also have to accept that most of our organizations, especially at the tactical or low end of the hierarchy, are being coached and led via innate traits instead of deliberately developed skills.

I think I would have been a much better leader if I had reflected and worked more deliberately on developing knowledge and skills in coaching and leading prior to the last five to eight years of my career. I think that there are a lot of reasons for this. But in the end, those reasons don't matter, like, at all! What I am stating is, to me, just fact. I would have been a better leader, or at least a better leader *earlier*, if I had taken more time to reflect on my skills and knowledge in a more deliberate way. This is not a criticism of my numerous mentors, who all tried endlessly to advise, teach, coach, and mentor me. It's a criticism of myself for not knowing that if

I had been more deliberate with this, I might have been much better. Be better. Journal, think, reflect, talk, confer, read…you will be a better coach and leader for it.

CHAPTER 38

Coach-Leader Duality of Perspective

Many of you may have started this journey seeing coaching and leading as two very separate things. Perhaps even now you still hold that mindset. Professional coaches, especially at the executive level, sometimes talk about being "out of the boat," implying that the people they are coaching are in a boat rowing but they as the coaches are not. Looking back at the fundamentals and TTPs and my initial inspiration for writing, it was the relationship between these two roles or concepts, leading and coaching, that spurred my interest. But I, too, had an underlying division between these roles in my mind—and in my life. I led teams at work, and I coached basketball at night and on weekends! See Figure 38.1.

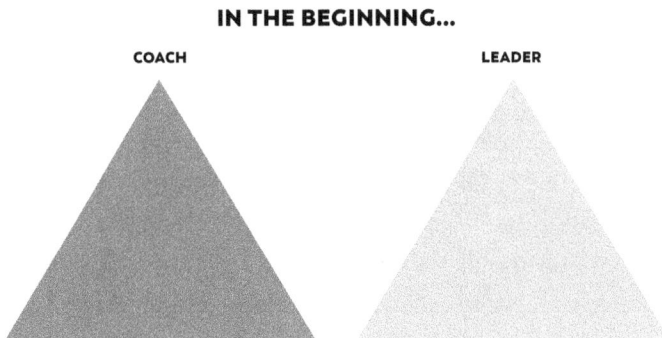

IN THE BEGINNING...

COACH

LEADER

Figure 38.1

As you read through the book, I hope that you saw that there was a ton of overlap between these two roles (see Figure 38.2). Some of the overlap was in the direct applicability of concepts. Things like trust, communication (listening) skills, and connection were obviously relevant to both. But it was while exploring many more of the facets of fundamentals and TTPs that concepts began applying dissimilarly to both. For example, scheduling was a very specific and arduous process that I had to master to be effective in the high-tempo world of being a general officer in the military. But the breakdown aspects of basketball practice planning and skills development, although the same scheduling concept, are applied very differently. Many fundamentals or TTPs are the same at their core principles but can be applied very differently to coaching or leading. This means the quiver of skills for coaches or leaders presented by this examination is even bigger than I had initially thought.

EVOLUTION!

COACH   LEADER

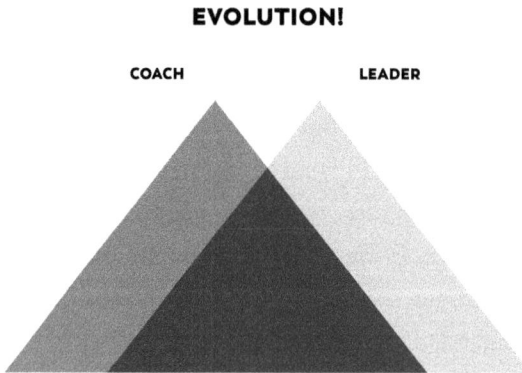

Figure 38.2

The other thing that made the fundamentals and TTPs align was my similar approach to both roles (see Figure 38.3). Even though they were different roles in my life, I approached coaching and leading from much the same perspective; therefore, the fundamentals and TTPs of executing on both were inextricably linked. So, since I saw connecting, emotions, and trust (just to name a few) as fundamental to inspiring young players as well as military subordinates, then the fundamentals and TTPs that I employed were also applicable to both. I guess the opposite could also be true. If an individual approached coaching from a very different standpoint, used very different styles and approaches to each, and saw them as two very distinct roles, then the arrows would be forcing all the fundamentals and TTPs to be dissimilar in their applicability to either role, many perhaps only being applicable to one or the other.

SIMILAR APPROACH!

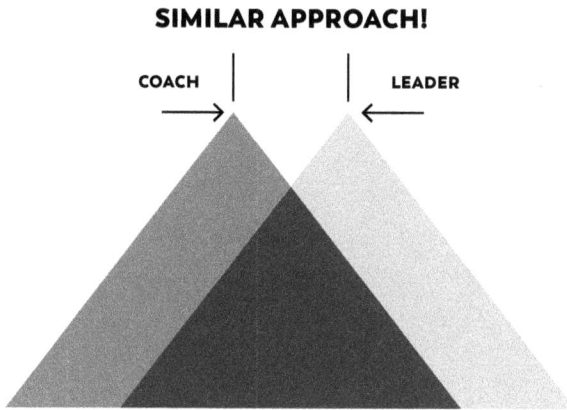

Figure 38.3

I think what this means for coaches and leaders is that, as you progress in your roles in either sphere, taking some time to self-assess and ask yourself if you are approaching your roles very differently may lead to some interesting insights. For example, a hard-nosed leader struggling at work to establish true connection with subordinate team members but having wild success in coaching his kids in sports might look at the differences in how he approaches these two different roles in his life. Maybe some of the fun-loving, people-centric, "life before performance" approaches that he uses while coaching his kids could be very informative in infusing a connection at work. A next step might be asking which of these distinct roles he feels is more authentic to his true self and why he has taken such different approaches in these two roles.

CHAPTER 39

Improve Myself...
Improve the Team

Y ou cannot improve your listening skills without being an example for others as to how to master those skills for themselves. Similarly, while working to improve any team, we learn so very much about ourselves. Ask any coach, teacher, or instructor, and they will tell you how much more they learn when trying to teach a skill compared to when they merely perform that skill themselves. In fact, the interesting dynamic in many of these facets became that the more I professed them and encouraged others I was mentoring to use them, the more effective I became at understanding and applying them myself. Huh. Neat!

The question I asked myself while looking through this paradigm at the fundamentals and TTPs was, "What am I holding as my focus while working on this issue?" Was it enabling the team, or working on myself? I know, not very academically rigorous. One of my dear friends, who is often the academic voice in my head, would caution me to the inherent biases that such a subjective framework would offer. But my terribly subjective list offered a very surprising reflection, which I think is revealing. Here is the breakdown:

MYSELF	MY TEAM
Self-Awareness	Trust
Communication...Listening	Vision
Balance	Teaching = Leading = Coaching
Creativity	Connection
Leading with Emotions	Connecting with the Material
Setting Intentions	Finding a Style
The Problem Is Me	Adjusting Approaches
Scheduling	The Role of Authority
Lead by Example	
Don't Be Templated	Service
Fear	Mentoring/Coaching Techniques
	Beginning, Starting—Basic Training
	Challenge; Aspirational Goals
	Coaching Wins and Losses
	Role of Recognition
	...And all of the rest of them!!! Yup, all of them. I know, riiiigggght?

Some of this seems self-evident. Of course, I was focused on myself when looking at self-awareness, setting intentions, or leading with emotions. But others surprised me. My reflection clearly was that scheduling was about enabling and being focused on myself at the pinnacle of the scheduling process. Even though this is a skill that I believe enables teams more than individuals, as I looked at it, the focus was on my own development. On the other hand, it was somewhat obvious that prioritization would be a team-focused TTP. But I was surprised by my reflection about finding a style. I know that finding a style is a very personal thing, but while I was analysing where my focus was while writing about it, it was clearly not on helping myself but rather on helping others in their own searches. Perhaps this is because I waited so long in my career to really have a hard look at what style I had. Maybe it's because I place more stock in a coach or leader's ability to adjust approaches to the situation and the people. Not sure. But in both the areas of finding a style and adjusting approaches, I felt that my focus was on the team first, and my skills and personal development took a second-tier role.

You will notice that in the table, about halfway down on the right, there is a blank slot. My initial take was that "Leading by Example" was focused on the team and what they needed from a leader. But the more I thought about it, and the more I reflected on my journey through leadership and what it meant to me, the more it became obvious that this aspect of leadership was central to my value system and not really about my team, but just about who I had to be. I could not lead or coach any other way; it would not have been authentic. In this way, what I was focused on when thinking and writing about this was myself. Yes, leaders eat last, and all of the other concepts embodied by setting a personal example have nothing to do with the coach or leader and everything to do with the team. But this concept, to me, is highly personal, and my reflections on it are focused inward, on my personal value system that I believe is rooted in a need to be of service. So, I moved it and left the blank to recognize my internal dilemma on this one.

Finally, in the overwhelming majority of the fundamentals and TTPs that I wrote on, I felt that I was focused on team or organizational development, not on myself as a coach or leader. That is not to say that the skills are not personal skills! Much to the contrary. Almost everything in the book is something that I feel each coach and leader can use to improve upon their skills at leading and coaching. But what I found was that the vast majority of the fundamentals and TTPs were things that focused me back on the team. For example, my approach to innovation was really about how to synergise lessons learned, new ideas, historical examples, and first principles into moving our team forward in effectiveness and efficiency.

The things that I tried to foster really had nothing to do with my personal skills, even though it was my methods and approach that were the levers to foster the creativity and advancement we were searching for. It was all focused on the team.

So here is an opportunity for you to get some very personalized reflections. Take the list of chapters and do the same thing for yourself. If you have some other leadership or coaching skills and knowledge that you think I have missed, add those things to the list. Then divide a paper into two columns like I did and ask yourself the following questions in order to bin them:

→ What were you holding in your mind while reading or thinking about that concept? Was it the team development and how you can coach or help others, or was it your personal development?

→ When you reflect on the concept or skill, are you thinking about how to apply it personally, or how to implement it as part of your team?

→ Which fundamentals and TTPs resonate with you on such a personal or visceral level that they are clearly value-based priorities for you?

Now, at the bottom of the page, in quick bullet points, start writing down the deductions that you come to from reviewing the list. Are the topics predominantly in one column or the other? Are there groupings of topics in each column that were easy to bin but others where you saw applicability on both sides? Why do you think that is?

If you hadn't developed a habit of journalling yet, by doing this you will have taken the first step toward true reflection on your coaching and leading skills.

CHAPTER 40

Linked Concepts and Sections

I n military operational planning, once objectives are set, end states are quantified, and intermediate objectives begin to be flushed out, patterns begin to emerge that link certain intermediate objectives together. Sometimes at the outset of operational planning, these patterns are already coalescing in the minds of planners. We call these "lines of operation." During the campaign in the Pacific in WWII, the line of operation from the Solomon Islands, Papua New Guinea, and the Philippines was synchronized with the island-hopping across the Gilbert and Marshall Islands. These patterns can be highly effective at helping us to understand their relationship to each other and to sequence and synchronize that which must occur, either conceptually, or in physical time and space. Some become conditions that need to be set before moving on to the next objective. Others are mutually supporting concepts like control of the air or setting of logistical lines of communication. I used this "lines of operation" approach to look at the linkages between the various fundamentals and TTPs in order to highlight patterns. These patterns can be revealing and can enhance the importance of the associated elements. For me, this was a very reflective process and one that I highly recommend. As you read these quick patterns, try to see if there are practical examples from your experiences where you would draw the same linkage, or if there are other patterns that your experiences would link together. (Write them down in the margins or in your journal.)

Teaching—Coaching Techniques—Mentoring—Communicating

One can draw a direct line between the techniques of teaching and coaching, many of the mentoring examples I have given, and the fundamental skill of communicating. When one views the relationship between coach and team, between leader and team, or between peers as *always* a relationship, then the techniques that were outlined in the sections above take on a more enhanced meaning. In seeing teaching as the never-ending process of improving everyone around us and ourselves, we see that a sense of humility and connection occurs. It is about the relationship. This carries right into the coaching and mentoring techniques, as we need to hold that relationship above the transactional issue of the moment. This is why the concept of the bridge in communicating is so powerful. If we focus on the relationship, then we see every encounter as another opportunity to establish the pillars of that bridge. This is why people who have worked together and have great relationships can communicate so easily, with a commonly understood vocabulary. Much of it can even be unspoken.

Vocabulary

One could argue that the establishment of a coherent vocabulary, one rooted in emotional agility, that provides a framework not only for solid communication, but for the establishment and execution of a comprehensive vision, should have been a section all its own. I feel like I kept returning to it, almost as something that I should have always done in advance. Prior to getting into a crisis, having to establish a connection in a pinch, or managing a poor-performing member of a team, establish a framework of vocabulary. Your vocabulary will obviously enable a more precise understanding between all elements of your team, allow for the accountability so key in trust, and root the team in the values that underpin the organization and, more importantly, the people on the team.

Inspired Execution... or... Vision—Connection—Priorities—Scheduling

I can draw a direct line between the creation of a vision and the scheduling function that is needed to execute and ensure success. Create the vision then gain a connection with the people executing the vision, prioritize the work then enable the team effectively using a rigorous scheduling process, and it works. But the spaces in between vision, connection, etc., are enabled by teaching, communicating, and mentoring. These are the "human spaces," not management tools. I think that I would label the entire process as "inspired execution." Indeed, in communicating, I like to think that to truly understand me, for me to effectively build that bridge, you need to get a glimpse of and feel my inspiration. I think in looking at the very "management tool" focus of the four sections I listed here, then trying to see how I applied them, it is truly an execution function that can only be done if the spark that the vision is based upon is woven throughout the entire process. If inspiration is matched with an effective tool to bring it to fruition, we have inspired execution.

Vision—Setting Intentions—Connection—Challenge

When it came time to set aspirational goals, to challenge the teams I was working with, if I had not done the work in advance, it would seem like flailing against a wall. I would frustrate my team, and, in turn, I wouldn't be happy with where we were going or how we were getting there. When I looked back at the times in which I achieved success in setting aspirational goals, this occurred because of the work done in advance of setting those goals. The link I draw here starts with establishing a vision. Yes, you must create that vision. But vision without buy-in from the team is not vision-ary…it's lonely. So that vision needs to be communicated so that the team, and the individuals on the team, feel a connection to it—and to you in leading and coaching them toward that vision.

Wedged between establishing the vision and connecting yourself and the vision to the team is setting intentions. This element, linked inherently to effective communication, was a key skill that enabled the connection. Prior to meeting with the team in communicating the vision, in mentor-ing and coaching individuals, even in updates and routine meetings, I set intentions that revolved around linking the work they were doing back to the overarching vision. I would set the intentions based upon the people and the type of meeting. This would allow me to focus on the results that I wanted from that specific encounter. It became key to connecting with people and connecting them and their work to the vision. (Sounds very in-spiration-like!) This was foundational to thereafter setting aspirational goals that challenged the team's performance. They needed to believe in what we were doing and trust and believe in me prior to setting challenge goals.

Self-Awareness—Leading with Emotions— Setting Intentions—The Problem Is Me

Probably the most personally insightful linkage in the various sections is the one that centres on my personal journey of discovery. It starts with an attempt at being self-aware as to what I am, and, more importantly, how I am undermining the collaboration and effectiveness of my team when I allow emotions on the surface to control my behaviours without space. The to-and-fro between creating that space and maintaining my authentic self by leading with emotions (the inherent way in which I tended to lead and inspire individuals and teams) was a very revealing process. The key skill that enabled me to navigate this better was setting intentions daily, for specific events, and overall, in a consistent fashion. Once I had a better grip on my surface emotions while still allowing myself to access those emotions, I could remain authentically inspiring. Thereafter, I had to recognize where my specific approach, preoccupation, emotional connection, or pet peeve was getting in the way of progress. This linkage is the most inwards-focused one of my development experiences. Although totally oriented around better enabling my teams, it was an individual process that I only looked outside to be accountable for progress.

Zoom Perspective—Connection— Communication—Adjusting Approaches

I love the concept of zoom perspective. The instant I heard the term, I intuitively knew it was a key skill. I love the connection between zoom perspective, vision, and priorities. The ability to zoom in and see the tactical and technical micro consequences, and then extrapolate them out to the larger macro objectives and vision with the intent of perhaps modifying priorities was, as I have said, intuitively brilliant. But what I was not prepared for was how zoom perspective enabled me to be better not merely in terms of managing the organization, but, more importantly, in coaching and leading the people on our team. By using the ability to zoom in, I could immerse myself in their environment. This enabled me to be in the moment and to better connect with them and to their issues and potential solutions. By listening well while zoomed in, I was not merely communicating (transmitting) my vision and demands on performance, but, more importantly, understanding and accepting their realities. This allowed me to adjust the mechanics of managing the organization, but, more importantly, it led me to a clearer understanding of what coaching and leading approaches were going to work best with these individuals or sections of my team. Too often we cheapen the zoom-in function as a fact-finding tour, a photo op, or a show of support, all with the intent to either gain information to adjust goals and objectives and the elements that affect them or to convince those on the bottom of the team that we care. By increasing our understanding at these levels, the real gold is that we can coach and lead better by using the best techniques and approaches specifically tailored for this section, these individuals, at that moment.

Random Thoughts and a Challenge

W e see the world through our personal lens, our own perspective. Each of us sees our workplaces, teams, colleagues, and organizations in different ways. Perhaps you see that the advances in workplace cultures that directly result in lower overall workloads and therefore less stress are worth any cost in terms of loss in performance. Perhaps you are like me, and you can see underperforming and lacklustre workplace cultures with leaders who are disconnected from their teams and do not see or internalize their role in making the required changes. No matter what you see in your leading and coaching roles, the ideas and concepts here, alongside the examples I have tried to use to bring them to life, can hopefully assist in some way to enhance your experience and provide some clarity on a path forward. If nothing else, you should take away the fundamental truth that leaders need to coach their teams to excellence, and coaches cannot abdicate their responsibilities to lead organizations to become better.

If I were going to prepare a team to take on a crucial mission, I would want to finish by focusing them on the key elements of the operation: the trust and confidence that they have in each other and that I have in them. So here goes. The fundamentals you have built by being open to learning, internalizing knowledge and skills by reflecting on your own performance, and allowing yourself the vulnerability that a humble student of leadership and coaching should have will hold you in good stead. When things get tough, remember these fundamentals, and remember that you are never alone in this if you are being true to yourself. The variety of situations and infinite characters of people you will deal with can never all be covered. But, by having a sense of right and remembering the examples and techniques I shared in this book, you will have a bank of knowledge and skills to reference. Trust in your own skills while remaining humble about your approach. Be confident in your values while being open to the collaboration that teams require to excel. Trust in your judgment regarding the approach you take in any given situation, and have faith that you will know when crisis direction is required. Never stop leading your teams, and never stop coaching them.

Not everything will go well. Even the most seasoned leaders fail, some catastrophically. *How* you coach and lead through adversity, *how* you set up the conditions for your teams to face adversity, *how* you foster the leadership and coaching development, inspiration, and skills from within your own teams…*these things* will define your success more than anything else.

My final thought is not a deep reflection; it is a challenge. It comes from pure humility. I know that much of what is written here is, in your opinion, incorrect. I know that you might disagree with my approach and see through some of the examples to tease out other traits, skills, factors, or truths that would undo the premises upon which they are based. I know that the list of fundamentals is incomplete, as is the list of TTPs. Therefore, the work here is incomplete. Perhaps I have missed a true fundamental or technique that is more revolutionary to coaching and leading. Perhaps my logic is flawed concerning those items that are linked, or rather the logic could be explained better in a different way. Even more to the point, maybe the fundamentals and TTPs in this book do not address the core problems that are manifesting in our teams and workplaces. Here is the challenge:

Write me. Write it yourself. Debate it. Talk about these things with colleagues or friends, coaches and leaders, followers all. The principal reason why I wanted to write these things down was not to have a book that people referred to, but to create a spark that got them to put this book down and then start leading, coaching, and talking openly about all the ways to bring out the best in our teams. I wanted to be of service. I want to always be of service. The service here is making leaders and coaches better. By volunteering to coach, by stepping up and leading well in work, life, sport, and community, we make our world a better place.

I would love to be proven wrong and have to write another book filled with your feedback and your musings and examples about how wrong I was. What a better place we would be in. *Aha!*

Acknowledgements

None of this happens by accident, or is done alone. There is a story behind every acknowledgement, because we are shaped by the people in our lives. I practice daily gratitude for the blessings of everyone mentioned here, and thousands others.

I am eternally grateful for the love and support of my Valy-girl. At my lowest lows, she has stood beside me, caressed the back of my neck, and gave me the reassurance that only a soul mate can do. She forgives my faults and gives me the constant encouragement that allows me to believe in myself. My love and affection for her knows no end. Foevo.

Mom and Dad. As a child adopted at birth, and a Dad, I now know the huge emotional commitment that my Mom and Dad made. I had no idea, and I still often completely forget, I am adopted. They were always the steadfast anchor in my life and that of our boys. I remember Mat saying that my parent's place (that my sister now lives in) was the only constant house he ever knew through all the moves, and that going there was like going home. I am who I am because of you. I love you.

My sister Ann. Man did we fight as kids. Now Val and I cannot imagine our lives without you. You have been a rock for me and the boys for decades. You and I discuss everything and anything. The more I live the more I agree with everything you say (yuck!!). Love ya sis.

Mathew. I am so proud of you and the man you are. You were my introduction to being a Dad and later a coach. I made mistakes and you were always ok with that. I love our Clancy boy discussions….that turn into heated political debates!! (Val has to leave the room!!) Laugh as much as you can. Enjoy this ride. It goes fast.

Ryan. I love you dearly my son. Our never-ending conversations about music, basketball, and life are the things of legends…just glad they are not recorded!! I have so many great memories of you skiing, playing guitar, cooking, and playing ball. It is good enough in this life just to be you. The path will reveal itself. Be open to the challenge…and the change.

Kim and Blair. Thank you can never be enough. You were always curious about what I was up to, and you are a wonderful part of our framily. We love your visits to the Williams Cottage! You are such an example of great parents, and of true hospitality. Never again a bottle of rum…..and I DON'T DANCE!

Gary and Lisa. Thank you eternally for welcoming me into your circle. You have been framily to us through thick and thin. Your backyard oasis and music filled house have been a godsend. I love you…..man.

My childhood best friends Stan, Bruce, Kevin, Ivan and Steve. You guys gave me a childhood surrounded by quality and value that formed the expectations for myself. Road hockey, basketball, football, epic hide and seek at night….. Thank you.

Marc, Big Jean, Tony, Claude, J and all your partners and families. I am much of what I am as a leader due to the early example you provided me and because of the incredible friends you are. We bonded over Air Cadets at 742, drill and a love of flying. Lifelong friends.

CMR Class of 89. You taught me what the phrase "I would give my life for you" meant. They were THE most formative five years for me. Man did I screw up a lot of things! Thank you for being my brothers and sisters in arms.

Ben my wingman, Michel and Garce. Our road to "wings" was hoed by humility interspersed with epic parties. Thank you for always reminding me that flying was FUN! Saskatchewan and Manitoba will never be the same. I think about us all almost dying while trying to cross the Bow River in Banff with our mountain bikes on our backs! And then seeing bonhomme Koolaid.

The Tac Hel family. My first mentor Herm Harrison, president and founder of the "I love Tac Hel club" who opened my eyes to this family. Alain Parent who shepherded me through my epic failures and mentored me in spite of myself. Chris Coates who pushed me to be better by always getting me to do the uncomfortable imperatives. (Save the beer!!) Rick Findley, Christian Drouin, Todd O'Malley, Marcel Duval, Paul Jefferies...leaders and friends. Jake my battle buddy; you were the second-half of myself I needed. To everyone I worked with, for, around....I apologise for being so blunt and overbearing at times, but am so proud of what YOU accomplish every day in the service of our nation. NHLTH

My NORAD family and American allies. Charles "Skip" Lucky who always took the time to mentor and listen. Gen Jacoby and Gen VenHerck, my country owes you a debt of gratitude. Andre Viens who provided me the consummate example of the gentleman General. "Tick" Pierce, Joe Southcott, Chris "Kathy" Ireland, Ed "Hertz" Vaughn, Bobbie "Magoo" Davis ... proud to fight alongside you. The Alaska ANR/ALCOM/11AF team, but especially Cory and Brooke Mendenhall, Tom Bussiere and Barb, Dave Wolfe and Daniel, we will always remember Alaska because of you and your friendship. My entire NORAD J3 team, but especially Dave "Oscar" Meyer and Pete "Coach" Fesler, I would follow you through fire brothers. Kevin "Fumez" Huyck .... No daylight brother.

Trevor, Heather and Hillary Teller. What great friends you are. We are so honoured by the treasured spot we share with y'all. Honourary Aunt and Uncle!

Canadian Army family. Thank you for not kicking this obstinate pilot out of your trusted inner circle. One of my most treasured memories was the Commander of the Canadian Army calling me "his Aviation Brigade Commander." My career favourite posting was the four years I spent as Directing Staff at Ft Frontenac. Send the best to teach, and your problems become manageable.

The RCAF family. Mike Hood who trusted me. Scotty Howden who listened to my rants. To my brother Michel Lalumiere, what an honour to serve beside you and get the second bar on our CDs together.

Kris, Allee and Axl …Ruger and Berlin. Awesome friends don't see distance, or rank. You taught me that. Thank you. (Remember High Pie!)

To Taffy who sat at my knee, shared my toast, my morning sandwich, our long walks, and was my co-pilot up and down the ALCAN and across the continent. Constant companion and loving soul. With the softest ears.

And to everyone else…yup…you know who you are. There is a part of you all inside these pages. Thank you.

To Julie and her team at Book Launchers (www.booklaunchers.com) I will forever be an advocate for you and your team to any writer wanting to get their book published. Thank you.

Rino Ferari and his team in Cobourg that provide all my stylish clothing, thank you. You make this tired warhorse look and feel great.

www.ingramcontent.com/pod-product-compliance
Lightning Source LLC
Chambersburg PA
CBHW071542210326
41597CB00019B/3094